Europe's Third World

Modern Economic and Social History Series

General Editor: Derek H. Aldcroft

Titles in the series include:

Railways in Britain and the United States, 1830–1940
Studies in Economic and Business History
Geoffrey Channon

Exchange Rates and Economic Policy in the 20th Century
Edited by Ross E. Catterall and Derek H. Aldcroft

Trade Unions and the Economy: 1870–2000
Derek H. Aldcroft and Michael J. Oliver

Spain
A Modern European Economy
Joseph Harrison and David Corkill

Britain and the Economic Problem of the Cold War
The Political Economy and the Economic Impact of the British Defence Effort, 1945–1955
Till Geiger

Industrial Reorganization and Government Policy in Interwar Britain
Julian Greaves

Merchants and Migrations
Germans and Americans in Connection, 1776–1835
Sam A. Mustafa

Industrial Clusters and Regional Business Networks in England, 1750–1970
Edited by John F. Wilson and Andrew Popp

Europe's Third World

The European Periphery in the Interwar Years

DEREK H. ALDCROFT

University of Leicester

ASHGATE

UNIVERSITY ... LYMOUTH

9007321250

© Derek H. Aldcroft, 2006

All rights reserved. No part of this publication may be reproduced, stored in a retrieval system, or transmitted in any form or by any means, electronic, mechanical, photocopying, recording or otherwise without the prior permission of the publisher.

Derek H. Aldcroft has asserted his moral right under the Copyright, Designs and Patents Act, 1988, to be identified as the author of this work.

Published by

Ashgate Publishing Limited
Gower House
Croft Road
Aldershot
Hants GU11 3HR
England

Ashgate Publishing Company
Suite 420
101 Cherry Street
Burlington
Vermont, 05401–4405
USA

Ashgate website: http://www.ashgate.com

British Library Cataloguing in Publication Data
Aldcroft, Derek Howard
Europe's Third World: The European Periphery in the Interwar Years – (Modern Economic and Social History).
1. Europe – History – 20th century. 2. Europe – Economic conditions – 20th century. 3. Europe – Social conditions – 20th century. I. Title
940'.09724

US Library of Congress Cataloging in Publication Data
Aldcroft, Derek Howard,
Europe's Third World: The European Periphery in the Interwar Years/ Derek H. Aldcroft.
p. cm. – (Modern Economic and Social History)
Includes bibliographical references and index.
1. Europe – History – 20th century. 2. Europe – Economic conditions – 20th century. 3. Europe – Social conditions – 20th century. I. Title. II. Series: Modern Economic and Social History Series.
D421.A425 2006
940'.09724–dc22 2005014115

ISBN 0 7546 0599 X

This book is printed on acid-free paper.

Printed and bound in Great Britain by MPG Books Ltd, Bodmin, Cornwall

For Steven
with sincere thanks

Contents

List of Tables

General Editor's Preface

Economic and social history has been a flourishing subject of scholarly study during recent decades. Not only has the volume of literature increased enormously but the range of interest in time, space and subject matter has broadened considerably so that today there are many more sub-branches of the discipline which have developed considerable status in their own right.

One of the aims of this new series is to encourage the publication of scholarly monographs on any aspect of modern economic and social history. The geographical coverage is world-wide and contributions on non-British themes will be especially welcome. While emphasis will be placed on works embodying original research, it is also intended that the series should provide the opportunity to publish studies of a more general and thematic nature which offer a reappraisal or critical analysis of major issues of debate.

Derek H. Aldcroft
University of Leicester, UK

Acknowledgements

Over the years I have had much assistance from various academic colleagues in this country and abroad.

A special thanks is due to friend and colleague Dr Steven Morewood of the University of Birmingham who has done service beyond the call of duty during my writing of this book. He has read and commented in detail on all the chapters, provided numerous references and source material, and generally acted as an unpaid adviser. His encyclopaedic knowledge of the twentieth century has saved me from many blunders. To him I extend my sincere gratitude and it is fitting that this volume is dedicated to him. I hope that he is not too disappointed with the final product, but at least I can blame him for any errors that remain!

I should also like to thank another friend and colleague, Dr Michael Oliver, who, while not having seen this work, has over the years been a most energetic sounding board, a provider of sources and a sympathetic listener.

Dr Joseph Harrison of Manchester University and Professor David Corkill of Manchester Metropolitan University kindly read the chapter on Spain and Portugal and offered many helpful suggestions and insights.

I would also like to take this opportunity to thank Tom Gray, History Editor at Ashgate Publishing, who has for many years given his support and encouragement, and also done so much to make the Modern Economic and Social History series a success. One could not wish for a more patient and understanding colleague.

Derek H. Aldcroft
University of Leicester

Introductory Note

Thirteen European countries are the focus of the present study: Poland and Hungary, the Baltic states (Estonia, Latvia and Lithuania), the Balkan countries of Albania, Bulgaria, Romania and Yugoslavia, and the Southern European or Mediterranean countries of Greece, Portugal, Spain and Turkey. The last of these was largely out of Europe by the interwar period but, as explained in Chapter 8, in view of its past history in Europe and its close if often stormy relationships with Greece, it seemed appropriate to consider Turkey alongside Greece and Albania. The choice of countries is not wholly arbitrary, as will become clear in Chapter 1, but briefly they were all backward nations, with high agrarian components and income levels but a fraction of those of Western European countries.

From time to time economic historians and economists pose thought-provoking yet tantalising questions on the issue of comparative development, such as why isn't the whole world developed (Easterlin 1981), or why is the West so rich while much of the rest of the world is so poor (Landes 1999); or, at a more micro level, Hobsbawm ponders why Albania is not as wealthy as Switzerland, given the superficially similar characteristics of the two countries (Hobsbawm 1994). Tantalising questions because quick and straightforward answers are not readily to hand; they can only be answered, and even then not necessarily simply, after a great deal of research into the dynamics of comparative development.

We do not propose to take on the whole world in this volume; the limit is one continent, focusing on the marginal or peripheral countries which failed to participate fully in the drive to modern economic growth through to 1914. But the real testing time came in the transwar period, not simply because of the somewhat inauspicious conditions for economic development in that period, but because many countries had to cope with quite different geographical and administrative entities following the vast reconfiguration of the map of Europe after the First World War. Nearly all, apart from Spain and Portugal, were new creations or differently constituted states as a result of the postwar settlement. The Baltic states threw off the Russian yoke; Poland re-emerged after nearly a century and a half of foreign tutelage; Yugoslavia was a new creation; while Bulgaria, Hungary, Romania, Greece, Turkey and Albania experienced substantial territorial and population changes.

CHAPTER ONE

Characteristics of the European Periphery

The definition of the periphery used in this volume is an economic rather than a geographic one. European peripheral countries are the poor ones, those that largely missed out on the industrial revolution of the nineteenth century which transformed the economies of Western Europe and the United States. As a working concept we have defined the impoverished peripherals as those countries which in the early twentieth century still had around one half or more of their population dependent on agriculture and with incomes per capita of less than 50 per cent of those of the advanced nations of Western Europe. On this basis, therefore, we would then encompass much of Eastern Europe (Poland, Hungary, Romania, Yugoslavia and Bulgaria), Spain, Portugal, Greece and Turkey in Southern Europe, along with the Baltic states of Estonia, Latvia and Lithuania, and ending up with little Albania. It so happens that most of these countries could also be classed as peripheral in a geographic sense and many of them were fairly small in terms of population.

The only debatable issue was whether or not to include Italy since, according to two Spanish scholars (Molinas and Prados de la Escosura 1989, 397), Italy and Spain had very similar incomes per head in 1910 and 1930. After careful consideration it was decided to exclude the former country. Other sources suggest that Italy had a higher per capita income than Spain; but, that apart, the depth of structural change in Italy was deeper than in the case of Spain, and more akin to the Western European pattern. Structural change and income per capita growth tended to go hand-in-hand in Italy, whereas in Spain structural adjustment lagged behind improvements in income per capita (see Molinas and Prados de la Escosura 1989, 397). More generally, one gets the impression from a reading of the evidence that Italy was a more mature country than Spain, with a stronger integration into the international economy and a more pronounced role in international affairs. Known as the least of the Great Powers and lacking significant natural resources, Italy was a successful belligerent in the First World War and subsequently, under Mussolini, became an aggressive military state. In fact, a country that by the late 1920s had the world's second largest air force, the third largest army and the fifth largest navy, and was soon to embark on imperialistic ventures, could scarcely be classed as a poor European peripheral country (Morewood 2005, 26).

A word about regional definitions is appropriate at this stage since these can be a source of confusion. This is especially the case with Eastern Europe or East-Central Europe, which can be a definitional nightmare. Broader definitions of East-Central Europe can include some twelve to fourteen countries. Kofman (1997, 3), for example, defines East-Central Europe to mean Austria, Czechoslovakia, Hungary, Poland, Lithuania, Latvia, Estonia, Romania, Yugoslavia, Albania, Bulgaria and Greece, which includes 10 of the countries covered in this volume. However, Greece can be listed under Southern Europe, while Bulgaria, Romania, Yugoslavia, Greece and Albania are also classed as Balkan countries. For simplicity we have adopted the following categories. The region frequently referred to as Eastern Europe includes six countries – Hungary, Poland, Bulgaria, Romania, Yugoslavia and Czechoslovakia. The last of these is not included in this volume since its level of development was more akin to that of the West than to that of the peripheral countries. The term Balkans is used throughout to refer to the three main Balkan countries of Bulgaria, Romania and Yugoslavia. Spain, Portugal and Greece are part of Southern Europe, which can also include Turkey by virtue of its small presence in Europe. The term Iberian Peninsula refers to Spain and Portugal. Turkey and Albania are normally mentioned separately, while Estonia, Latvia and Lithuania come under the heading of the Baltic states.

Most of the 13 countries covered in this volume had several features in common. A large proportion of the population was dependent on the primary sector, principally agriculture, for their livelihood. This ranged from 45–50 per cent in the case of Southern Europe (Spain, Portugal and Greece), between 50 and 60 per cent in the case of Hungary, Poland and the Baltic provinces, excepting Lithuania, to 70–81 per cent in the Balkans (Bulgaria, Romania and Yugoslavia), Albania and Turkey (see Table 1.1). Almost everywhere agricultural systems and methods of production were backward and fairly unyielding; by Western standards productivity levels were very low, while medieval-type strip farming was still quite common in some regions, especially in the Balkan countries. Most operations in peasant agriculture were performed by human labour or by animal-drawn implements. Peasant life was not a pleasant one and general living conditions were often very primitive (Bideleux and Jeffries 1998, 449–52). Land ownership patterns varied a great deal and there were many changes in the course of the period (see later chapters), but few countries, apart perhaps from the Baltic states, emerged with patterns of land ownership and cultivation that made possible more efficient farming practices, though productivity levels still fell well short of those in Western countries.

Table 1.1 Population and Income Levels for Selected Countries

Country	Population in 1920 (000s)	Population in 1939 (000s)	% population dependent on agriculture, circa 1930–34	Growth rates of population 1920–39	Illiteracy rate: % of 7–10 year olds 1930–34	GNP per head in 1929 (US 1960 dollars)
Turkey	*13,648	17,500	81	2.10a	90.0	–
Albania	804	1,064	80	1.50	80.0	–
Yugoslavia	11,985	15,703	76	1.43	45.2	341
Bulgaria	4,847	6,305	75	1.30	31.4	306
Romania	15,635	20,045	72	1.27	42.0	331
Lithuania	2,116	2,597	70	1.10	37.0b	–
Poland	26,829	34,848	60	1.44	23.1	350
Estonia	1,105	1,122	56	0.10	4.0	–
Latvia	1,596	1,951	55	1.00	13.5	–
Hungary	7,990	9,129	51	0.76	8.8	–
Spain	21,303	25,600	50	0.90	31.0	455
Portugal	6,033	7,659	46	1.50	59.0	320
Greece	5,017	7,201	46	1.93	40.8	390
Sweden	5,904	6,341	31	0.30	0.1	897
Denmark	3,289	3,851	30	0.80	–	945
France	39,210	41,950	29	0.30	8.0	982
Norway	2,650	2,937	27	0.50	–	1033
Switzerland	3,880	4,206	22	0.40	–	1265
Germany	61,153	69,640	20	0.70	–	770
Netherlands	6,865	8,834	18	1.40	–	1008
Belgium	7,466	8,396	15	0.70	9.0	1098
England and Wales	37,887	41,660	5	0.49	0.0	1038

Notes: * 1927; (a) 1927–39; (b) 1923.

Sources: Polonsky 1975, 172; Kirk 1946, 24; Kaser and Radice 1985, 93, 532; Moore 1945, 26; Kirk 1946, 24; Bairoch 1976, 297; Hope 1994, 53–54; Hale 1981, 18; private communication from Irena Bakula of Riga, Latvia.

The backwardness of agriculture can be measured by the low levels of productivity as against Western standards. In terms of both land area and persons engaged in agriculture productivity levels were but a fraction of those in Western Europe (see Table 1.2). It follows therefore that there was enormous potential surplus population in agriculture, except in Estonia and Latvia, had agricultural practices conformed more closely to best practice techniques of Western Europe (see Table 1.3). In some cases marginal productivities on the land were probably zero or negative, which implies that drawing people out of agriculture would have raised the average productivity level. The only problem here was that unless commensurate changes were taking place in the rest of the economy there was nowhere for redundant agricultural labour to find employment.

Table 1.2 Indices of Agricultural Productivity in Calorie Units (average 1931–35, Europe* = 100)

	Per person dependent on agriculture	Per male engaged in agriculture	Per hectare of of agricultural land
Albania	22	25	70
Bulgaria	47	55	80
Estonia	99	103	69
Greece	50	48	77
Hungary	78	75	87
Latvia	111	103	80
Lithuania	73	74	69
Poland	49	56	75
Portugal	53	53	47
Romania	48	53	69
Spain	88	94	53
Turkey	35	39	–
Yugoslavia	38	43	69
Denmark	354	323	236
Sweden	146	134	118
Austria	134	128	153
France	174	160	109
Germany	195	191	181
Netherlands	259	237	377
Switzerland	194	167	371
England and Wales	319	240	193

Note: * Excluding USSR and Turkey.

Source: Moore 1945, 35.

Table 1.3 'Surplus' Agricultural Population Assuming Existing Production and European Average Per Capita Level (circa 1930)

Country	Surplus Population %
Albania	77.7
Bulgaria	53.0
Estonia	0.4
Greece	50.3
Hungary	22.4
Latvia	–10.9
Lithuania	27.3
Poland	51.3
Portugal	46.9
Romania	51.4
Spain	11.9
Turkey	65.0
Yugoslavia	61.5

Source: Moore 1945, 63–64.

Low levels of efficiency in farming inevitably led to pressure on land resources, a situation intensified by the rapid population growth during the interwar period, which came at the most inopportune time as far as the peripheral countries were concerned. Apart from the exceptional case of Estonia, most countries had population growth rates well in excess of those in Western Europe. In Albania, Turkey, Portugal, Greece, Poland and the Balkans, population was growing at well over 1 per cent per annum in the interwar period, compared with only 0.5 per cent for England and Wales, 0.7 per cent in Belgium and Germany, and as low as 0.3 per cent in France and Sweden (see Table 1.1). Much of this rapid expansion can be attributed to the very high birth rates at a time when death rates were falling rapidly, due to health and medical improvements. But in some countries, as for instance Romania and Greece, populations were augmented considerably by large additions resulting from territorial gains and population migrations following the postwar peace settlements. Greece had an influx of well over a million expatriate Greeks (adding possibly one quarter to her population total), the main contingent coming from Turkey following the Greek defeat in Asia Minor in 1922, as well as smaller numbers from Balkan countries. In return Turkey received some 400,000 of its own nationals from Greece.

Despite the exchange of populations following the war and the reduction in minority status by the peace treaty settlements, many of the

Baltic and East European countries still had large minority populations. Table 1.4 gives a breakdown of the ethnic composition of the countries in question, with the predominant group given in bold type. Apart from Albania, 10 per cent or more of the populations of these countries consisted of ethnic minorities, while in the case of Poland and Romania the proportion was as high as 30 per cent. The new Hungarian state on the other hand, while more homogenous in ethnic terms, had some three million of its nationals living as minorities outwith its borders. In some countries there were up to a dozen or more different minority groups. The worst case was that of Yugoslavia. Though Slavic interests accounted for more than three quarters of the population, this figure masks the actual diversity and the potential for conflict. The two main groups, the Serbs and the Croats, were scarcely the most congenial of partners, nor for that matter were the Slovenes. Moreover, the main Serbo-Croat contingent included a not inconsiderable number of Bosnian Muslims, Macedonians, Bulgarians and Montenegrins. Altogether there were over a dozen assorted minority interests, including Germans, Magyars, Romanians, Albanians, Turks, Poles, Italians, Gypsies, Bulgarians, Czechs/Slovaks and Macedonians, none of whom could assimilate easily one with another. Moreover, most of them suffered minority discrimination and persecution at one time or another at the hands of the dominant Serbs. In fact the ethnic problems of the new Yugoslav state were exacerbated by the fact that the Serbs, who represented about 40 per cent of the population, tended to monopolise the positions of power within government and administration and paid lip-service to the interests of their minority nationals. As Berend comments, 'No other country in Europe – except the Soviet Union, which had preserved the old multinational empire – possessed such a diverse population' (Berend 1998, 171).

Perhaps even more fascinating were the tiny pockets of ethnic groups left over from a bygone age. In Poland there were small numbers of Tartars, while nomads and semi-nomads, for example the Vlachs, were to be found in the Balkan countries (Crampton and Crampton 1996, 2). More significant from the point of view of political developments were the pockets of Germans and Jews in many countries. Linguistic divisions, though a guide to ethnicity, are even more complex because of much inter-linguistic mixing in some regions. Religious affiliations were equally complex. Though the most important were Protestant, Roman Catholic, Orthodox, Greek Catholic and Muslim, there were also many smaller religious sects.

This 'ethnological soufflé', as Tiltman (1934, 266) called it, was bound to give rise to serious problems, some of which have persisted to the present day. Minority nationality problems were in fact 'one of the most acute causes of tension in east Europe throughout the interwar period' (Hauner 1985, 68). It is true that the countries with significant minority interests were enjoined, under the League of Nations minority treaties which they signed, to observe good behaviour towards their alien residents and to avoid the exercise of discrimination. In practice there was a notable reluctance to abide by their obligations. Generally speaking, 'the states were mainly concerned with interpreting the provisions in the most restrictive possible sense and used every device to vitiate their effect' (Robinson et al. 1943, 264). In few cases, therefore, were minority groups accorded equality of treatment in government and administration, and in the dispensation of economic and social services.

As well as being predominantly agrarian-based, the populations of these countries were very illiterate judged by Western standards. About half the countries had illiteracy levels of 40 per cent or more in the early 1930s; in Portugal the rate was nearly 60 per cent and in the case of Albania and Turkey it was as high as 80–90 per cent. Only the Baltic states – excepting again Lithuania – Hungary, and to a lesser extent Poland had relatively high levels of literacy (see Table 1.1). Everywhere illiteracy was considerably higher among females than among males.

High agrarian dependence inevitably meant that modern industry played a relatively small role in the economies of the peripheral countries. At the extreme, Turkey and Albania probably had less than 10 per cent of their labour forces employed in this sector, and even then much of it consisted of small-scale domestic or workshop manufacture. The Balkan countries fared little better in this regard, whereas Poland and Hungary had developed more substantial industrial interests before 1914. The Baltic states also had a thriving industrial sector before 1914 which mainly served the Russian market, though much of it was subsequently lost as a result of war and revolution. Yet however small and insignificant the industrial sector, most countries had experienced some modern development before 1914, even if only through the backwash effects of Western development and the influx of Western capital and technology. True industrial development was often highly concentrated spatially, sometimes forming islands of capitalism in a sea of primitivism, while the level of efficiency fell well short of Western standards (see Berend and Ranki 1982).

One feature of the limited industrial development was the marked presence of foreign capital in modern joint stock enterprise. This was true both before and after the war despite attempts by nationalist politicians to extend the practice of nostrification principally through increased state holdings. Some 50 per cent of the total Latvian stock capital was in foreign hands in 1925, while by the early 1930s the proportions of joint stock capital owned abroad in Poland was two

Table 1.4 Ethnic Composition of Peripheral Countries circa 1930 (%)

	Albania	Bulgaria	Estonia	Hungary	Latvia	Lithuania	Poland	Romania	Turkey	Yugoslavia
Albanians	**92.0**									3.6
Arabs									1.0	
Bulgarians		**87.0**						2.1		
Byelorussians							3.9			
Croats				0.5						
Czechs							0.1			
Estonians			**86.0**							
Germans			2.0	6.9	3.0	4.0	3.9	4.2		3.6
Greeks	5.0									
Gypsies								1.5		0.5
Hungarians				**89.6**				8.6		
Italians										0.1
Jews		1.0			5.0	7.0	7.8	4.1		0.1
Kurds									8.0	
Latvians					**77.0**					
Lithuanians						**81.0**	0.3			
Macedonians Magyars										3.4
Other Slavs										1.4
Others	2.0	2.0		0.7	2.0	2.0	0.3	2.2	5.0	0.2
Poles					2.0	3.0	**69.2**			
Romanians				0.3				**70.8**		

Table 1.4 *concluded*

	Albania	Bulgaria	Estonia	Hungary	Latvia	Lithuania	Poland	Romania	Turkey	Yugoslavia
Rumanians and Vlachs										1.0
Russians			12.0		11.0	3.0	0.2	2.3		
Ruthenians							14.3			
Serbs				0.2						
Serbo-Croats	1.0									**77.0**
Slovaks				1.8						
Slovenes										8.1
Turks		10.0						0.9	**86.0**	1.0
Ukrainians/ Ruthenians								3.3		

Sources: Polonsky 1975; Crampton and Crampton 1996; Robinson et al. 1943.

fifths, one half in Hungary and three fifths in Bulgaria (Hinkkanen-Lievonen 1983, 335). Most other countries had a relatively high proportion of foreign capital in modern enterprise, both in industrial undertakings as well as in raw material and mineral extraction, a reflection of the low level of domestic accumulation. In some sectors foreign ownership was dominant, as in the case of the Romanian oil industry.

Retarded industrial development also meant a low level of urbanisation. The rural–urban split of population was in many cases almost the reverse of that in West European countries. One or two countries, notably Hungary, Greece and Spain, had relatively high levels of urbanisation, but even in these cases it was still only about half the Western level. Otherwise, the urban proportion was a third or one quarter of that in the West, and even less in the case of Albania and Turkey (see Table 1.5).

Table 1.5 Rural/Urban Distribution of Population (circa early 1930s)

Country	Rural	Urban
Albania	88.2	11.8
Bulgaria	78.6	21.4
Estonia	71.0	29.0
Greece	57.5	42.5
Hungary	57.5	42.5
Latvia	65.4	34.6
Lithuania	76.9	23.1
Poland	72.8	27.2
Portugal	80.9	19.1
Romania	79.8	20.2
Spain	51.5	48.5
Yugoslavia	77.7	22.3
Belgium	19.5	80.5
England and Wales	20.0	80.0
Germany	30.1	69.9
Netherlands	20.5	79.5

Sources: Hauner 1985, 83; Kirk 1946, 14.

The trade orientation of European peripheral countries was consistent with their low level of development. Export–product ratios were fairly low by Western standards, especially for Spain, Portugal, Greece, Bulgaria, Serbia, Turkey and Albania, which indicates a relative lack of integration in the international economy. On the other hand, low export–product ratios would lessen the strength of the dependency theory (see Hanson 1986, 83, 93 and Chapter 2 of the present volume). However, Hungary and Romania, along with the Baltic states, had somewhat higher ratios before 1914, though in the case of the Baltic states this was very much a consequence of their serving the Russian market.

The composition of trade reflected the domestic economic structure of these countries. Primary commodities tended to dominate the export trade, sometimes with heavy dependence on one or two products. In the case of Greece, tobacco accounted for some 55 per cent of all exports in 1926–30, while three commodities (tobacco, dried fruit and wine) made up about 80 per cent of total exports (Freris 1986, 87). Romania's dependence was almost as great, since cereals and forest and petroleum products accounted for over 77 per cent of all exports. In Bulgaria cereals, tobacco, and eggs and livestock accounted for 73 per cent, while for Yugoslavia cereals, livestock and forest products made up 59 per cent (Lampe and Jackson 1982, 368–69). Finished goods, on the other hand, formed a very small component of exports, especially in the Balkans and in Albania and Turkey, though in the case of Poland and Hungary they were more substantial at about 20–25 per cent (Polonsky 1975, 178). Conversely, imports consisted mainly of manufactured and semi-manufactured goods, though some countries also had a not insignificant food import component. The fact that some of the countries were dependent on food imports despite their large agrarian interests is eloquent testimony to the failure of their agrarian systems to respond to the needs of rapidly growing populations.

Another feature of the peripheral countries was their poor infrastructure facilities, which was partly a consequence of their low level of urbanisation and their relative poverty. Based on five separate measures, that is, transport, communications, housing supply, health care, and educational and cultural services, the European peripherals generally scored badly, with Spain, Bulgaria, Romania, Portugal, Turkey and Albania bringing up the rear (see Table 1.6). While low incomes and a limited tax base inevitably reduced the scope for state expenditure on these facilities, it should also be noted that a relatively high proportion of government budgets was devoted to military activities, administrative costs and debt service. Thus by Western standards the provision of housing, sanitation, health care, welfare services and educational facilities was very poor in the peripheral countries of Europe.

Table 1.6 Infrastructure Levels Based on Five Components*

Rank	c.1920	Score	Rank	c.1937	Score
1	Denmark	75.3	1	United States	83.5
2	Switzerland	70.9	2	Sweden	79.2
3	Australia	63.0	3	Denmark	74.2
4	Norway	62.3	4	New Zealand	73.1
5	Netherlands	59.5	5	UK	70.3
20	Greece	23.7	20	Hungary	21.4
21	Hungary	20.0	21	Poland	18.8
22	Yugoslavia	16.3	22	Greece	18.3
23	Poland	16.3	23	Spain	17.0
24	Spain	15.2	24	Yugoslavia	14.3
25	Bulgaria	14.2	25	Bulgaria	13.9
26	Romania	10.8	26	Romania	13.5
27	Portugal	9.2	27	Portugal	13.1
28	Turkey	0.3	28	Turkey	9.3

Note: * Transport, communications, housing supply, health care, and educational and cultural services.

Source: Ehrlich 1985, 326.

One notable feature lacking in the European peripheral countries was the existence of a strong and acquisitive middle class element in society. There were landowners and peasantry, clergy and bureaucrats, soldiers and politicians, but no substantial petty and middling bourgeoisie which had been the driving force in mercantile and industrial pursuits in Western countries, as had the yeoman farmer in the agrarian sector. According to Berend (1998, 32), 'The relative weakness of the modern middle class constituted one of the most outstanding aspects of the structure of society.' The societies of the peripheral countries were noted for their rigid social stratification and limited social mobility and their apparent olympian indifference to the tenets of economic modernisation. In part the lacuna was filled by non-indigenous elements, especially the Germans and the Jews, who played key roles in trade, industry and finance in much of Eastern Europe and the Baltic states. But they could never become complete substitutes for home-grown middle class products since they were always regarded as minority intruders. This was especially the case with the Jews, whose differences in social and religious beliefs, together with their preponderating influence in fields of economic and financial activities, despite apparent assimilation in some cases, marked them out as targets for anti-Semitic behaviour on the part of the native residents (see Berend 1998, 33–39). In Poland, Hungary, Romania and the Baltic states, as well as in Czechoslovakia, there was growing animosity towards the Jewish communities throughout the interwar years, which facilitated Hitler's plan for their eventual elimination (Mendelsohn 1983, 257).

When considering the impoverished nations of Europe, it is important to bear in mind their political experience. With the exception of Spain and Portugal all of them can be classed as new or reconstituted states arising out of the aftermath of the First World War. Large territorial and population shifts occurred as a result of the postwar settlements, including those arising from subsequent conflicts notably that between Turkey and Greece. Virtually all these states adopted new constitutions and set up parliamentary regimes, in some cases where none had existed before. But consolidating and stabilising the new creations proved a difficult task given the weak, often corrupt and unstable administrations, the inexperience in democratic methods, and the problem of reconciling divergent interests, many of which arose from the ethnic and religious diversity of the populations, especially in Eastern Europe. Often the result was a plethora of parties, frequent changes in governments and general political instability. Perhaps not surprisingly, therefore, it was not long before democracy began to falter. The new democracies were overwhelmed by forces of the right and one by one they succumbed to authoritarian rule. Whereas in 1920 nearly all European countries could be classed as democracies, by the end of the interwar period 16 of the 28 European states had been taken over by some form of dictatorship or authoritarian regime which had largely dispensed with the trappings of democracy (Lee 1987, xi–xv; Newman 1970, 21–22).

Apart from the totalitarian states of Italy and Germany, it was the peripheral countries that accounted for most of these tyrannical regimes. All had succumbed to some form of authoritarian rule by 1938. More often than not this arose as a response to unstable parliamentary government and party conflict or as a defence against the threat of communism. In the case of Southern Europe (Italy, Spain, Portugal, Greece and Turkey), Wallerstein interprets the swing to authoritarian government in these countries as a reaction to their lagging behind developmentally and the quest to capture past glories through the cult of the state and economic nationalism (Wallerstein 1985, 37). Few if any of the new regimes could be regarded as popular dictatorships since their support was largely drawn from military groups, top bureaucrats, landowning and upper classes, and in some cases royal circles (Valenta 1974, 1433). Despite the lack of popular support many took Hitler's Germany as their role model and tried to imitate fascist traits.

The first to succumb was Hungary when in 1920 Horthy took control of the country in the counter-revolution following the short-lived Bolshevik regime of Bela Kun in the previous year, while in 1926 Pilsudski gained control of Poland. Several of the authoritarian regimes were of the monarchical variety. President Zogu of Albania proclaimed himself self-styled monarch in 1928 with almost unlimited powers and remained in power through to the Second World War. In Yugoslavia King Alexander assumed control of the country in 1929 as did King Boris in Bulgaria in 1934, while Romania followed suit in 1938 when King Carol dispensed with parliamentary government. In the final Balkan state, Greece, a semi-fascist regime was set up in 1936 by General Metaxas under which no opposition was permitted.

Of the remaining peripheral countries, the Baltic states adopted rather milder authoritarian versions: Lithuania came under the control of Smetona in 1926, and Latvia and Estonia fell to Ulmanis and Päts respectively in 1934. Turkey was effectively ruled by Kemal Atatürk from 1923 until his death in 1938, having assumed dictatorial powers on his assumption of the presidency of the new Turkish Republic set up in 1923. Finally, there is the example of the Iberian countries of Spain and Portugal. The latter was effectively controlled by Dr Oliveira Salazar from 1928 when he became minister of finance and he remained dictator until 1968. Spain's final capitulation to the authoritarian right took longer. General Primo de Rivera ruled as Spanish dictator between 1923 and 1930, but he was succeeded by a republican government. It was not until 1939, when General Franco defeated the republican forces in the Spanish Civil War, that dictatorship was resumed.

By the interwar period, therefore, many of the European peripheral countries had structural characteristics which either relegated them to a low level of development or reflected their economic backwardness. And, as might be expected, these very characteristics were not helped by the hostile economic climate of the interwar period. This does not mean, however, that their economies were totally static either before 1914 or afterwards. In fact, during the long nineteenth century there were changes and signs of progress in most of the peripheral countries as the influence of Western development seeped, albeit almost imperceptibly at times, south and east through the continent of Europe. Before examining the interwar experience in more detail, therefore, we first take a look at peripheral Europe in the context of nineteenth century development.

CHAPTER TWO

Peripheral Europe Before 1914

Economic development is a complex and puzzling phenomenon. There is no telling precisely when, where and how it will happen – why some countries and regions become rich while others remain desperately poor. The classical notion that free factor flows would lead to convergence in development has long since been confounded by the glaring disparities in levels of income that now prevail across the globe. Economists and economic historians have shed many words on this topic but still it remains something of a mystery.

On a global scale the most tantalising issue is why Eastern civilisations, once very advanced, lost out to the West; and why in Europe the Iberian and Mediterranean countries gave way to Northern Europe. On the other hand, if North America's potential was more obvious, that of Australia certainly was not. A large and seemingly barren and inhospitable country, so far from anywhere, became one of the richest nations in the world within decades of the arrival of the first major contingent of settlers, who at the time were regarded as the scum of the earth.[1] On a smaller canvas there are any number of development oddities. For example, who would have thought that the tiny and inhospitable island of Nauru in the Pacific would one day have one of the highest per capita incomes in the world on the basis of bird droppings (a source of phosphate fertilisers), later to be complemented by money laundering for the Russian Mafia (MacMillan 2003, 114)? Or that Mauritius, a small and unpromising African island, would shine forth like a beacon, in sharp contrast to most of its mainland neighbours across the water?

European development is not without its own puzzles – as Hobsbawm (1994) inferred when he queried why Albania was not as rich as Switzerland, given that the two countries had similar characteristics: resource poor, sparsely populated, mountainous. That Europe, or at least part of it, came to dominate the political, economic

---

[1] But far from being a blot on the landscape they transformed it. As David Monroe commented in 1842: 'The extraordinary rapid growth which has followed upon this settlement of the scum of the Earth on the shores of Australia would almost make it appear that in colonizing it is as in gardening, the more of your foundations consist of dung the more rapid and striking is the production ...' Quoted in Statham (1992, 205). Statham (1990, 43–63) shows the importance of the much maligned New South Wales [Officer] Corps in getting things going.

and cultural life of much of the world in its heyday in the nineteenth century is not open to question. When it emerged from the Dark Ages it steadily extended its control and influence over the vast majority of the earth's surface, 7 per cent in 1500 to 84 per cent in 1914 (Tilly 1992, 183). In the words of Carlo Cipolla (1981, 300), 'The history of any remote corner of the world after 1500 cannot be properly understood without taking into account the impact of European culture, economy and technology ... *Sans l'Europe l'histoire moderne est inconcevable.*'

The core–periphery debate

Yet for all its supremacy Europe itself was a continent deeply divided, politically, socially and economically. The core of modern development lay in the north-west corner, while to the south and east there was persistent lagging: from the Iberian Peninsula along the Mediterranean, into the Balkans up through European Russia, and back into Poland and the Baltic states. The dividing line was Austria-Hungary, not quite up to Western standards, but far better than the periphery here outlined. Not all peripheral countries in a geographic sense were impoverished. There were exceptions to this geographical categorisation of course. The Scandinavian countries would not fall into this category, nor would Switzerland. More doubtful cases are Finland and Italy (see Arrighi 1985).

Such was the lagging in these countries that some historians have tended to regard Europe's peripheral states as also-rans in the process of modern development, dependent for much of the time on the core nations of the West. In her study of peasant farming Doreen Warriner (1964, 75) reduced the economic history of East/South-eastern Europe to a mere footnote.[2] Chirot (1976, 9), in his work on southern Romania, saw the periphery, or at least Eastern Europe, as something akin to a colony of the core before the First World War: 'In a sense, then, Eastern Europe became a colony of Western Europe.' Similarly Hershlag (1968, 31–32), in a somewhat wider context, referred to the semi-colonial status of some nations: 'the richer preferred to keep the less fortunate, retarded areas in a state of underdevelopment and economic dependency as long as international conditions permitted' (cf. Lampe and Jackson 1982; Hinkkanen-Lievonen 1983, 335–36). Ranki (1985, 64) expressed a similar view about the Balkans, which he claimed were integrated into the world economic system in a way that kept them

---

2 'In the economic history of the nineteenth century Eastern Europe did not amount to more than a footnote' (Warriner 1964, 75).

underdeveloped and structurally backward, not unlike the enclave economies of the Third World (Senghaas 1985, 187). Tomasevich (1955, 212–13) saw capitalism in the South Slav lands not as an indigenous development, but as basically an appendage of Central and Western European capitalism introduced primarily by foreigners. But, 'Whether its representatives were foreigners or nationals, capitalism in the South Slav areas remained essentially rapacious and exploitative rather than creative, a corrupting crust rather than a well-developed economic system.' Writing in the 1960s Spulber (1966, 7–8) likened the East European countries to the developing nations of Asia and Africa. Even Spain was seen as an economic colony of the advanced nations by the economic nationalists of the 1920s (Harrison 1985, 36).

The core–periphery debate, with its Marxist overtones, is a complex one which has been applied more generally to twentieth century lesser developed countries. However, as the above illustrations indicate, several writers feel that it is not without relevance to nineteenth century Europe.

The main tenets of the thesis is that peripheral countries are poor, less civilised and concentrate on low technology primary commodity production by virtue of their dependence on richer countries, which in turn exploit the international division of labour for their own benefit, thereby reinforcing the peripheral states' dependent role in the international economy. There is therefore a certain degree of inevitability in the process. As some countries develop industrially and become wealthy while others lag behind, the latter will tend to take on the characteristics which bracket them as dependent economies. These characteristics include the following:

1. Concentration on the production of primary commodities a large part of which are exported to the richer core in unprocessed form.
2. Dependence on imports of manufactured consumer goods and capital equipment.
3. Heavy reliance on foreign technology, know-how, skilled expertise and capital.
4. More generally the situation may give rise to 'a condition of cultural, psychological, social and political dependence' (Colman and Nixson 1994, 48), which in the European context is especially relevant given the political subordination of many peripheral regions to imperial masters.

Poor countries have generally laid the blame for their unfortunate circumstances on the capitalist exploiters of the West for, as Landes (1999, 252) notes, 'It feels better that way.' But the nineteenth century situation cannot be regarded as one of complete suppression of modern development in peripheral regions by the advanced core. Berend and Ranki (1982, 9), admit that the relationship was fundamentally an unequal one which tended to benefit the core while often proving destructive to the periphery, but it could also be beneficial to the latter by acting as 'an inducement to development, serving – under appropriate conditions – to lift the area from its peripheral position'. On the other hand, Landes feels that the core–periphery is a mistaken metaphor and that lagging development was an internal problem rather than one generated by dependency:

> Europe's development gradient ran from west to east and north to south, from educated to illiterate populations, from representative to despotic institutions, from equality to hierarchy, and so on. It was not resources or money that made the difference; nor mistreatment by outsiders. It was what lay inside – culture, values, initiative. These peoples came to have freedom enough. They just didn't know what to do with it.
>
> (Landes 1999, 252–53)

The core–periphery analogy is complicated in its application to Europe since it was not simply a question of an East–West, North–South split. It was in fact replicated at a more micro level in many regional and local guises. For example, the Habsburg dynasty itself had an East–West gradient, with the more industrialised western half serving as a market for the products of the agrarian-based eastern sector, while the Balkans were in turn dependent on Austria-Hungary's large domestic market. At a more local level, the developing industrial/commercial centres such as Budapest, Bucharest, Sofia, Istanbul, Athens, Barcelona, Madrid and Lisbon acted as core magnets for the more backward agricultural hinterlands. In some cases there was even a reversal of the stereotyped roles. The nascent industrial sectors in the Baltic states, Poland and Finland served as suppliers to the more backward imperial regime of Russia (see Berend 2003, 139).

The core–periphery/dependency theory can also be somewhat misleading if it is put in a politico/economic context since economic subordination was not synonymous with political status. Some peripheral countries had a more independent existence than others. Spain, Portugal and Greece after 1830 were autonomous countries in their own right yet they were clearly laggards in development. And while much of the rest of peripheral Europe was in thrall to the old and crumbling empires of Ottoman Turkey, Russia and Austro-Hungary, political dependency did not always mean economic subservience. The Baltic states and the western parts of Poland were more advanced than their political master and became important industrial suppliers to

Russia, whereas by contrast the Balkans could never really throw off the Ottoman yoke even when they secured independence (Chirot 1989a, 7–9). One should also note that the export orientation of many so-called dependent regions was in fact lower than that of the leading Western countries. Apart from Hungary and Romania, which had export–product ratios of around 20 per cent in 1910, many of the peripheral countries had low percentages: Greece 5.6, Portugal 5.6, Spain 8.4, Bulgaria 6.5, Serbia 8.8 (Hanson 1986, 83, 93).

Another point to bear in mind is that peripheral or marginal areas have changed over time and some of the later laggards were once at the cutting edge of development. But what is noticeable is that there have always been marginal areas or marginal countries, even though they may not always be the same ones throughout time. Why they persist is a difficult problem to explain. A classical view would suggest that there should be convergence as the marginal efficiency of factors declines in the core zones relative to the outlier areas and hence factors of production should flow accordingly to exploit the gains in the latter. However, in practice this does not happen since barriers arise to equalisation.

The concept of the core–periphery division within Europe is not simply a nineteenth-century phenomenon. As Pollard notes, there has always been a marginal Europe, but the players have changed hands over the centuries. Greece and Rome were the power points of civilisation in their heyday. England, Wales and Scotland, along with the Scandinavian countries and Hungary, were the peripheral lands in the period when the prosperous core was located in Italy, Flanders, the Rhineland and southern Germany (Pollard 1997, 10, 267). At what stage the 'golden triangle' of North-west Europe emerged as the key centre of economic activity is still open to debate. Many writers would argue that the European advances can be located well before the eighteenth century and that there is evidence to suggest that Western Europe at least was well in the lead before the industrial revolution. As already noted, Cipolla (1981, 300) felt that global history after 1500 could not be properly understood without taking into account the impact of European culture, economy and technology. Landes (1969, 13–14) believes that western Europe was already comparatively rich before the industrial revolution by comparison with other regions of the world and it was this that made it ready for the breakthrough into modern economic growth. This lead, he argues, was the product of centuries of slow accumulation and rise in incomes per head. McNeill (1963, 653; 1979, 376) traced the roots of European dominance back to the sixteenth century and maintained that by 1700 the wealth and power at Europe's command clearly surpassed anything that other civilised communities of the earth could muster. Snooks (1996, 258) is even more emphatic: 'By 1500 Europe had equalled, if not exceeded, the technological achievement of any former or contemporary civilisation.' Similarly, Jones (1981, 41, 183) argues that a decisive gap between Europe and Asia was emerging before modern industrialisation. There is, to be sure, a wealth of detail on Europe's burgeoning industrial and technological capabilities from 1600 onwards which lends support to the notion of Europe's rising pre-eminence (see Goodman and Honeyman 1988; Chirot 1985, 192–93).

Yet some doubts persist. In his recent and often controversial study of early modern Europe, Musgrave (1999, chs 5, 7) not only questions the primacy of Europe *vis-à-vis* Asia but also raises doubts about the conventional thinking regarding the leading position of North-west Europe. He argues that it was Europe, rather than Asia, that was underdeveloped in the early modern period, and that the Europeans came to Asia as marginal players and utilised the highly developed commercial structure already there. He also takes issue with the traditional notion that Western Europe, or rather Northern Europe in his North–South divide, was at the cutting edge of development. Until well into the eighteenth century Europe's industrial heartland was still located in the South, which looked nearer to an industrial revolution than the more backward North. The problem with this interpretation is how to explain why the roles were suddenly reversed. Musgrave's answer is that this transformation came about because of the series of heroic and risky gambles in technology which tipped the scales in the North's favour.

Musgrave's thesis would not apply to Eastern Europe, however. According to Good (1993, 1), the gap between East and West Europe has a long history and the polarisation between the two can be traced back to the early modern period when 'proto-industrialization sprouted in rural areas of Western Europe and the "second serfdom" took hold in Eastern Europe'. Chirot (1989a, 5), while reluctant to reject the dependency theory outright, argues that Eastern Europe was already seriously behind the West in 1500 or 1600 and that the Balkans, Poland and Hungary eventually became economic adjuncts of the West.

On the other hand, Bairoch's regional breakdown of incomes does not appear to indicate great disparities in income levels across the globe until after the middle of the eighteenth century or possibly later. It can be seen from Table 2.1 that in 1750 Western Europe had no commanding lead globally in terms of per capita income and that if anything it was North America which was in pole position. Nor does Eastern Europe seem to be trailing very far behind. The difference in income levels between Western and Eastern Europe was around 15 per cent and, though there are no separate figures for Southern Europe, it is possible that the difference was of even smaller magnitude. Spain in 1800 had an income per capita very close to the combined average of Britain and France (Tortella 1994, 2). Thereafter Western Europe forged ahead, along with North America. By 1830 Western Europe had an income per capita 38 per cent greater than that of Eastern Europe; this widened to 64 per cent in 1860 and to close on 80 per cent at the turn of the century, by which time Spain's per capita income had declined to just over half the British and French levels and Portugal's was less than a third (Tortella 1994, 2). The disparity between the richest and poorest countries was considerably larger. The four wealthiest countries (Britain, Switzerland, Denmark and Belgium) had an average income per capita three times greater than that of the four poorest European countries (Greece, Poland, Bulgaria and Serbia). Taking eight countries at both extremes narrows the gap somewhat, but the rich nations were still some two and a half times better off than the poorest. All the latter were located in Southern and Eastern Europe, whereas the wealthiest were in the north-west corner of the continent.

Table 2.1 Real GNP Per Capita for Different Regions (1960 US dollars)

	Western Europe	Eastern Europe	North America	Developed countries	Third World	World
1750	190	165	230	182	188	187
1800	215	177	239	198	188	191
1830	270	196	322	237	183	197
1860	379	231	536	324	174	220
1880	455	279	724	406	176	250
1900	588	328	1052	540	175	301
1913	693	412	1333	662	192	364
1928	784	426	1657	781	194	405
1938	868	566	1527	856	202	433

Source: Bairoch 1981, 7, 12.

The backwash of Western development

Whatever the exact timing of the global divide, there can be no doubt that by the latter half of the nineteenth century the countries of Southern and Eastern Europe were peripheral players as far as modern economic development is concerned. Not that peripheral Europe remained completely unaffected by developments in the West. As Berend (2003, 137) notes, 'The fringe of an unprecedented European prosperity carried the sleepy, stagnant, unindustrialized countries along.' Western influence came through many channels, via trade, imported capital, the influx of foreign workers and entrepreneurs, foreign technology, the construction of railways and the creation of Western-style institutions as, for example, in banking. In the later nineteenth century the underdeveloped countries of Europe tried to foster industrialisation by tariff protection and other forms of state assistance, especially in Hungary and the Balkans.

The process was a slow and erratic one, and it often led to lop-sided and sometimes inefficient development. Where Western enterprise and capital were directly involved it was often concentrated in the exploitation of minerals and raw materials for use in the investing nations' own markets. This was true of the pyrites and mining concerns in Spain, which became foreign enclaves of development with most of the cash benefits being drained off by the overseas operators, and perhaps even more so in the resource exploitation in the Balkan countries. The development of the Romanian oil industry was dominated by foreign companies, while 40 per cent of Western industrial investment in Serbia went into the extractive industries (Berend 2003, 157). Railway construction was also heavily dependent on outside capital and enterprise. However, much of the imported capital was indirect in the form of loans to state governments which were used for military purposes, to cover budgetary deficits and for building up the state apparatus, and only a small proportion found its way into what might be termed productive investments. As a result of official profligacy most of the Balkan countries were insolvent by the end of the nineteenth century.

Given the poverty of these countries modernisation was inevitably very dependent on Western assistance in one form or another, but this had the unfortunate effect of leading to unbalanced development either in the form of foreign dominated enclaves, especially in resource extraction, or in the shape of heavy dependence on specific sectors, notably agrarian, in order to serve Western markets. Thus Hungary and much of the Balkans became the granary of Europe in the latter half of the nineteenth century. However, cereal monoculture regions or countries heavily dependent on a handful of agricultural products were rendered very vulnerable to market changes. This was especially so in the case of cereals when American producers invaded Western Europe in the later nineteenth century. In this respect the Balkan countries were more vulnerable than either Hungary or Poland, the latter having a more diversified economic structure.

Table 2.2 Growth Rates of GDP Per Capita 1870–1910

Country	1870–1910
Austria	1.44
Czechoslovakia	1.59
Hungary	2.15
Poland	1.53
Portugal	0.30
Romania	1.85
Spain	1.37
Yugoslavia	1.74
Belgium	1.03
Denmark	1.55
France	1.09
Germany	1.63
Netherlands	0.90
Norway	1.11
Sweden	1.49
Switzerland	1.18
UK	1.00

Source: Good 1993, 24.

Within marginal Europe there was of course considerable divergence in economic performance and the extent of industrialisation. The degree of political subordination was not necessarily a good indicator of the rate of progress. While Balkan backwardness might reflect relics of Ottoman rule and influence even after independence was secured, the same excuse cannot be used for the Iberian Peninsula, that is, Spain and Portugal, which had once waxed high in the European firmament. Pollard (1981, 243) believes that both the Iberian and Balkan Peninsulas did not get beyond the beginnings of the industrialisation process except in very limited sectors and regions, and even then it was not internationally competitive. By contrast the Baltic countries did better industrially than their political master and became important industrial suppliers to the less developed Russian Empire. Poland too, despite its subordination to three countries, developed a worthwhile industrial base. Hungary, as part of the Dual Monarchy, also had a more diversified economic structure, though falling behind its more advanced partner.

In the decades before the First World War most of the peripheral countries probably kept pace with or, in some cases, exceeded the economic performance of the richer nations further west (see Table 2.2). It should be noted of course that they started from a very low base and also that estimates of domestic output expansion for this period do vary somewhat. But even so they still remained largely agrarian and raw material producing countries where islands of capitalism or industry floated on a sea of primitivism.

The low levels of income per capita by the end of the long nineteenth century tell their own story. They were only a fraction of those of the most advanced countries of the West, one half or less and possibly as low as 20 per cent in the case of Albania and Turkey. For those none too happy with the reliability of national income estimates for this period there are plenty of other indicators to illustrate the degree of backwardness. Data on levels of industrialisation, railway mileage and agricultural productivity confirm how far these countries lagged behind the West. Per capita levels of industrialisation (see Table 2.3) were a very small fraction of those of the UK, Belgium and Germany, and the same is true of the data on density of railway development (see Table 2.4). The most telling statistics are the very low levels of goods transported and journeys made per inhabitant compared with those in Western Europe.

Table 2.3 Per Capita Levels of Industrialisation (UK in 1900 = 100) (triennial averages, except 1913)

	1800	1830	1860	1880	1900	1913
Austria-Hungary	7	8	11	15	23	32
Bulgaria	5	5	5	6	8	10
Greece	5	5	6	7	9	10
Portugal	7	7	8	10	12	14
Romania	5	5	6	7	9	13
Russia	6	7	8	10	15	20
Serbia	5	5	6	7	9	12
Spain	7	8	11	14	19	22
Belgium	10	14	28	43	56	88
France	9	12	20	28	39	59
Germany	8	9	15	25	52	85
Netherlands	9	9	11	14	22	28
Sweden	8	9	15	24	41	67
Switzerland	10	16	26	39	67	87
UK	16	25	64	87	100	115
Australia	–	–	6	8	11	19
Canada	5	6	7	10	24	46
Japan	7	7	7	9	12	20
New Zealand	–	–	4	5	8	13
United States	9	14	21	38	69	126

Source: Bairoch 1991, 3.

Table 2.4 Railway Development circa 1911

	Land area per 1 km. of railway (in sq. kms)	Length of railway per 100,000 inhabitants (in kms)	Weight of goods transported per inhabitant (in 100,000 tons per annum)	No. of railway journeys per inhabitant per annum
Bulgaria	49.98	44.6	0.53	0.8
Greece	41.74	59.8	0.28	3.5
Hungary	15.73	110.0	3.00	5.6
Portugal	31.16	48.1	0.81	2.5
Romania	37.66	34.3	1.30	1.6
Serbia	51.21	32.6	0.26	0.3
Spain	34.14	74.2	1.46	2.5
Great Britain	9.70	71.3	8.18	21.9
Germany	8.72	95.5	9.50	25.3
France	13.20	103.7	3.09	12.6
Belgium	6.30	63.0	10.89	26.8
Switzerland	9.12	120.8	4.84	31.0
Sweden	32.32	252.5	6.89	10.9
Denmark	10.37	133.9	2.66	11.0
West Europe	10.14	90.2	8.18	21.9
South Europe	25.14	61.0	1.37	3.3
Central and East Europe	*20.49	50.4	1.59	1.7
Periphery total	*27.53	59.4	1.66	2.5

Note: * Excludes Russia.

Source: Berend and Ranki 1982, 100.

The why and wherefore of peripheral backwardness has been much debated in recent years and many explanations have been advanced to account for the lagging. In the light of Western development the most pertinent would seem to be the drag of the agrarian sector, the limited human resource development and the quality of statecraft and institutional constraints. To these issues we now turn.

The limiting role of agriculture

Since agriculture tends to bulk large in the economies of less developed or pre-industrial societies, it is generally acknowledged that it has a vital role to play in the process of modernisation (Reynolds 1985, 406; World Bank 1993, 109–10). While Western experience demonstrates the growing importance of the industrial sector, nevertheless without corresponding changes in agriculture the modernisation process could have been aborted. Agriculture fulfilled various functions, including acting as a source of labour and capital accumulation, earning foreign exchange through exports, providing food for an expanding population and supplying a growing market for industrial products. The last of these especially presupposes an improvement in the efficiency of agriculture and rising rural incomes.

Agriculture was not of course completely static in the peripheral areas of Europe during the nineteenth century. We know that primary commodities constituted a predominant share of exports and that export volumes were expanding. There are many examples of peripheral countries responding to Western demands – for example Hungarian wheat and flour, Romanian wheat, Greek currants, Serbian plums, Portuguese wine, and in raw materials and minerals, Baltic timber and Romanian oil, though in the case of Albania it is hard to find much unless we include tortoises! But generally speaking this type of development was extensive rather than intensive, utilising surplus land and resources and exploiting the peasantry, while backward linkages to the rest of the economy were limited since much of the processing of export products was carried out abroad.

In an important sense this pattern of agricultural development effectively led to a freezing of modes of production and landholding tenures: big estates, especially in Hungary, Poland and Spain, and a large mass of dependent peasantry working small plots, in some cases under conditions which can be termed neo-serfdom following emancipation.

Nor was the system conducive to rapid productivity growth. Palairet (1997, 361–62) reckons that in the Balkan provinces of Bulgaria, Serbia, Bosnia, Macedonia and Montenegro productivity in farming (output per capita) was declining from the later nineteenth century. The data in Tables 2.5 and 2.6 suggest that productivity growth fell short of that in Western countries over the long haul and that levels of productivity by 1910 were only a fraction of those in the advanced countries.

Agriculture at the periphery of Europe was not a dynamic sector. If anything it acted as a drag on economic development. In the Iberian Peninsula, for example, the agrarian sector has been seen as one of the main restraints to economic modernisation (Tortella 1994, 5–9), and the

Table 2.5 Indices of Agricultural Productivity (in millions of direct calories per male agricultural worker) 1830–1910

	1830	1860	1880	1900	1910
Austro-Hungary	5.0	6.2	8.6	10.3	11.9
Bulgaria	–	6.0	7.9	7.8	10.4
Greece	–	4.9	4.9	5.0	4.7
Portugal	–	4.1	3.5	3.5	3.7
Romania	–	6.7	8.0	11.3	13.9
Serbia	–	7.1	7.5	8.1	9.2
Spain	4.9	6.1	6.2	8.1	9.1
Belgium	8.1	10.9	13.8	18.1	21.3
Denmark	10.9	20.0	27.4	35.0	39.8
France	7.9	12.2	13.7	16.9	17.7
Germany	7.8	12.2	16.0	25.5	30.6
Netherlands	9.3	10.8	12.2	15.8	19.0
Sweden	6.0	8.4	10.3	12.2	15.3
Switzerland	6.4	9.0	10.7	12.7	13.9
UK	13.5	18.0	19.2	21.3	24.1
Australia	–	20.2	31.0	32.9	50.4
New Zealand	–	32.9	41.3	51.0	59.4
United States	20.8	26.1	35.0	40.7	47.0

Source: Bairoch 1991, 12.

same could be said for most of peripheral Europe. General poverty prevailed among the peasantry throughout the nineteenth century due to heavy taxation, antiquated tenure systems, lack of capital and know-how, and the force of tradition and custom (Warriner 1965, 6–7). There was no great structural transformation after emancipation and the formal removal of feudal restrictions. In fact many relics of feudalism persisted, including strip farming and traditional modes of production and behaviour. The production methods of many peasants in the South Slav lands, for example, were positively medieval and yields were very low; and with increasing population the man–land ratio deteriorated so that land hunger became a problem even before the interwar years (Tomasevich 1955, 211). Even in a country such as Hungary, which probably experienced more transformation in the agrarian sector than most countries in response to export markets for wheat and flour, old habits and the traditional way of life remained ingrained among the peasant classes for many years to come, which helped to perpetuate

Table 2.6 Annual Rate of Growth of Productivity in Agriculture 1830–1910

	1830–1860	1860–1910	1890–1910	1830–1910
Austro-Hungary	0.70	1.41	1.20	1.09
Bulgaria	–	1.67	0.23	*1.09
Greece	–	0.01	–0.29	*–0.11
Portugal	–	–0.50	0.15	*–0.24
Romania	0.21	1.60	1.27	1.00
Serbia	–	0.38	0.75	*0.53
Spain	0.70	0.23	1.72	0.78
Belgium	1.01	1.00	1.87	1.22
Denmark	2.05	1.40	1.36	1.63
France	1.46	0.57	0.99	1.01
Germany	1.52	1.37	2.56	1.73
Netherlands	0.51	0.75	1.72	0.90
Sweden	1.13	1.01	1.51	1.18
Switzerland	1.13	0.85	0.92	0.97
UK	0.96	0.43	0.81	0.72
Australia	–	2.36	1.09	*1.84
New Zealand	–	1.21	1.16	*1.19
United States	0.75	1.34	0.95	1.02

Note: * 1860–1910.

Source: Bairoch 1989, 331.

social rigidity, resistance to change and general backwardness. By the interwar years it was still possible to comment as follows:

> there was a feudal, or even pagan view of the world among the peasants, and a corresponding moral view, thus, a backwardness, centuries behind modern life and work techniques. There was animal-like identification with the home, with work; backward views on health care, apathy, lack of understanding of a new way of life ... There was only one matter on which all the peasants agreed; namely, they regarded the whole outside world, the world that surrounded and oppressed them for centuries, as hostile, alien, and one that could not be understood.
>
> (Quoted in Held 1980, 278).

Thus the problem in the peripheral countries was not so much that they were resource poor or that they were predominantly agrarian, since there were several countries – for example Canada, Australia, New Zealand and Denmark – which had grown rich on the basis of exploiting their primary assets. Rather, as Pollard (1998, 75) notes, it was the specific backwardness of agriculture and the 'poverty and underdeveloped resources in relation to the technology available at the time'. The limited extent of capitalist development meant that there were few opportunities outwith agriculture for the growing numbers on the land. Thus people were forced to remain on the land thereby accentuating the land–population problem, driving down yields to a point where marginal productivities were either very low or zero. This problem became even more acute in the interwar period when population growth rates accelerated and markets for agrarian produce deteriorated. Industrialisation then became a high priority.

Education and literacy

Though it is generally recognised that the relationship between education and economic growth is a complex and sometimes tenuous one, nevertheless it is also widely believed – and the historical evidence lends some support to this contention – that countries deficient in educational provision will face great difficulty in unlocking the door to modern economic growth (for a global review see Aldcroft 1998). This makes sense since the dissemination of new ideas and new ways of doing things, and the spread of new technology which underpins growth, depend to a large extent on whether the population has acquired the aptitudes, skills and motivation for the exploitation of modern techniques and new forms of organisation, or what Abramovitz (1989, 46–48) has termed 'social capability'. This capability cannot be achieved without a certain degree of literacy and formal education in society as a whole. More than that, the quality must be satisfactory; it should be secular and rationalistic as opposed to narrow and ritualistic, otherwise it will not produce the desired results (Abramovitz 1989, 25–26).

One noticeable feature of almost all past developed countries is that they had a relatively high rate of literacy or educational attainment at the start of modern economic growth, while there was a sustained effort to improve the human capital stock subsequently. This was certainly the case in North America, Western Europe, Japan and later the East Asian countries, and for the most part the type of educational provision was of the rational and secular variety. Several studies have noted the connection between education or literacy levels at a given point in time and the future course of per capita income. In a wide-ranging analysis, seeking to explain why the whole world was not developed, Easterlin (1981) argued that it was the spread of rational education that produced the motivational response among Western nations. Using primary school enrolments for a diverse range of countries, he presented a persuasive case for the importance of education as a modernising force. The spread of mass education of a secular and rationalistic type not only helped to foster attitudes and attributes conducive to the acquisition of new technology and improved methods of production, but also it heralded an important shift in political power away from feudal elites, together with a break in traditional values and cultures which allowed greater scope for the ambitions of a wider section of the population.

Sandberg (1982, 688) also explored the longer-term relationships between education and income using a wide sample of European countries. Literacy levels in 1850 were found to be 'an amazingly good predictor of *per capita* income in the 1970s'. Using adult literacy rates as a proxy for human resource stocks, he found that countries which were highly literate at the start of the period, even though poor, were generally the ones that eventually attained higher levels of per capita income. Conversely, the lower the initial per capita stock of human resources, the slower the rate of modernisation was likely to be, as in the case of Southern and Eastern Europe.

A more rigorous study by Barro (1991) covering 98 countries over the period 1960–85 tended to confirm these conclusions. He found that the real per capita growth rate was positively correlated with the initial stock of human capital (proxied by 1960 school enrolment ratios) and negatively related to initial (1960) levels of real GDP per capita. In other words, poor countries had the potential to catch up with richer nations providing they had initially high levels of human capital provision relative to their levels of per capita GDP, but not otherwise (Barro 1991, 437).

While some question marks are bound to remain on this issue, and especially regarding the proxy indicators used in the studies to measure educational input, the results do seem to indicate that early educational attainment is important for achieving modern economic growth. The reasoning is logical and confirms what we said earlier, that to exploit opportunities countries require an articulate and mobile labour force, with the ability to utilise new technology, and a ready supply of enterprising and acquisitive individuals, as well as 'a more rational and more receptive approach to life on the part of the population' (Cipolla 1969, 102). Without an improvement in the human resource stock these attributes are unlikely to emerge.

Returning to the European context we find that from as early as the mid-seventeenth century less than one half of the adult population of major Western European cities was still illiterate (Cipolla 1981, 76), though elsewhere in Europe the situation was far less promising. By the mid-nineteenth century virtually all the West European countries, as well as the Scandinavian, had adult literacy levels above 70 per cent. But in Eastern and Southern Europe literacy levels were below 50 per cent, and in many cases much less. In the case of Bosnia, for example, the literacy level was only about 12 per cent of the population by the early twentieth century (Berend 2003, 177). Significantly, the under-achievers in literacy and education include all peripheral countries covered in this volume, namely Spain, Portugal, Hungary, Romania, Yugoslavia, Greece, Bulgaria, Poland, Albania, Turkey and the Baltic states.

It was not only the quantity of education that was the problem in the more backward areas, for in many cases the quality too left much to be desired. A good illustration of this point is the case of Spain which, though it increased its educational provision during the nineteenth century, yet by 1900 well over half the population was still illiterate and modern economic growth was conspicuous by its absence. The main impediment here was that most educational provision was under the influence of the Roman Catholic Church, which laid much emphasis on the creed and the catechism to the neglect of secular instruction (Easterlin 1981, 10). Núñez (1990, 135), in demonstrating the adverse effects of educational provision in Spain, also shows that the ramifications of educational change can be very wide-ranging and one of its main contributions may be 'a better disposition towards change and social mobility in a very general sense'. The lack of good human capital development has been cited as one of the main constraints to economic modernisation in Spain. Similar strictures can be made about Portuguese educational provision (see Tortella 1994).

Thus we may safely conclude that an important factor in the economic lead of Western Europe was the head-start it achieved in educational provision. Peripheral Europe was seriously disadvantaged in this respect and its low literacy levels may be compared with those of African countries at the mid-twentieth century.

Government and institutions

Government and institutions, or what Hall and Jones (1999, 84) refer to as 'social infrastructure', have long been recognised as important attributes to the process of modern development. Though the link between politics and economics is a complex one, as Good recognised in reference to the Austro-Hungarian Empire, the rewards from untangling the relationship may be substantial: 'Once we unravel the link, we will understand better why the Empire disappeared in 1919 and why after 1750 some European countries grew rapidly, others more slowly, and still others hardly at all' (Good 1991, 239).

Western development experience might have been very different had political and institutional systems not been adapted to the needs of a modern society. For example, in order that economic enterprise may flourish it is essential that institutional and legal frameworks protect individual property rights, enforce contracts, minimise the costs of economic transactions and facilitate resource flows. In addition, social institutions should be such that they protect citizens from excessive diversion of the product of their labour, either by the state itself or by private agents, through thievery, protection rackets, taxation or state extraction. Now while circumstances of poverty, stagnation and unruly conditions may call for greater state intervention to provide a milieu conducive to economic enterprise and individual initiative, there is always the danger that governments and institutions may fall into the wrong hands – that is, into the clutches of corrupt elite groups whose main aim is to divert public funds for their own benefit – in which case poverty and backwardness will continue to prevail (see Janos 1989, 327). Such situations have been described as 'negative sovereignty', where states exist in name only and institutions and bureaucracies are inefficient and corrupt and often unstable. The antithesis, 'positive sovereignty', is more likely to flourish under pluralistic, democratic regimes, producing a social infrastructure more conducive to economic development (Jackson 1990, 1–21).

Many examples can be quoted from history where states and institutions have been inimical to economic progress. In much of Eurasia state structures and institutions changed little and remained basically feudal and repressive. The great dynasties of India, China and the Ottoman Empire were little more than military despotisms bent on preserving their power by extracting tribute from impoverished subjects who were condemned to little more than subsistence. Little encouragement was given to individual initiative since this would have undermined the basis of feudal power. The overhead costs of the upkeep of the army, the central government and a parasitic aristocratic elite were heavy and tended to weaken the strength of these empires in much the same way as had occurred in the later Roman Empire (Kahn 1979, 30–31).

Nearer home, the conditions in medieval Europe were not much more auspicious for economic progress under the fragmented control of individual rulers. Pillage, plunder and exaction were the meat of everyday life. Fortunately Europe escaped the clutches of monolithic dynastic rulers and in time a system of nation states emerged which provided an environment more conducive to modern enterprise and personal endeavour as graft, corruption, thievery and confiscatory taxation were reduced to a minimum, while the legal framework sanctified economic and commercial transactions. The process took many centuries to complete and much of Eastern Europe and the rest of the world still laboured under negative sovereignty reminiscent of the Dark Ages in Europe and the East.

Indeed, in many parts of peripheral Europe governments and administrations closely resembled those in post-colonial African countries of the latter half of the twentieth century. Exploitation, bribery, corruption, thievery and thuggery, vestiges of feudalism, and traditional modes of behaviour and thought were rife throughout the Balkans including Greece and Albania, Turkey, and the Iberian countries and were by no means absent elsewhere, and they lingered on well into the twentieth century (Fischer-Galati 1970; Crampton 1987). The worst examples of degenerate government probably occurred in the Balkans and this was true even after independence had been gained. Corrupt and despotic rulers continued to impose heavy taxes on their subjects, and in the process the state drew more human and fiscal resources away from productive investment than it itself contributed, except for those wasted on forms of 'symbolic modernisation' (Berend and Ranki 1982, 69–71). Following emancipation in Romania, 'excessive exploitation of the peasantry continued unabated and, indeed, probably increased after the emancipation there' (Blum 1978, 438). The same was true in the South Slav lands (Tomasevich 1955, 213). The case of Bulgaria provides an object lesson in public corruption, bribery, financial scandals and exploitation. Liberation from the clutches of the Turks did little to improve the lot of the peasants who constituted around 80 per cent of the population. They were seen mainly as a source of revenue to meet the rapid growth of state expenditure arising mainly from debt servicing, the armed forces, an overblown bureaucracy and ostentatious public works. A large part of the money raised through foreign loans was used for such purposes. While the peasants bore the burden, they received little in return, since the small part of state spending that was devoted to 'modernisation' was 'of a decorative rather than self-sustaining variety', much of it concentrated in the urban areas, especially Sofia, in the form of parks, public buildings, museums, trams and electric lighting to which the peasants had little access. To compound their misery many peasants were the victims of unscrupulous usurers and were forced to pay astronomical rates of interest in some cases (Bell 1977, 8–16).

That the states and institutions of peripheral countries were captured by corrupt and self-seeking elites can be explained in part by the role of the middle classes. Whereas in Western Europe the rising middle classes sought outlets for their energies in mercantile and industrial pursuits and even in agricultural improvement, as did the frustrated samurai in Japan, in the peripheral states there were fewer opportunities for the dispossessed middle and better educated strata of society to exercise their talents. In any case many of them despised the market place and so sought refuge in politics and public office rather than in economic activities (see Janos 1989, 336).

Public sector employment provided an escape route from the vagaries of the market and also gave the elites secure and reasonably lucrative occupations in which they could match the standards of their contemporaries in Western Europe. Like their later counterparts in Africa, they built bureaucracies, armies, public buildings and showplaces in imitation of the West but without the resource base to support them (Chirot 1989b, 10–11). As a consequence public employment expanded rapidly in many peripheral countries, often exceeding 5 per cent of the labour force compared with 2.4 per cent in Germany and 1.5 per cent in England, and absorbing some 25–40 per cent of state budgets (Janos 1989, 338).

However, it was not so much the size of the cohorts in administration that created problems but the fact that they managed to dispense state resources liberally and in directions that did little to boost economic development. Apart from the large amount consumed by official salaries, the other main heads of budgetary expenditure were spent on the armed forces, ostentatious and show projects and, later, debt servicing. Only about one fifth of the money raised through loans on behalf of Balkan governments found its way into productive activities (Lampe 1989, 200–201). Faced with rising expenditure and a limited and inefficient tax base resort was had to foreign borrowing, but at a price. External debt rose rapidly from the 1870s, the largest debtors – in descending order of magnitude on a per capita basis – being Portugal, Spain, Italy, Greece, Romania, Serbia and Russia. The servicing of these debts absorbed from between 20 and 35 per cent of budgetary revenue by the turn of the century and several countries were by this time insolvent. When new foreign loans to service past debt became increasingly difficult to negotiate, the authorities turned their attention to milking the indigent population. The situation has been described as follows:

> In Eastern Europe, as well as in Iberia, tax collection drives sometimes took the form of military campaigns, in the course of which troops would occupy entire villages, search the houses of delinquent taxpayers, and proceed to remove anything of value. Even short of such methods, revenue raising remained brutal business that generally relied on arbitrary assessments or levies on such staples as salt, kerosene, liquor, and tobacco ...
>
> (Janos 1989, 340)

In essence the system involved income transfer from the poor to the richer members of society so that the elites could have the means to ape the life-style of their counterparts in the West, just as post-colonial leaders in Africa have been doing for the last half century. Janos describes the process as follows:

> the peripheral state became a grand instrument of income equalization, not, to be sure, among the various economic strata of peripheral societies, but between the elites of the backward and the advanced industrial societies of the Continent.
>
> (Janos 1989, 341–42)

Since the system aroused considerable discontent it could only be kept going by bribery, corruption, repression and the degeneration of parliamentary systems, that is, by ensuring sympathetic candidates were elected. In Spain, Portugal, Hungary and the Balkans political and electoral fraud became commonplace. So too did repression, since the heavy burdens placed on the agrarian proletariat inevitably led to an alienated and rebellious peasantry in much of peripheral Europe. In fact from the 1890s 'the frustrations of the peasantry kept the societies of the European periphery in a virtual state of civil war' (Janos 1989, 345), which moved governments to devise new instruments of coercion in an attempt to preserve the traditional power structure. The challenge was such that:

> All over the European South and East, the countryside was turned into an armed camp, as governments organised special forces of rural gendarmes that, with their military uniforms, equipment, and tactics, were not so much conventional constabularies as armies of occupation within their own nations.
>
> (Janos 1989, 347)

which Janos argues led to stagnation or decline in agrarian production throughout much of peripheral Europe.

The consequences of such strategies came home to roost in time. They did little to solve the budgetary problems or to transform peasant agriculture, but instead the burdens of the peasantry increased and rural living standards stagnated or declined. Social unrest and nationalistic tensions inevitably followed. While attempts at modernisation were made from time to time, as in the laws to encourage industry, it was very difficult to graft modern capitalism on to an alien landscape. As in the case of the South Slav lands, capitalism could never come to full fruition because it

> was not an economic system which grew out of the internal structure of the economy, but rather, it was an appendage of Central and Western European capitalism and it was introduced into the South Slav lands primarily by foreigners. Whether its representatives were foreigners or nationals, capitalism in the South Slav areas remained essentially rapacious and exploitative rather than creative, a corrupting crust rather than a well-developed economic system.
>
> (Tomasevich 1955, 213)

Thus states and institutions in peripheral Europe had much in common with those in present-day African countries. Where governments and officials cannot be trusted, where bribery and corruption are endemic, and where legal frameworks cannot secure property rights and commercial agreements, then transaction costs will be high and this will discourage enterprise and development. After all, when the risk and reward patterns so clearly favour the politically astute and those with the right connections at the expense of individuals of enterprise and initiative, who in their right mind would risk their assets (Landes 1990, 10; Batou 1990, 465)?

There is little doubt that in virtually all the peripheral countries, apart perhaps from Albania, there were some signs of development and change throughout the long nineteenth century. There are many examples of progress in agriculture and the seeds of modern industrialisation. Several peripheral economies were also growing at a respectable rate, even if at times erratically. Yet when all is said and done, much of the change was of a marginal type and by 1914 all of the peripheral countries could be classed as underdeveloped. Agrarian employment was still dominant and structural change had made very little impact on them. Referring to the eastern and southern provinces of the Austro-Hungarian Empire and the Balkans Berend (2003, 180) writes: 'The phase of modern structural changes remained a distant goal in the overwhelmingly agricultural and raw materials-producing countries. Despite its economic progress and advances, the region humiliatingly failed to modernize.' Lampe (1989, 202) came to a rather similar conclusion with regard to the Balkan region: 'The sweeping structural changes that turn growth into development would not appear in the Balkans until after the Second World War.' As we shall see, well before then there were to be dramatic shifts in the peripheral landscape as a consequence of the changes wrought by the First World War.

CHAPTER THREE

Peripheral Europe in the Interwar Setting

The Great War marked a turning point in the history of Europe – one might say it marked the end of an era. Europe's power and influence in the global arena waned visibly in the ensuing decades as political and economic forces worked against it. The map of Europe was transformed following the postwar peace settlement. The great empires which had once manipulated the European power system were gone. In their place emerged several weakened national powers and a motley collection of new or reconstituted states, mostly small, backward and weak, which struggled, in a hostile economic climate and against the political machinations of the larger nations, to retain their independent identity. These were the countries which constituted peripheral Europe.

New states for old

It was probably only a matter of time before the old order of prewar Europe was undermined because of national rivalries, nationalism and greater participation in government. Apart from Germany, the older empires were rotten from within and were crumbling visibly before 1914. The Ottoman Empire was at its last gasp in Europe; it had steadily lost territory during the nineteenth century and, following the destructive Balkan Wars of 1912–13, when Serbia, Greece and Albania had made substantial gains at its expense, it was left with only a toehold on the mainland. The same wars signalled the virtual end of the Austro-Hungarian Monarchy as a great power, long the 'sick man of Europe'. Despite its creditable economic performance it was surrounded by virulent nationalist forces on all frontiers which it had been powerless to accommodate within its imperial structure. Revolutionary forces and social ferment in Russia were also having a similar disintegrating effect on the Romanov Empire. Thus, even without a general war, it seems very likely that much of the imperial control of Europe would still have crumbled in short order (Overy 1994, 7–8; Taylor 1948, 228–29).

The war in effect completed the process of imperial disintegration. As most of the European empires faded away (Austro-Hungarian,

Romanov, Turkish and German),[1] many lively and independent states emerged from the ruins. Even before the formal peacemaking exercise got under way, aspiring contenders were laying claims to former imperial territories and many of these were later confirmed by the peacemakers in the treaties concluded with the ex-enemy powers.[2]

The result was the largest redrawing of the map of Europe ever to take place. Most countries were affected in one way or another except for the neutrals. Apart from Spain and Portugal all the peripheral nations considered in this volume gained or lost something. The Baltic states secured their release from Russian control while Albania's prewar independence was confirmed, but only just, much to the chagrin of Italy and Greece. The ex-enemy powers were cut down to size so that, for example, both parts of the Dual Monarchy – Austria and Hungary – became shadows of their former selves. Turkey managed to retain a toehold in Europe and Bulgaria's frontiers of 1914 were more or less confirmed which meant that she sacrificed most of the gains made in the First Balkan War. Poland was resurrected as a united and independent national state from the component parts which had been under German, Austrian and Russian control since the partitions of the later eighteenth century. Serbia, along with Croatia, Slovenia, Bosnia and Herzegovina, Montenegro and one or two other bits and pieces, formed the new Kingdom of the Serbs, Croats and Slovenes, mercifully shortened to the more manageable title of Yugoslavia in 1929. The most spectacular beneficiary was Romania, which was rewarded somewhat lavishly for being an unreliable ally of the Western allies, by gaining large tracts of territory at the expense of Russia, Hungary and Bulgaria. As a result the size of the country more than doubled in terms of both area and population. Greece, which had joined the Allied side late in the conflict, was also another significant gainer, though falling short of its original aspirations. She secured western Thrace from Bulgaria and was allowed to occupy Smyrna (Izmir), from which Greek forces subsequently moved inland in an effort to thwart the ambitions of the resurgent Turkish nationalists (Kemalists). This resulted in the disastrous Asia Minor campaign.[3]

---

1 The British and French empires were left standing as victors but their fulcrum point lay beyond Europe.

2 The main one was of course the Treaty of Versailles concluded with Germany on 28 June 1919. Most of the new territorial arrangements were mapped out at the Paris Peace Conference in the first half of 1919. Subsequently treaties were concluded with Austria (St Germain 10 September 1919), Bulgaria (Neuilly 27 November 1919), Hungary (Trianon 4 June 1920) and Turkey (Sèvres 10 August 1920, superseded in 1923 by the Treaty of Lausanne).

3 In actual fact both western and eastern Thrace (the latter from Turkey) were initially awarded to Greece and handed over to her in 1920, following the signing of the Treaty of Sèvres (10 August 1920) which the Turks refused to ratify formally. Prior to this

The peacemaking exercise has not generally been regarded as a success story. From Keynes's attacks onwards it has received a bad press and there have been only a few apologists. It did have many faults and it probably raised more problems than it solved. However, in all fairness one has to bear in mind that the hands of the peacemakers were to some extent tied not only by the fact that aspiring nations had already laid claims and occupied territories before the peacemakers had begun their task, but also by the fact that they were inundated by demands from nearly every country for special treatment and it was a case of juggling these claims in the attempt to satisfy all alike. 'All that the Conference could do was to register accomplished facts and delimit the frontiers of the new states, and even in this task its hands were far from free' (Cobban 1944, 15). If possible the peacemakers were inclined to reward or punish states according to whether or not they had supported the winning side. In the end no one was satisfied with the final outcome. Nor did it help matters either that the chief negotiators, Woodrow Wilson and Lloyd George, leaders of the United States and Great Britain respectively, had only a hazy notion of the geographic configuration of some parts of Europe.

The new geographical configuration of Europe resulted in the creation of a multitude of small and weak states and left many national minorities under alien rule. Though the peace settlement reduced minority status compared with before the war around one third of the inhabitants of East European successor states were left stateless in the sense that they constituted national minorities. In the case of Hungary nearly a third of its citizens were located outwith its borders. The fact that nations were defined largely in ethnic terms served to heighten national perceptions of ethnic perfection, giving rise to demands for ridding nations of 'alien' elements, who had once lived and worked fairly peacefully together, and fostering claims for the reconciliation of expatriates. 'Ethnic nationalism was to become an important force in fascist movements in these countries' (Bideleux and Jeffries 1998, 491).

Greece had been encouraged by the Allies to occupy the prized port of Smyrna on the coast of Asia Minor, which she did in May 1919. Subsequently, in order to consolidate claims on Turkish territory, Greek forces, with the approval of Lloyd George, moved inland into Asia Minor (June 1920) towards Turkish nationalist forces which had been grouping under the leadership of Atatürk in the interior. By August 1920 they had penetrated some 250 miles inland up to the edge of the Anatolian plateau. A further advance towards Ankara, the headquarters of the Turkish forces, proved too much for the Greeks. They were soundly trounced in a Turkish counter-attack, and Turkish troops then moved on to Smyrna and ransacked the Greek quarters. An armistice was concluded in October 1922 which allowed Turkey to regain eastern Thrace and retain Constantinople and Smyrna, subsequently confirmed under the terms of the Treaty of Lausanne in 1923, which more or less overturned the provisions of the Treaty of Sèvres which had favoured Greek claims.

Ethnic rivalry and rightward political forces were grist to Germany's ambition to extend its influence in Europe. The political vacuum created in Central/East Europe provided an ideal opportunity for a determined predator since the new and reconstituted states were 'extremely weak reeds to place in the path of Germany, and they possessed few features that would lead to any hope of their being anything but satellites ... of Germany, Hitler or no Hitler'. The battle for control of the region enjoined France and Germany almost from the first moment of peace, with Germany's claims fortified by her ignominious treatment at the peace table. But that is part of another story (Newman 1968, 27, 58, 105, 201).

Reconstruction issues

Perhaps the most pertinent criticism of the peacemaking arrangements was the lack of a solid postwar relief plan for Europe. Keynes, in his vitriolic denunciation of the peace settlement, noted with dismay that no provision had been made for the reconstruction and rehabilitation of stricken Europe (Keynes 1919, 211). Once the peacemakers had redrawn the boundaries and punished the vanquished, they concluded their deliberations in the belief that Europe could look after itself. But there was scant prospect of that. By the end of hostilities much of Europe was literally destitute. There were severe shortages of almost everything, food, raw materials and equipment, and also a lack of hard currency to purchase supplies from the United States. Economic activity and trade had sunk to very low levels: in 1919, for example, industrial production on average was running at about half prewar levels and agricultural output was down by roughly one third (League of Nations 1943a, 46). Many parts of Europe were desperately in need of external assistance for the immediate task of dealing with starving populations, let alone addressing the longer-term issue of starting on the process of reconstructing devastated areas. The League of Nations, in one of its later reports, captured the plight of Europe as follows:

> All countries in Europe were suffering from a lack of working capital and from a loss through wear and tear or physical destruction of fixed capital ... stocks (of food, raw materials and manufactured goods) had been exhausted during the war ... Durable consumers' goods were likewise largely worn out, destroyed or in need of repair. Housebuilding and repair in particular had been practically at a standstill during the war, and in the war zones whole towns and villages had been devastated ... much of the machinery had not been replaced and in certain areas machinery had been deliberately destroyed by retreating armies ... The mechanism of transportation

> was particularly affected. Railway rolling stock was in a deplorable condition all over Central and Eastern Europe ... The state of roadbeds was often inadequate for rapid traffic, and many bridges were in a dangerous state.
>
> (League of Nations 1943b, 7–9)

The scale of the operation is difficult to comprehend fully since the ramifications of four years of hostilities had been so far-reaching. It was not simply a matter of making good physical losses and restoring former levels of output. The war had affected every conceivable aspect of economic and social life in every European country – even the neutrals, though obviously to a much lesser extent. Apart from the setback to economic activity, physical devastation was fairly widespread, population losses were severe, former markets had been lost, government finances and currencies were in disarray, and transport systems were in a chaotic state. Added to this there were the tasks of assimilating the new territorial arrangements, setting up constitutions, and unifying economic, legal and administrative systems. All this at a time when resources were very short, people were starving, social and revolutionary ferment was widespread, and border conflicts over territory and populations were common.

The peripheral countries, apart from Spain and Portugal, were in a far worse position than the major powers. The Baltic states had lost their main market and were engaged in disputes with Germany and the Soviet Union. Greece was in confrontation with Turkey, while Albania was fearful of losing its independence. Hungary was trying to get to grips with a much reduced size whereas for Romania the reverse situation was the case. For Poland and Yugoslavia, the two most severely devastated countries, there was the task of welding together disparate economic systems. Eastern Europe as a whole was in a very bad way, and at the close of the war its economic and social system was on the point of collapse (Rothschild 1974, 16).

Clearly there was an urgent need for outside relief. In the immediate postwar period some assistance was made available to stricken Europe by the allied powers, mainly from American sources. From the Armistice in November 1918 until the summer of the following year a relief programme was organised under the auspices of the Supreme Economic Council, with the bulk of the supplies coming from the United States. Most of the relief consisted of food provision together with a small amount of clothing, and 20 European countries were recipients of supplies, largely on a credit basis, though ex-enemy countries were expected to pay in cash. The official relief programme was short-lived, however, being terminated in August 1919. Thereafter relief activities were mainly confined to private and semi-official bodies which dispensed small amounts of aid, again mainly in the form of foodstuffs (League of Nations 1943b, 34; 1943c, 12).

Needless to say the aid programme was totally inadequate and it pales into insignificance with that organised after the Second World War. Though most of the relief was in the form of food, hunger and poverty remained acute throughout much of Europe in the early postwar years. Estimates suggest that American food supplies were sufficient to feed every child in Central and Eastern Europe for one month only. There was virtually no provision for providing Europe with raw materials and equipment which were needed to restore supply capability, let alone assistance for rebuilding damaged infrastructures. Both the United States and Britain recognised that something needed to be done if European countries were to recover, but little further action was forthcoming.

The absence of sustained aid meant that countries were forced to seek their own salvation. To obtain supplies of commodities they could draw on their meagre currency reserves or negotiate private credits. Unfortunately both of these solutions were limited, the latter drying up after 1920. The position was exacerbated by the postwar boom in commodity prices caused by the global scramble for raw materials and food, which meant that much of continental Europe was 'starved of primary products' (League of Nations 1946a, 71). Many countries, especially in Central and Eastern Europe, were importing in 1919 and 1920 at levels of about one third those of prewar times, with negligible volumes of raw materials and equipment (League of Nations 1943b, 19; Orde 1990, 111).

In desperation governments were forced into more extreme measures in order to cope with relief and reconstruction and to ease the pressure of political and social disorders. Most countries retained their wartime trade controls, ran budgetary deficits, and allowed currencies to depreciate and inflation to take its course. Such strategies did provide some temporary if cosmetic relief and sometimes imparted an artificial stimulus to economic activity and employment. But the consequences could be disastrous. Poland and Hungary, along with Germany and Austria, suffered the ravages of hyperinflation; their currencies became valueless and had to be replaced by new units of account. What they gained in the inflationary period they lost in the stabilisation phase when real incomes, employment and economic activity in general were checked. In effect the process of reconstruction had virtually to begin again.

Most of the peripheral countries experienced bouts of inflation and currency depreciation on a more modest level and it was often some time before financial stability could be achieved. The details of stabilisation dates and levels are listed in Table 3.1. It took nearly a decade before the process was complete, by which time the postwar gold exchange standard was on the point of disintegration. Restoration values were but a mere fraction of prewar levels. Only Spain and Turkey remained on floating exchange rate regimes throughout the 1920s.

Table 3.1 Dates and Levels at which Currencies Stabilised after 1918

Country	Date of stabilisation[1]	Percentage of prewar rate
Albania[2]	–	–
Bulgaria	1924 (1928)	3.7
Estonia	1924 (1927)	1.1
Greece	1928	6.7
Hungary	1924	new currency
Latvia	1921	0.8
Lithuania	1922	–
Poland	1926 (1927)[3]	new currency
Portugal	1929 (1931)	4.6
Romania	1927 (1929)	3.0
Spain	floating rate	–
Turkey	floating rate	–
Yugoslavia	1925 (1931)	9.1

Notes:
[1] Dates of *de jure* stabilisation where different from those of *de facto* stabilisation are shown in brackets.
[2] Albania was the only European country which remained effectively on the gold standard throughout the war and postwar period. Foreign gold coins, foreign silver coins and bank notes were used as a mean of payment until a national currency was introduced for the first time in the later 1920s.
[3] Poland initially stabilised the gold value of its currency in 1924 but was forced to abandon it the following year.

Source: League of Nations 1946a, 92–93.

The failure to organise an adequate programme of relief for Europe undoubtedly delayed its recovery. While some advance on the very low levels of activity recorded shortly after the war was inevitable, by 1920 many countries fell well short of their peacetime levels of output in both industry and agriculture. Even by 1925 economic activity in Eastern Europe was still not fully restored to prewar levels (League of Nations 1943b, 12).

The longer-term consequences of delayed recovery and financial reconstruction are worth noting. When conditions did become more stable several countries were forced to rely heavily on capital imports which left them in a vulnerable position when commodity prices collapsed in the early 1930s (see below). Secondly, the failure of the allied powers to alleviate conditions in Europe in the early postwar years did little to further the cause of parliamentary democracy. Many citizens became disenchanted with pluralistic government, especially those who had lost savings in the turmoil of inflation. Denise Artaud (1973, 16) argues that financial reconstruction was at the root of the problem and the delay in bridging what was essentially a dollar gap in the transitional period proved fatal. Ruth Henig (1995, 39–40) goes further and suggests that the failure of the US authorities to assist in the regeneration of Europe with liberal credit facilities was an important element in the absence of lasting peace on the continent.

Fragile stability

Conditions were somewhat more propitious for sustained development in the latter half of the 1920s. By the middle of the decade political and economic conditions were more stable than in the early postwar years. The evacuation of the Ruhr in 1923 and the revised reparations settlement with Germany in the following year, the negotiated agreements on inter-allied war debts, and the signing of the Locarno Pact in 1925 (between Britain, France, Germany and Italy), which guaranteed the existing Franco-German border, all helped to raise international confidence and reduce political tensions and suspicions of future conflict. There were also improvements on the economic front. Most of the great inflations had run their course and financial reconstruction and currency stabilisation had made steady progress. The return of Britain and the Dominions to the gold standard in 1925 strengthened the international monetary system. Primary commodity prices were also much firmer following the sharp setback after the postwar boom. Though reconstruction and recovery were not fully complete in all countries, progress had been such that there was now the prospect that 'real progress [could] take the place of a painful struggle to regain a plateau of prosperity which had been lost ...' (Loveday 1931, 47). Currency, debt and financial issues, though by no means fully resolved, ceased to dominate the international economic scene as they had done in the first half of the decade.

Accordingly, there was a strong advance in economic activity worldwide in the years 1925–29, which in absolute terms was equivalent to that in the decade through to 1925. World industrial production and the volume of international trade advanced by some 20–21 per cent, an annual compound growth of around 5 per cent a year, which was quite impressive by historical standards. Total primary output rose by over 10 per cent, that is, 2.6 per cent per annum or nearly double the rate between 1913 and 1925, the pace being set by raw materials production, which rose by 21 per cent whereas food production only advanced by 6 per cent.

Europe shared equally in this expansion and if anything agricultural Europe, more or less synonymous with the periphery,[4] probably did slightly better than the average and certainly matched the performance of the industrial West. Industrial or manufacturing production in agricultural Europe rose by over 22 per cent between 1925 and 1929 and the output of primary products was better than the world average (Loveday 1931, 49). Most countries, apart from Poland, were able to surpass their prewar levels of output by the end of the decade.

Despite the progress in the peripheral countries there was no great structural transformation of their economies, which remained backward and economically vulnerable. By Western standards both agriculture and industry were highly inefficient, and the policies employed to encourage industrialisation tended to foster inefficiency and high cost enterprises. Moreover, agricultural Europe remained very sensitive to events in the international economy because of its heavy dependence on the exports of primary products at favourable prices, and for some countries their increasing dependence on foreign capital. The economies of agricultural Europe were thus based on rather shaky foundations.

Though there were some impressive gains in manufacturing production in the later 1920s, these were from a very low base, so that the industrial sector was still a very limited source of employment. Industrial development was encouraged by a range of state inducements including subsidies, tax reliefs, import controls, high tariffs and export bounties. The strategy towards greater self-sufficiency through import substitution was accompanied by the extension of state enterprise and, in some cases, the takeover of foreign assets (nostrification).

The policy of import substitution and greater self-sufficiency, which became even more pronounced in the following decade, was not an unqualified success. It was soundly criticised by Pollard (1981, 289) on the grounds that it inevitably led to 'high-cost, inefficient, technically backward industries pushing inferior goods which could survive only by constant protection and official support and therefore generated massive corruption', and which 'placed an intolerable burden on the peasantry and on the state budget alike, and removed what little chance there had been of success as specialist primary producers'. Such strictures may appear somewhat harsh in view of the pressing need to transform

[4] The term 'agricultural Europe' is usually taken to refer to the following countries: Bulgaria, Estonia, Finland, Greece, Hungary, Italy, Latvia, Lithuania, Poland, Portugal, Romania, Spain and Yugoslavia.

agrarian economies but they are not without some substance. It has also been suggested that scarce resources were squandered on projects of dubious quality, including arms production, building works and transportation facilities, some of which were designed for prestige purposes, which in turn placed a heavy burden on agriculture in the form of taxation with the result that the agrarian sector was starved of resources to improve its performance (Hertz 1947, 102–103).

Industrial progress did not lead to any great structural transformation of the economies in question. Even within the industrial sector itself much of the development was concentrated on branches such as textiles, clothing and food processing, rather than on newer growth sectors. Nor was there much evidence that industry kept pace with modern technical changes and new methods of production. In fact, with one or two exceptions, industry was scarcely affected by Western developments in business organisation, new methods of production and factory layout and management, mechanisation and mass production, or in the use of new forms of energy such as electricity. Even in the case of larger-scale enterprises the techniques of production and level of efficiency were well behind those of Western counterparts. In fact the limited nature of domestic markets and the difficulty of securing export orders often forced large firms to adopt measures that were technically and organisationally outdated. In the case of the Hungarian iron and steel and heavy engineering sectors, for example, they have been described as not much better than 'general stores' whose plants produced many varied items in small batches (Berend and Ranki 1974a, 238–40; 1974b, 134–42). The dual nature of the production process was very noticeable, with many small workshops or manufactories catering for the domestic market, alongside a few large concerns of indifferent quality with a very limited ability to compete in the international market.

Despite the creditable performance of the international economy during the later 1920s, the structures of prosperity were not based on very secure foundations. Marks (1976, 108) describes the era as 'a period of surface harmony and apparent economic prosperity', while in Beyen's (1951, 3) words these were 'years of hope and vigour', which 'ended in despair'. There were certainly signs of underlying weaknesses within particular economies and the same may be said for the working of the international economy, especially the monetary system. Such shortcomings as there were became all too apparent once the basis of prosperity was undermined with the collapse of international lending and the downturn of the American economy at the end of the decade.

The peripheral countries were especially vulnerable to shocks in the international economy since sustained prosperity in the global economy was essential if they were to break out of their structural bottlenecks. They were dependent above all on a favourable market for primary commodities, especially agrarian, trade expansion and the development of new markets, and the availability of foreign capital.

The problem in agriculture

Agriculture was clearly the main problem area and not simply because of price factors. Since it was still such a large component in most peripheral countries the state of prosperity was inevitably bound up with this sector. Unfortunately it did not play a dynamic role in most of these economies. Output expansion was slow and productivity levels for many crops remained below those of prewar times (Berend 1985, 168–70).

The main problem in agriculture was the need for structural reform to raise levels of efficiency. Diversification of the product base was one solution and there were signs of this taking place in the Baltic countries and even in parts of the Balkans. But it was a slow process and at the end of the decade there was still a long way to go before agriculture could match the standards of Western countries. There were so many obstacles to surmount. A combination of peasant self-sufficiency, small holdings, overpopulation on the land, primitive techniques, lack of capital and education, and heavy indebtedness inevitably made for inefficiency. Such problems defied easy solutions in an environment hostile to peasant interests, for example high taxation, and one in which the peasantry itself was opposed to radical change (Rothschild 1974, 331; Fischer-Galati 1970, 40). Land reforms carried out in the postwar years may have intensified some of the problems in so far as they resulted in greater fragmentation of holdings and solidified an already very traditional and conservative peasantry.

The structure and methods of agriculture thus remained remarkably static except on larger estates. Methods of cultivation were traditional, with strip farming still common and often a lack of even the most basic implements. In some cases the relative backwardness of agriculture *vis-à-vis* that in Western countries may actually have increased during the 1920s (Berend and Ranki 1974b, 123–32).

It is therefore not surprising that the agrarian sector could not act as a catalyst for the rest of the economy. It was of little help in terms of capital accumulation and very limited as a market for industrial goods, while its foreign exchange earning capacity was highly erratic and very vulnerable to the vagaries of the international market (see below). In fact as far as capital accumulation is concerned the agrarian sector probably acted as a drag on the rest of the economy because of its own heavy indebtedness. As Moore explains:

> The widespread prevalence of high indebtedness relative to assets and income indicates not only that self-capitalization in agriculture is low, but also that far from accumulating capital the peasant is frequently in the position of steadily depleting his resources and of borrowing to postpone the time of complete insolvency. In fact, whether the capital depletion takes the form of soil exhaustion and obsolescence of equipment or the form of growing indebtedness, it is clear that the process may be a spiral escaped only by capital originating outside of the agricultural organization.
>
> (Moore 1945, 97)

Thus, notwithstanding its absolute importance in the economies of peripheral Europe, agriculture made little if any contribution to the transformation of their economies. Indeed, the opposite may well have been the case, at least in East European countries, as Berend observes:

> Whereas agriculture had been the prime mover of economic dynamism from the sixties to the eighties of the previous century, it became the most vulnerable point in the economy, the main constraint on the growth and the socio-economic transformation which were so crucially needed.
>
> (Berend 1985, 209)

As noted earlier, the dominating factor in the prosperity of the peripheral countries was the state of agriculture and in turn this sector was the main determinant of their trade potential. Agricultural commodities, along with raw materials, accounted for the bulk of foreign trade. In the case of Hungary and the Balkan countries, for example, foodstuffs accounted for one half to two thirds of all exports (Drabek 1985, 470–74). Cereal and cereal products constituted the largest element, even though dependence on these items had diminished as alternative export crops such as dairy products, fruit and vegetables, poultry and livestock, tobacco and forest products were developed for the international market (Lampe and Jackson 1982, 368–69). If raw materials are included then some three quarters of all exports consisted of primary commodities.

The heavy dependence on commodity exports left the peripheral countries very exposed to the vicissitudes of the international market in primary products. Commodity markets are notoriously volatile, especially in price, and since some of the agrarian exports had inelastic demand and supply curves, quite small changes in either demand or supply could produce very large movements in prices. Two main problems faced producers in the postwar decade: the first was the increasingly hostile market environment in importing countries as they sought to protect their own agrarian producers; while secondly there was the tendency for international commodity prices to weaken, resulting in a deterioration in the terms of trade in primary producing countries.

The most difficult market was that for cereals, especially wheat, due to the enormous expansion of production in North America, Australia and the Argentine during the war and early postwar years when European production was curtailed, and then the subsequent recovery of European output during the course of the 1920s. By the end of the decade, with bumper crops in Canada and Europe together with the re-emergence of Soviet Russia into the international wheat market, the world was awash with wheat. The situation was exacerbated by the fact that the consumption of wheat per head in the more advanced countries was declining due to dietary changes. Global demand therefore failed to match supply potential. In the years 1924–29 world wheat output (excluding Soviet Russia) rose by almost 17 per cent above the prewar average in 1909–14, whereas world consumption was barely 11 per cent higher. Hence stocks of wheat in the main producing regions were rising steadily from 1925 onwards and prices weakened accordingly. By mid-1929 world stocks were listed at 28 million tons, twice the average of the early 1920s, and equivalent to more than one year's exports of the main producing regions (Tracey 1964, 118).

Thus the international market for grain exporters was not a happy one in the 1920s and certainly not for those competing with much more efficient overseas producers. Cereal exports from peripheral countries were much lower than before the war, and in the difficult postwar years, 1919–25, Eastern Europe had been a net importer. One reason for the decline was the enhanced domestic consumption due to population growth. The second factor was the tightening of markets of the importing countries due to protection and reduced consumption. But the major factor was the switch in the sourcing of cereal imports to cheaper producers. Before 1914 Eastern Europe still provided around one half of the wheat supplies of the industrialised West, whereas by 1929 the bulk of the grain was derived from North America (Overy 1994, 27).

For other agricultural products, for example fruit and vegetables and dairy and animal products, the international market was more favourable, one reason why some countries, such as the Baltic states and the Balkans, attempted to diversify their production structures to grasp more promising opportunities. The demand for many raw materials and minerals was also strong for much of the 1920s, especially for Romanian oil, Yugoslav metal ores and Baltic forestry products. Even so, the price structure for commodities in general was by no means wholly favourable to primary producers throughout the decade. Though there had been a general firming of commodity prices following the postwar slump, the latter half of the 1920s saw renewed weakness and a reversal of the terms of trade for primary producers. After 1923 world food prices fell almost continuously, with the exception of 1927, while raw material prices peaked in 1925 and then declined more rapidly than food prices through to 1929. In 1926 tobacco prices also dipped sharply, which hit Bulgaria badly since over one third of her exports were derived from this product (Crampton 1987, 104).

The overall position can be summarised briefly. World commodity prices fell by over 15 per cent between 1925 and 1929, with a fall of 18.8 per cent in raw material prices and 14.1 per cent in food prices (1923–29). Since the price of manufactures declined by less than 11 per cent, the terms of trade deterioration for primary producers was of the order of 5 per cent. But over the longer term, that is, from 1913 to 1929, the deterioration in the terms of trade of primary producers was more than twice as great at just over 11 per cent (Drabek 1985, 475). The worst affected country was Turkey which suffered a terms of trade deterioration of no less than 20 per cent in the later 1920s (Keyder 1981, 82–83). While not all primary producers were affected so severely there is little doubt that, in general, markets were already becoming difficult before the collapse in the subsequent depression. The situation was most acute for cereal growers since grain prices had by the end of the decade fallen considerably compared with the years 1923–25 (Ranki 1983a, 51–52).

It could be argued that reliance on primary commodity exports was a dead-end for many countries even without the disaster of the Great Depression. In the case of Hungary, for example, Ellis (1941, 75) argued that the writing was on the wall given the increasing self-sufficiency in the country's chief markets for grain coupled with competition from American suppliers. Weakening markets and prices not only affected external balances adversely, but also meant that the ability to import capital and to service debt was impaired. Moreover, the concentration on primary production, whether agricultural products or raw materials, created relatively few forward and backward linkages to the rest of the economy since much of the processing of products was carried out abroad. Such arguments are perhaps somewhat academic, however, since events were soon to intercede to demonstrate just how vulnerable primary producers were to the march of international forces.

Debt burdens

The other major problem which affected many peripheral countries was the rising burden of external debt. In the later 1920s, when international conditions became more stable, these countries borrowed heavily on external account, as did many other countries elsewhere, especially in Latin America and the Dominions.

The need for foreign capital was not in doubt given the low level of internal accumulation, which in some cases was lower than before the war. In Hungary, for example, domestic accumulation averaged only 5–6 per cent of national income, about half the prewar level, and even in the peak year the proportion was only 8 per cent (Berend 1974, 184). The shortfall was probably even worse in the Balkan countries of Bulgaria, Greece, Romania and Yugoslavia, and in Turkey. Thus external capital was clearly needed to finance development and structural transformation. This requirement was satisfied by a stream of official loans and private capital from the United States and Great Britain, which replaced Germany and France as the chief creditors. The total amounts exceeded the prewar volumes and accounted for over 50 per cent of the financing of these economies. In Hungary foreign capital was about equal to domestic accumulation and in the case of Poland the ratio of domestic to foreign capital was 4:6, with nearly 40 per cent of the total capital of joint stock companies being of foreign origin (Wellisz 1938, 148; Rose 1939, 194). Foreign participation was even higher in Bulgaria and Yugoslavia: in the former case 72.3 per cent of the national debt and 48 per cent of equity capital was owned by foreigners, while for Yugoslavia the respective shares were 82.5 and 44 per cent (Logio 1936, 140; Berend 1974, 186).

Lethbridge (1985, 557) argues that in the case of the East European countries foreign capital made a significant contribution to their economies. But one must question whether the large capital inflow was in the best interests of the debtor countries. Borrowing from abroad was expensive, the proceeds were often used unproductively, and the rising servicing costs proved fatal once the flow of foreign capital ceased and economic conditions globally turned sour.

One of the main issues with regard to the use of foreign capital is whether the borrowing country can service the debt costs, a problem that has plagued many countries before and since. To maintain solvency it behoves borrowing countries to ensure that sufficient funds are channelled into exchange-earning activities in the first instance so that debts can be serviced, and hopefully amortised in due course. Continued borrowing is not a problem, however, as long as the current servicing costs can be comfortably met.

This patently was not the case with the peripheral borrowers. Only a relatively small proportion of the loan proceeds found their way into productive and/or exchange-earning activities. The larger part of imported funds was used for financing non-essential imports and social infrastructures, the accumulation of private balances abroad, and the payment of interest and dividends (Political and Economic Planning 1945, 110). Estimates of the end-use balance of payments distribution of capital imports for Hungary, Bulgaria, Yugoslavia and Poland tend to confirm this general pattern. Of the $604.6 million inflow of both long- and short-term capital between 1924 and 1928 ($238 million of which was short-term), one half was used to finance a surplus of goods and services, one tenth for the purchase of gold, while most of the remainder went to meet interest and dividend payments on foreign debt (Nötel 1974, 79).

The Hungarian experience provides more detailed illustration of the end-use of capital inflows. During the years 1924–29 capital imports (both long- and short-term) were about equal to domestic accumulation. Of the long-term capital, some 40 per cent went to repaying former debts including some dating from before the war, 25 per cent was used for financing consumption, 15 per cent was invested in social infrastructure projects undertaken by municipal governments, including public health, education and housing, while only 20 per cent found its way into productive investment (Berend 1974, 186–7). Rothschild (1974, 168–9) accuses Hungary's rulers of soliciting credits that were too large relative to the capacity of the country to deal with them.

Two other problems related to foreign debt should be mentioned. First, the cost of capital was relatively high and most of it was in the form of fixed interest securities, rather than in equity issues. Nominal rates of interest were around 6–9 per cent, but the real rates were often much higher when account is taken of the deep discounts on the sale of new issues, depending on the creditworthiness of the borrowers (Political and Economic Planning 1945, 110). The big disadvantage of such issues was that the debt costs remained fixed when incomes declined. Secondly, a significant part of the capital inflows consisted of short-term advances which national credit systems of the recipient countries tended to convert from short-term credits into long-term domestic loans. Hungary and Poland, with about half their total debt in short-term form, were the most serious offenders in this respect, though many countries had quite large short-term credits. Moreover, short-term foreign liabilities constituted 20–40 per cent of commercial bank deposits in most Eastern and Central European countries (Macartney 1937, 466; Williams 1963, 94). This left the countries very exposed when economic conditions deteriorated and short-term funds were scuttling to safer havens.

It can be argued therefore that even before the disastrous events of the early 1930s the debt burden of some of the peripheral countries was becoming untenable. The position was especially acute in Eastern Europe and less so in the Baltic states. Capital imports were increasingly required to plug the gaps in the balance of payments as servicing costs put an increasing strain on external accounts. The reasons for the deterioration have been explained by Nötel as follows:

> Export expansion in these overwhelmingly agricultural countries remained extremely irregular and rather modest in most cases. Import expansion, under the pressure of long-repressed import demand, outpaced export expansion whenever not restrained by inflation or currency management. Deficits increased and surpluses vanished, in consequence, not only on trade accounts but also on trade and services accounts.
>
> (Nötel 1986, 185)

As can be seen from Table 3.2, an increasing proportion of export earnings were required to service the transfer of profits, interest and dividends abroad and this share rose dramatically once export earnings collapsed in the early 1930s. At the same time outpayments for capital services were absorbing an ever larger share of net capital inflows: 40 per cent in the case of Hungary, 28 per cent for Poland and 70 per cent in Estonia in 1928. By the following year total inflows of capital only just about matched outgoings in interest and dividends, partly as a result of the downturn in American lending from the middle of 1928. Within two years capital inflows had virtually dried up, commodity prices were falling rapidly and the tenuous position of borrowing countries was cruelly exposed.

Table 3.2 Debt Servicing as a Percentage of Export Earnings 1926–32

Country	1926	1928	1931/32
Bulgaria	8.5	12.3	22.0
Greece	–	32.0	44.0
Hungary	11.1	17.9	48.0
Poland	7.5	11.3	27.0
Romania	9.4	14.6	36.0
Yugoslavia	11.5	18.1	36.0

Source: Aldcroft 2001, 177.

In reality debtor insolvency was hastened rather than caused by the collapse of lending and the onset of depression in the early 1930s (Bandera 1964, 110–15). Even had international events not taken over there would likely have been a reaction in time given the increasingly insupportable debt burdens of the borrowing countries. The seeds of insolvency had been sown before the depression struck and since there was no obvious means of liquidating the growing burden of external debt the day of judgment was only a matter of time.

Crisis in the early 1930s

Just as many European countries must have felt that they were getting back to an even keel and making some real progress, the picture was rudely shattered by the biggest economic crisis in recorded history. For three years or more the world was engulfed in economic and financial turmoil from which few countries emerged unscathed. In the aftermath the international economic system was vastly different from what had prevailed before.

The detailed events and causes of the Great Depression must be sought elsewhere since space precludes a blow-by-blow account. In any case it is doubtful whether any such full retelling would serve a useful purpose or provide a coherent analysis of the crisis which, in Landes (1969, 372) words, 'does justice to the rush of disasters, tumbling one upon another; or ... illuminates the confusion of events'. Nevertheless, it is essential to sketch in the main background as it relates to the experience of the European peripheral countries.

Europe as a whole was affected very severely by the depression. Though there were variations in intensity most countries experienced steep declines in output, prices, employment and trade volumes, while balance of payments problems, currency crises and financial insecurity were widespread (for details see Aldcroft 1997, 49–52). Agricultural Europe probably fared worst of all because of the massive fall in commodity prices, the debt problem and the limited scope for adjustment given the low level of development (see Berend 1998, 271).

The big fall in primary product prices was little short of catastrophic for many less developed European countries. Overall they declined by roughly 60 per cent between 1929 and 1933, whereas prices of manufactures fell on average by about 41 per cent, which meant that the terms of trade of primary producers declined by around one quarter (Drabek 1985, 475). This contrasts with the position in Western industrial countries, especially large food importers such as Britain, which benefited considerably from the global fall in commodity prices.

Though the price decline was of similar magnitude for both food and raw materials, there were some marked variations among different commodities. Cereals were by far the worst affected. Wheat prices slumped to less than a third of the peak seen in the 1920s, whereas prices for meat and dairy products held up somewhat better. Commodity prices only recovered slowly after the slump and even by the eve of the Second World War they were still well down on pre-depression levels.

Paradoxically, farmers initially made the situation worse by producing more and dumping it on to an already glutted world market in an attempt to restore their revenues (Timoshenko 1933, 92, 96). This strategy met with very limited success since after 1930 external market conditions deteriorated very rapidly and export volumes plummeted as trade outlets dried up. Consequently, export receipts dropped sharply through a combination of price and quantity factors. In the case of Romania, for example, they fell by no less than 73 per cent, while export earnings for agricultural exporters in general declined to 40 per cent of the 1929 level. The enormous shrinkage in export earnings entailed a serious loss of international purchasing power and a rising burden of debt servicing (see Table 3.2). Since international debt servicing costs remained fixed in nominal terms, the debt servicing power of export earnings fell by between one half and two thirds in Hungary and the Balkan countries (Nötel 1986, 217–19).

For farm producers and peasants the price collapse was devastating. Agrarian incomes in many countries declined by one half or more and the situation was made worse by the price scissors gap that opened up between agricultural and industrial prices. The price of goods purchased by peasants rarely fell by more than a third, whereas the price at which they sold their produce fell by almost double that amount (Seton-Watson 1946, 82, 122; Roberts 1951, 71, 177). At times the gap was so wide that farmers had to release nearly twice the prewar amount of grain and cattle to secure the same quantity of manufactured articles (Hertz 1947, 194).

With diminished incomes and rising debt burdens many peasants teetered on the verge of bankruptcy. In Hungary 60 per cent of the land of smallholders was fully mortgaged and interest paid on agricultural loans amounted to more than 25 per cent of yearly income. In Yugoslavia one third or more of rural households were heavily in debt and their total indebtedness was equivalent to 80–90 per cent of their annual cash incomes (Rothschild 1974, 271). Indeed, throughout Eastern Europe agrarian indebtedness was a pervasive problem. One contemporary observer, Tiltman, who made an extensive tour of the region, reckoned that 70 per cent of all peasant holdings in Eastern Europe were threatened by debts and that many peasants were worse off in terms of real purchasing power than they had been before the war (Tiltman 1934, 118–20, 169, 249). The plight of the peasantry was aggravated by the high interest rates charged for loans and by heavy taxation. For some life became too difficult and they were forced to sell up and leave the land.

The worst of it was that recovery was so slow and hesitant. Prices remained at rock bottom for several years and even in the later 1930s commodity prices were still well below either 1929 or 1913 levels. Hence there was not much incentive to improve and modernise agriculture. Productivity stagnated and the basic structure of agricultural production and exports was little changed. As Berend records, traditional crops predominated in many countries: the output of seven main traditional crops in Central and Eastern Europe was 17 per cent greater in the years 1934–38 compared with 1909–13. 'All in all, the countries of the region could not adapt to changing market conditions of the thirties either by reducing costs or by making structural changes in production. Institutional, cultural-educational, and economic obstacles were too strong' (Berend 1998, 259). Among the peripheral countries only the Baltic states made a determined effort to adapt agricultural production to cater for export markets in their dairy and meat products, principally for the British and German markets.

The final blow to the economic solvency of many peripheral countries was the financial crisis of the early 1930s. This was especially the case with those countries which had become overburdened with debt in the later 1920s and were saddled with large debt service payments and short-term credits, which became insupportable as incomes and exchange earnings declined and the source of foreign credits dried up. New loans were essential to maintain payments on previous debts. To take the example of Hungary: 40 per cent of all loans to the country between 1924 and 1931 were used for servicing past debts and by 1929 all new credits were being used for that purpose (Berend 1998, 260–61).

With the collapse of export purchasing power, the end of foreign credits, and the loss of exchange reserves and flight of capital, many borrowing countries became literally insolvent. The financial situation was made even worse by the accompanying banking crisis in Central Europe, culminating in the collapse of the Austrian Credit-Anstalt in May 1931, because a substantial proportion of the equity capital of East European banks was owned by foreigners, notably Germans and Austrians. Even the Baltic states, though not heavy debtors, were nevertheless hit badly by the financial crisis in Central Europe and the subsequent collapse of sterling in September 1931, which led to the withdrawal of German and other foreign capital and precipitated a domestic withdrawal of funds, while the devaluation of sterling created near panic since a large part of the reserves of the Baltic states were in sterling currency.

The general scramble for liquidity in the summer of 1931 and the calling-in of short-term credits were the final straw. Nötel has described the sequence as follows:

> The financial crisis of mid-1931, superimposed upon the protracted export crisis in both commodities and manufactures, transformed the haunting spectre of the collapse of national currencies, within a few months or weeks, into an immediately threatening and practically unescapable reality for most east European countries. The sudden shift from continuing, even if irregular, capital imports to fast-spreading capital withdrawal and flight – with the balance-of-payments position already weakened by the sharp and long-lasting fall in export receipts and the rising or at least maintained debt service – in all countries threatened to exhaust, or actually exhausted, the rapidly shrinking proceeds and reserves of foreign exchange.
>
> (Nötel 1986, 227)

In sum, prospects for peripheral countries looked very bleak indeed at the start of the 1930s. Superimposed on their long-standing structural problems they now had to grapple with the task of salvaging their economies from the ravages created by the economic and financial crisis. Their efforts on both counts were met with only limited success.

Policy reactions to the crisis

In the dire circumstances of the time, it was inevitable that emergency action would have to be taken to avoid complete collapse. Economic commentators have often been critical of the restrictive and autarchic measures adopted in the 1930s which, it is argued, were income destructive (Friedman 1974). However, one may ask what was the alternative? Desperate problems required desperate remedies, uninspired by logic or ideological motives, in a global *sauve-qui-peut* situation.

Despite its alleged shortcomings, economic policy in the 1930s had some degree of logic. There were several factors which helped to shape the policy response. Strange as it may seem in the circumstances, one was the fear of rekindling inflation, a threat which contemporaries associated with budgetary deficits and currency depreciation. Accordingly, depression and financial crisis were met with a drive for fiscal prudence and currency stabilisation, even though these policies were detrimental to economic recovery. Secondly, many peripheral countries were anxious to restore international confidence in their economies in the hope that this would encourage a resumption of foreign lending. Debtor countries were therefore reluctant initially to default on their loans, though in time default or the negotiation of moratoria became unavoidable. For similar reasons there was an equal reluctance to allow their currencies to depreciate since this would weaken international confidence by raising the spectre of inflation, while it would also increase the nominal value of debt service costs in domestic currency (Bandera 1964, 119). To restore trade balances it was also necessary to cut imports drastically since it was almost impossible to raise the level of exports.

A longer-term issue bearing on policy strategy was the growing force of nationalism. This of course was not especially new but it gathered increasing momentum in the 1930s, and not simply as a reaction to the crisis itself. The trend towards increased state intervention and a policy of import-substitution and autarchy seemed to offer a more realistic solution to the problems of agrarian peripheral countries than the liberal capitalism associated with bourgeois democracy. The latter was discredited in the eyes of right-wing political forces who exploited nationalistic sentiments in both the economic and political spheres. Moreover, focusing on national sentiment helped to facilitate the diversion of social unrest. In the event, it was to prove a high cost strategy since it eased the way for German infiltration in many of the peripheral countries (Macartney and Palmer 1962, 285–88).

One final factor shaping policy was rearmament. This became an increasingly dominant issue in the latter half of the decade as international tension increased with Germany's defence plans. From the mid-1930s many state-sponsored industrial projects in peripheral Europe had strategic considerations and defence needs in mind. In scale many of these no doubt went far beyond normal security needs, but this was understandable given the unease of governments as to the precise nature of Germany's intentions.

During the course of the decade there were some subtle shifts in policy direction. In the early 1930s the focus was on orthodox and defensive measures – not surprisingly, since the main objective at this point was to prevent complete financial collapse, while at the same time providing a modicum of relief for the most distressed sectors of the population so as to limit the danger of serious social upheaval. Once the immediate crisis was past there was some relaxation in the tight policy stance on both the external and domestic policy fronts, with a move towards more constructive measures of development, though still very much within an autarchic framework.

The immediate task was to tackle the external problem in order to avoid complete insolvency. Most European countries in fact took action to defend their external accounts soon after the start of the crisis. In practice this meant that virtually every conceivable form of trade and payments restriction barring blockade was utilised so that by the mid-1930s trade and commercial policy, and of course trade volumes, had sunk to an historical nadir (Friedman 1978, 158).

In contrast to many Western countries, the peripheral nations did not abandon gold and devalue their currencies, which would have allowed more room for manoeuvre on the domestic policy front. Instead they resorted to exchange control to maintain the value of their currencies. As can be seen from Table 3.3, most peripheral countries, apart from Poland, imposed exchange control in the early 1930s. The need to check capital flight, conserve foreign exchange and bring about the restoration of confidence were the main motives behind the strategy.

Debt burdens were also considerably eased by partial or complete suspension of their servicing in 1931 and 1932. Subsequently further relief was secured through negotiated agreements with major creditors on the capital sums and terms of repayment, the overall effect of which was to lessen substantially the debt outstanding and the servicing costs (Condliffe 1941, 243–44).

Table 3.3 Exchange Rates in the 1930s

Country	Official suspension of gold standard	Introduction of exchange control	Depreciation or devaluation in relation to gold	Extent of depreciation by early 1935 (%)
Albania	–	–	–	–
Bulgaria	–	15/10/31	–	–
Estonia	28/6/33	18/11/31	6/33	42
Greece	26/4/32	28/9/31	4/32	57
Hungary	–	17/7/31	–	–
Latvia	28/9/36	8/10/31	9/36	–
Lithuania	–	1/10/35	–	–
Poland	–	26/4/36	–	–
Portugal	31/12/31	21/10/22	10/31	42
Romania	–	18/5/32	7/35	–
Spain	–	18/5/31	1920	45
Turkey	–	26/2/30	1915	–
Yugoslavia	–	7/10/31	7/32	23

Notes:

Bulgaria, Hungary, Romania and Yugoslavia were, along with Austria and Germany, members of the Reichsmark bloc.

Portugal, along with the Baltic states, became members of the sterling area.

Poland was a member of the gold bloc until 1936, as was Greece between June 1933 and September 1936 when she joined the sterling area.

Turkey pegged its currency to sterling between March 1930 and September 1931, then to the French franc until September 1936 and then back to sterling.

Sources: Bank for International Settlements 1935, 9; League of Nations 1937, 111–13.

On the surface, trade restrictions and exchange control served their immediate purpose. Capital outflows were checked, trade balances improved and currency instability was obviated. But there were costs involved. Exchange control tended to raise domestic prices and it made exporting more difficult in so far as it maintained artificial and overvalued currencies. It has been estimated that East European currencies were overvalued in relation to sterling and the dollar by up to as much as 60 per cent (Nötel 1986, 229). Moreover, protection of currencies limited the scope for expansionary fiscal policies given the need to compress domestic costs and prices. As with the gold bloc members, countries that practised exchange control had a worse trade and income performance than those countries which had left gold and devalued their currencies (Harris 1936, 103; Ellis 1941, 152).

Recognition of the disadvantages of external controls led to some relaxation from 1934 onwards, principally in the modification of exchange control. This was done by concealed measures of devaluation, the use of multiple exchange rates and export bonuses, so that exporters received more domestic currency from their export sales than they would otherwise have done using the official rates of exchange. The terms of the premia varied from country to country with a range between 20 and 50 per cent. Yet even with this relief most exchange control countries still suffered from overvaluation relative to free market currencies (Lampe and Jackson 1982, 464–65; Royal Institute of International Affairs 1936, 85–86; League of Nations 1941, 171).

The upshot of the closer affinity among exchange control countries in trade and payments was the spread of clearing agreements. These agreements entailed the bilateral balancing of claims between the countries concerned, thereby minimising the use of free foreign exchange. The first negotiated agreement was concluded between Austria and Yugoslavia in January 1932, to be followed by a raft of similar agreements between Central and East European countries, and to a lesser extent the Baltic states. By the end of the 1930s much of the trade of Germany, Austria, Italy, Hungary, the Balkans, Greece, Albania and Turkey was conducted by means of bilateral clearing (Berend 1998, 270).

One of the inevitable consequences of such trading relationships was of course the growing economic and political influence of Nazi Germany in many of the peripheral countries. Germany became the major trading partner of the Balkan and Baltic states, Hungary, Albania and Turkey. Whether these countries gained from the increasing domination of Germany is an issue which has been debated frequently, but somewhat inconclusively. It was difficult to resist Germany's encroachment since she was one of the few countries prepared to buy agrarian products and other commodities at prices above those ruling in the world market, while supplying much needed equipment in return. On the other hand, it has been argued that Germany exploited these countries for her own strategic purposes to gain access to food and raw materials, no doubt motivated by the desire to avoid a repetition of the blockade tactics of the Royal Navy which occurred in the First World War. In the process her trading partners piled up large blocked Reichsmark balances which could only be used to purchase German goods some of which, aspirins and cuckoo clocks being the famous examples, were allegedly dumped in large quantities on her erstwhile suppliers. According to contemporary reports, Yugoslavia is said to have received enough aspirins from Germany to last a decade, while Romania was even more lavishly supplied, with aspirins to relieve 500 years of headaches! (Einzig 1938, 26; Jones 1937, 76–77).

Whether such stories are true or false, the fact remains that there were some gains to be gleaned from the German connection. Germany's trading relationships were by no means totally exploitive and they did help to relieve these countries from the lingering effects of the Great Depression. In the glutted commodity markets of the 1930s, especially for agrarian products, the German outlet was invaluable. On the other hand, increasing trade dependence on Nazi Germany may have slowed down structural change and diversification of production and also retarded reintegration into the world economy. In so far as countries became locked in to serving the needs of the German war machine with primary products the incentive to shift away from commodity production was obviously lessened (Berend 1998, 276). However, this conclusion needs to be tempered by the fact that the more isolationist, state-induced import substitution policies were, in some cases, bringing about a degree of structural change. In the case of Hungary, for example, the import of finished goods fell from 40 to 27 per cent of total imports between 1929 and 1937, continuing a trend established in the previous decade (Berend 1998, 271).

In the long run, of course, it all ended in disaster. Germany's economic influence was but a prelude to political and military domination. Germany in fact used her trade connections as a smoke-screen in South-eastern Europe to infiltrate Nazi agents who spread the political gospel. Under commercial disguise, political agents were widely employed throughout the region and by the end of the decade Nazi 'commercial' agents were thick on the ground. Contemporary accounts record the case of a German soya-bean company in Romania employing no less than 3000 commercial agents to spread the Nazi gospel, while in Bulgaria German military experts dominated the army

(Jones 1937, 64, 82). By this time it was too late to disengage and one by one the unfortunate countries were swallowed up in the Nazi military machine.

Though state intervention in the economy increased during the 1930s there was little prospect initially of governments doing very much to alleviate the depression through active fiscal and monetary policy. For one thing the dire state of public finances precluded such a strategy as revenues collapsed under the impact of recession, while expenditure commitments proved difficult to curtail quickly. Yields from indirect taxes and dues fell by at least one third in many countries and those from direct taxes declined by more than one half during the course of the depression (Schönfeld 1975, 197–98). Thus governments were more concerned about devising ways of dealing with budgetary deficits via expenditure control or tax increases than they were in stimulating activity and employment by fiscal means. Moreover, at the time the classical goals of budgetary equilibrium and currency stability were still seen as over-riding priorities to ensure financial prudence and restore confidence at home and abroad (Spigler 1986, 141). And, given the overvaluation of many currencies, compression of the domestic price and cost structure was required in order to achieve international competitiveness.

Accordingly, monetary and fiscal policies were highly deflationary in the early 1930s. The most extreme case was that of Poland where deflationary policies were vital in view of the large budgetary deficits and the attempt to maintain the value of the zloty without resorting to exchange control. Total budgetary expenditure was reduced by one third between 1930 and 1934, while stringent credit controls were imposed by the banks (Landau 1984, 129–30; Gorecki 1935, 109; Taylor 1952, 43). The strategy was very much influenced by the French example, where the authorities were forced to undertake severe internal compression due to the overvalued currency which was still attached to gold. As in the French case, Polish policy undoubtedly helped to intensify and prolong the depression, and it was not until 1936 that the strategy was reversed (Smith 1936, 168–78; Zweig 1944, 54–56; Korbonski 1992, 251).

Similar policies were followed in most other countries with varying degrees of intensity. The Hungarian government believed that a rigid deflationary stance was necessary if foreign investment was to be attracted to the country again, while Yugoslavia's retrenchment policy relied heavily on French advice (Polonsky 1975, 56–57). However, despite adherence to orthodox fiscal policies it behoved governments to maintain or increase some expenditures on public works and unemployment relief in order to ease the social impact of the crisis.

Towards the middle of the decade there were signs of some respite in sight. Yugoslavia was the first country to change course when in 1934–35 cheaper money and reflationary government expenditure on public works signalled an end to the policy of retrenchment (Royal Institute of International Affairs 1936, 128). Other countries soon followed suit and some, notably Hungary, the Baltic states and Turkey, initiated large programmes of state investment. The shift in policy stance was made possible by the gradual improvement in economic conditions and public finances, though increasingly important as time went on was the pressure of defence needs as international tension escalated in the latter half of the decade. As Hauner observes in relation to Eastern Europe:

> The rising military expenditures and investments thus constituted one of the most effective instruments of state interventionist policies, by means of which the majority of east European states sought after the depression to reactivate a whole range of economic sectors, particularly domestic savings, which in turn were to contribute to the strengthening of the defence potential.
>
> (Hauner 1986, 50)

By the end of the 1930s defence spending accounted for up to one third of public expenditure in several countries and as much as one half in the case of Poland (Overy 1989, 5). The increasingly hostile international climate of the period and the threat of aggression on the part of the two major totalitarian powers, Soviet Russia and Nazi Germany, prompted governments to take precautionary measures to protect themselves. Poland was potentially the most threatened country, being the most friendless and disliked of the new states, and in danger from both Germany and Russia which had scores to settle with her relating to frontier boundaries. Poland therefore was determined to become an effective military power at whatever the cost to general welfare.

In the event no amount of military preparedness could protect the smaller nations from the naked aggression of the superstates. It is questionable moreover whether heavy concentration on defence expenditure was ultimately in the best interests of their economies. Overy (1989, 4–5) is very sceptical as far as Poland is concerned, arguing that the quest for military might weakened an already fragile economy and gave rise to financial insecurity, low living standards and social unrest – one reason, no doubt, why the death of Pilsudski in 1935 ushered in what amounted to a military regime under the banner of a front organisation, the Camp of National Unity. In the end Poland's best efforts on the military front proved utterly futile when faced with the Nazi onslaught in 1939.

Moreover, when one considers the poor state of infrastructure facilities in most of the peripheral countries, one may also question the validity of the large share of public expenditure allocated to the defence sector. Services such as water, electricity, transport and communications, not to mention housing, health care and education, were far behind those in the West and in some cases little better than those in some of today's African countries. And, although there was evidence of improvement during the course of the interwar years, by the end of the period social infrastructure facilities had probably slipped further behind those of Western countries (Ehrlich 1973, 22; 1985, 369).

If we take into account the taxation side of the equation there is even more room for concern. Generally speaking, taxation systems were highly regressive and lacked both equity and logic. They were also badly administered. Yugoslavia may have been at the extreme end of the spectrum in this respect but serves to illustrate the point. Indirect taxes in that particular country accounted for some three quarters of state revenues and the administration of tax gathering was designed to suit more the convenience of the bureaucracy than the needs of economic and social welfare. As Tomasevich (1955, 688) explains, the principles of collecting public revenues were those 'of charging its citizens as often as possible and as heavily as possible; taking the money where it could find it, and getting it from those who make the least outcry, rather than according to the principle of the ability to pay'.

Regressive fiscal systems tend to be a feature of backward countries and in this respect peripheral Europe was no exception. The hardest hit were the low income groups and inevitably this meant the peasantry suffered (Jelavich 1983, 241). In the three main Balkan countries some 50 per cent of the total cash income of peasant households was absorbed in taxation of one form or another. In view of the extremely low incomes prevailing at the time this was a very steep imposition and one which must surely have discouraged investment and improvement in agriculture. Yet the inequities of taxation systems were so blatant. More prosperous groups outwith the agrarian sector, for example government officials, rent receivers and businessmen, often escaped with very light burdens. The distortions in the tax system were also remarkable. Owners of urban housing in Yugoslavia, for example, paid little tax on their rental income and even enjoyed preferential interest on mortgage loans. One consequence was that a large share of capital formation, over 50 per cent, consisted of residential property (Tomasevich 1955, 686–87). This was a very high proportion given the scarcity of capital, the poor infrastructure facilities and the fact that much of the property was for high class rental rather than for low income group needs. But it was by no means an uncommon feature in other Balkan countries. The distorting effects of taxation anomalies were widespread throughout South-eastern Europe and, according to one report, the structure and administration of taxation systems were ripe for reform: 'There are few spheres of public policy in which a constructive approach would yield speedier results' (Political and Economic Planning 1945, 124).

The international background, both political and economic, was scarcely the most auspicious of environments for latercomers to modern development. No sooner had the European peripheral nations recuperated from the effects of the Great War than they were engulfed by depression and financial crisis. And if that were not enough, before they had the chance to recover properly from the catastrophe of the early 1930s, the international political scene deteriorated visibly so that in the latter half of the 1930s defence requirements became a dominating factor in government policy.

The chapters which follow explain how each of the 13 peripheral countries coped with their own internal problems against the background of international events.

CHAPTER FOUR

The Balkan States

This first group of peripheral states consisted of three nations with but one thing in common: an overwhelmingly agrarian structure generating low incomes for a poor peasantry. Otherwise they were as different as chalk and cheese. Bulgaria was a small compact nation of robust peasant farmers and with a strong national identity. Yugoslavia, by contrast, was a conglomerate nation with little identity, forged out of slabs of territory belonging to different countries, resulting in a multi-ethnic pot-pourri almost as bad as that of the old Austro-Hungarian Empire. Finally, postwar Romania comprised a much expanded country and a proud people, whose citizens have been dubbed 'the Neapolitans of the Balkans' (MacMillan 2003, 147).

Bulgaria

For five centuries Bulgaria was under Ottoman rule until the state was restored as a principality under Turkish sovereignty by the Treaty of Berlin in 1878 (*de jure* independence being finally achieved in 1908). This was in a much reduced form from the 'Big Bulgaria' proposed by Russia following its recent defeat of Turkey. Nevertheless, its neighbours, Serbia, Greece and Romania, still found it far too big for their liking. Its subsequent history down to the First World War was therefore a turbulent one, culminating in the Balkan Wars of 1912–13, which more or less ended 'Turkey in Europe'. Despite its contribution to the defeat of Turkey, Bulgaria failed to capture the spoils of war. The gains made in the first Balkan War of 1912 were reversed in the second conflict of the following year when her former allies deserted her. By the Treaty of Bucharest in August 1913 she was forced to renounce claims to eastern Thrace and the southern Dobrudja, while Serbian and Greek control of much of Macedonia was confirmed.

Thus the vision of a 'Greater Bulgaria' under King Ferdinand I seemed to be fading and one reason for the country's joining the Central Powers in the war of 1914–18 was that it appeared to offer the best opportunity of recovering the lost provinces of Macedonia, southern Dobrudja and Thrace. But it was not to be. Despite some early successes in which Bulgaria managed to seize the coveted lands, by 1918 the country was exhausted and forced to surrender. Ferdinand abdicated to return to his passion of bird-watching, and was succeeded by Boris III whose chief interest was driving trains. He was considered a weak and incompetent monarch but in fact lasted far longer than many people would have predicted (MacMillan 2003, 147).

In territorial terms the peacemakers dealt with Bulgaria fairly lightly. By the Treaty of Neuilly of November 1919 the territorial frontiers with Romania, Yugoslavia and Greece were defined and these denied Bulgaria claims to Macedonia (given instead to Greece and Yugoslavia), Thrace (to Greece and Turkey) and the southern Dobrudja (to Romania), leaving it without any access to the Aegean. In effect the provisions more or less confirmed the frontiers obtaining in 1914 which had been cut back severely the previous year following the Balkan Wars (Temperley 1921, 459). Bulgaria's territory in square kilometres was reduced by under 10 per cent, from 111,800 to 103,146, between 1914 and 1921, while her population rose slightly from 4.75 to 4.91 millions due to the influx of refugees from the lost lands.

In striking contrast to Yugoslavia, Bulgaria had the advantage of being a fairly compact nation from an ethnic point of view. Some 85 per cent of the population was Bulgarian and orthodox. The only significant minority group consisted of Turks (just over 10 per cent) left over from Ottoman rule. There was of course a large expatriate population of around one million Bulgars (16 per cent of the population) located in lands ceded to other countries. This was somewhat lower than the expatriate populations of either Hungary or Albania, but it certainly did little to convince Bulgaria of the justice of the settlement and like Hungary it supported revisionism. It also gave rise to a refugee problem as Bulgars migrated back to their homeland, some 450,000 eventually resettling. Thus, apart from accommodating these migrants, Bulgaria had no great integration problems arising from territorial changes or assimilation of large numbers of minority nationalities.

The financial provisions of the treaty were more onerous. Substantial debt burdens in the form of reparations and related debts were imposed by the treaty. The reparations bill alone was fixed at 2250 million gold francs, equivalent to nearly one quarter of the national wealth of Bulgaria, and even higher with the inclusion of other debt demanded by the treaty to cover prewar Ottoman debts. The annual payments required to extinguish this debt over a 37-year period were 105 million gold francs, which was equal to over half the prewar budget (Pasvolsky 1930, 65–67; Bell 1977, 194). Payments were due to start in 1921 but in fact nothing was paid until 1923 apart from some deliveries in kind, mainly livestock and coal. Following protests by the government the debt was scaled down and divided into two parts, only on one of which (550 million gold francs) would immediate repayment begin, in annual instalments of 5 million francs rising to 10 million in 1930. At the peak, the reduced obligations absorbed some 8 per cent of budgetary expenditure (1928–29), by which time Bulgaria had paid 41 million gold francs plus 100 million in kind (Lampe 1986, 62; Pasvolsky 1930, 148). In 1932, in accordance with the Lausanne Agreement on international debts, war debt and reparation payments effectively came to an end (Royal Institute of International Affairs 1936, 38–9).

At the conclusion of hostilities Bulgaria was in no fit state to pay anything, let alone an enormous reparations bill. For a small and very poor nation the country had shown great resilience, though at a high cost to the economy and its human resource base. Some 900,000 men were drafted into the forces (40 per cent of the male population) and war losses were the highest of all the belligerent countries on a per capita basis: 100,000 killed and 300,000 casualties (Bell 1977, 122).

But what really defeated Bulgaria was the loss of resources to the Central Powers and the setback to domestic output. Towards the end of the war the economy was on the brink of collapse and the population and troops facing starvation (Pundeff 1992, 79–80). Deliveries of foodstuffs and raw materials to Germany, together with seizure by German soldiers, declining harvests and government requisition of fodder and livestock, left the civilian population severely short of life's necessities. Grain harvested fell by over 50 per cent during the years 1915–18, due to the depletion of farm labour and a contraction in the area under cultivation. Industry, which had initially been boosted by wartime demands, eventually suffered from labour and raw materials shortages; so much so that by 1918 it was estimated that less than one third of large-scale manufacturing concerns were able to operate regularly, while small workshops were going out of business (Lampe 1986, 44; Bell 1977, 123). Some relief came with deliveries from the American Relief Administration immediately after the war, but being an ex-enemy country Bulgaria had to pay for these in hard cash.

Given the dire economic situation it was to be some time before Bulgaria could achieve financial stability and restore the currency. Unbalanced budgets, trade deficits and shortages had led to a large rise in prices during the war and a further big increase took place through to 1923, when the index stood at 3045 with 1913 as 100. The immediate cause was the large rise in the money supply much of which was to cover budgetary shortfalls as a result of large extraordinary expenditures at a time when revenue collection was limited. The rate of exchange fell accordingly and the expectations of large reparation payments between 1921 and 1923 also had an adverse effect. But the exchange rate did not fully reflect the rate of internal inflation, for the government imposed exchange control in December 1918 which served to maintain the rate artificially above its true market rate (Berov 1983, 491–95).

It was not until 1924 that the government managed to check the growth in the money supply and reduce budgetary deficits by imposing a severe deflationary policy. Inflation was brought under control and the exchange rate stabilised *de facto* in 1924. Improvements in the trade balance, an influx of short-term credits and two international loans, one for the settlement of refugees in 1926 and the other in 1928 specifically for stabilisation purposes, allowed Bulgaria to complete the transition to the gold exchange standard (League of Nations 1946a, 130–31). The lev was stabilised at 3.7 per cent of its prewar par value.

Given the severe problems facing the country in the early postwar years, Bulgaria appears to have made a quite remarkable performance in the 1920s – the more so in that before 1914 it was one of the least industrialised and most backward of European countries, with the exception of Albania. The prewar attempt at modernisation was very limited, described by Berend (1998, 130) as 'a humiliating failure' – a judgment that may seem perhaps a little unfair, but the country's industrial base was still very small so that any subsequent growth may seem more spectacular for that reason. Berov's statistics suggest that the Bulgarian economy was almost back to the prewar level by 1923; overall output was slightly down but industrial production, which recorded a dramatic jump between 1919 and 1923, was 53 per cent higher than in 1910–12, stockbreeding 10 per cent higher, but agricultural production 15 per cent down (Berov 1983, 495–96). After that there were some equally impressive gains so that industrial production by the end of the decade had more than doubled, while crop production had increased by around one quarter (Lampe 1986, 53; Crampton 1987, 139–44).

The gains in industry were especially marked in foodstuffs, textiles, chemicals, construction materials and metal products. Even so, modern industry's share of national income was only around 5 per cent in the 1920s compared with 2.7 per cent before the war, and was more than outweighed by rural and artisan manufacture (Lampe 1986, 71). How far this burst of industrial growth was due to government policies is difficult to estimate precisely. The new tariff laws did not come into effect until 1926, when there were steep increases in duties for manufactures and semi-manufactures and for foodstuffs. And as Lampe (1986, 72) notes, except in the case of sugar and cement the highest levels of protection do not correspond with the highest rates of growth, with the two most expansive sectors, chemicals and metallurgy, being less well protected. The new legislation on industrial encouragement of 1928, extending already existing laws dating back to before the war, does not seem to have been of great moment. Apart from renewing tax and tariff exemptions, the main change was a reduction in rail freight rates of one quarter. In any case, the legislation came too late to have much effect on performance in the 1920s.

It would be convenient to conclude that the lack of a major land problem was the reason for Bulgaria's relative success on the agrarian front. But in fact this would not be entirely correct. It is true that Bulgaria avoided major upheavals in land redistribution since it was already a country of small peasant holdings, with an absence of large estates and few landless labourers. It thus enjoyed a compact situation and a seemingly idyllic egalitarian structure. The percentage of agricultural land in holdings over 50 hectares was only 1.6 per cent (1930), while two thirds consisted of plots between 1 and 10 hectares and the rest in holdings of up to 50 hectares (Moore 1945, 82). But this structure contained its own problems. Many of the units were far too small to be really viable even with the most up-to-date working methods, and in time they got smaller as plots were subdivided to make provision for the increase in population including the influx of refugees. Land reform laws that were passed in 1920 and 1924 exacerbated the problem since they set limits to the maximum size of holdings and distributed land to landless families (Kovatcheff 1934, 441–72). The average size of holding declined from 7 to 4 hectares over the period 1900–1940 (Hoffman 1972, 49).

The second problem was that many holdings consisted of a collection of strips not all of which were continuous. On average holdings consisted of 10 strips which could be some distance apart, even in the next village. Though some efforts were made to eliminate this spatial diffusion of strips, the patchwork quilt character of Bulgarian farming remained a prominent feature throughout the period. A further problem was the increasing overpopulation on the land and underemployment despite the low level of technology. Estimates suggest that up to two thirds of the rural population was surplus to requirements (Moore 1945, 207).

Yet though compared with Western countries yields per hectare and per man were very low, the Bulgarian peasant, by his diligence and enterprise, produced the highest yield rates in the Balkan peninsula (Rothschild 1974, 331). Moreover, there were signs of enterprise in terms of crop diversification away from the heavy reliance on cereals. This change was most marked in the case of tobacco which became an important crop in the 1920s, and when prices weakened in this commodity there was a shift to other crops and industrial products (see below).

The farming community was badly hit by the fall in commodity prices in the Great Depression. According to Logio (1936, 138–39), the prices of agricultural products sank to a low of 34.4 at the start of 1934

(1929 = 100), whereas the index for local manufactured articles was 88 and that for imported goods 82. This meant that peasants had to give up about two and a half times their own produce in exchange for the latter goods. Export earnings also fell heavily; by 1933 they were less than half the 1929 level (Lampe 1986, 78).

The fall in export earnings had serious repercussions for debt servicing. In the latter half of the 1920s Bulgaria, like many other East European countries, had run up heavy foreign debts. Much of the borrowing consisted of short-term credits which were recycled by the banks into long-term investments, thereby creating a liquidity problem for financial institutions once the flow of overseas funding dried up (Pasvolsky 1930, 248–50). Debt servicing costs as a percentage of export earnings rose from 12.3 per cent in 1928 to 22 per cent in 1931/32 (Drabek 1985, 425; Nötel 1986, 223). The government promptly took action following the international financial crisis of the summer of 1931; on 15 October 1931 it imposed exchange control, soon to be followed by the control of foreign trade. By 1933 the Bulgarian National Bank had to authorise all imports and by the mid-1930s it was also allocating quotas and issuing import licences (Crampton 1987, 141–42).

The public finances were also affected adversely. There was a large fall in revenue yields whereas initially expenditures were maintained so that budgetary deficits widened. To deal with the mounting crisis the government imposed a deflationary policy, with cutbacks in expenditure and increases in taxes. Civil service salaries were reduced as were profit rates on public contracts. A surtax was introduced and in November 1931 duties on imports of raw materials and machinery (many formerly zero rated) were raised and made permanent the following year. Corporate taxation was also raised and in March 1933 the tax on industrial enterprises was more than doubled.

Despite the difficult conditions the government did make an early and concerted effort to help the farming community. In fact agriculture became the focus of relief policy, more so than in other countries. In December 1930 a Cereals Purchasing Board was established to control the purchase and export of cereals with the objective of stabilising prices. The marketing of other agricultural products, such as hemp, cotton, flax, rice and silk cocoons, was taken on by the state banks.

From March 1932 measures were taken to protect farmers with debts from going bankrupt. Debt burdens were reduced, interest rates cut, the land tax was lowered and state banks were given the power to buy properties of insolvent farmers for resale on favourable terms. In 1933–34 public works were started to relieve unemployment (Spigler 1986, 129–30).

The policies were not very well coordinated and some of them were inconsistent. The increased expenditure involved also made it more difficult to balance the budget. Nevertheless, they did make some contribution to relieving the hard pressed agrarian sector.

In fact, in the circumstances agriculture performed quite well in the 1930s. By the end of the decade crop output and even livestock production had more than recovered to the pre-depression levels. Crop values per capita were in fact 22 per cent higher (Lampe 1986, 84–85). The pressure on grain and tobacco prices encouraged a shift to alternative crops such as fruit farming and market gardening, dairy and poultry produce, industrial crops and stockbreeding, all of which expanded rapidly in the 1930s. The government encouraged this diversification, as did the cooperative organisations which purchased about one third of agricultural produce and supplied credit to farmers. Possibly three fifths of farmers had dealings with cooperative institutions (Crampton 1987, 138–39).

Yet despite the diversification, Bulgarian agriculture still remained very backward. The proportion of land devoted to cereals was still very high (about two thirds), the highest in Eastern Europe, as was the amount of land left fallow. Wheat, tobacco and eggs accounted for over 50 per cent of export earnings (Hoffman 1972, 55). The use of modern machinery was very limited, despite state efforts to encourage its adoption, while chemical fertilisers were fairly rare.

As with other East European countries, Bulgaria's trade was drawn into the German orbit during the 1930s – in fact more so than most, since by 1938 Germany dominated the trade of Bulgaria, with 59 per cent for exports and 52 per cent for imports, compared with under a quarter in 1929 (Hiden 1977, 173). Following the imposition of exchange control in 1931 there was a rapid move to clearing; by the mid-1930s 76 per cent of exports were transacted under clearing arrangements and 88 per cent by 1939. Bulgaria had a relatively close affinity with Germany and German military experts came to dominate the Bulgarian army (Jones 1937, 64, 82). Who gained the most from these arrangements is a much debated issue. German purchases of Bulgarian exports (nearly all agricultural) doubled between 1930 and 1938, though Lampe (1986, 84–91) doubts whether bilateral trade was superior to a multilateral variant. On the other hand, Ritschl (2001) rejects the notion that small countries were exploited by Nazi Germany's foreign trade policies. Had it not been for the German market one suspects that Bulgarian exports would not have almost returned to their pre-depression level on a per capita basis (Lampe 1986, 90).

Industrialisation under a policy of import substitution seemed the only way forward in the harsh climate of the 1930s. Real industrial output was maintained quite well through the depression and rose by over 50 per cent between 1929 and 1938, a more creditable performance than either Yugoslavia or Romania, and far better than the average for all Europe.

Yet despite some impressive growth rates in certain industrial sectors, the overall economic structure did not change very much. Manufactured goods accounted for less than 5 per cent of export values (much of it processed food) and modern industry for only about 5–6 per cent of national income and 8 per cent of the labour force, not very much different from the 1920s, and the lowest shares in South-east Europe apart from Albania. Much of the growth came from smaller enterprises established in the 1930s rather than from larger concerns or state-assisted (tax and tariff exemptions) enterprises. One reason for this may well have been the steady decline in the scope of the encouraged industry sector; many sectors were withdrawn altogether while the number of encouraged enterprises fell from 1145 to 854 between 1931 and 1937 (Lampe 1986, 95). Whether this was propitious from the long-term development point of view, given that scale economies and technical progress are usually associated with size, is a debatable point, though at the early stages of development small acorns may hold important portents for the future.

In contrast to agriculture and foreign trade, the state's direct influence in industry appears to have waned somewhat in the 1930s. Even the increase in armament expenditure at the end of the decade did not involve a significant change in state policy in terms of resource mobilisation and direct control of industry. Having been fairly stable between 1929 and 1935, defence expenditure rose by some 70 per cent between 1935 and 1938, to absorb 24.8 per cent of total public expenditure, double that of 1935 (Hauner 1986, 57). In fact much of the increase in expenditure was absorbed in buying motor vehicle equipment and machinery from Nazi Germany, rather than being spent on domestic military installations.

The state's direct role in the economy was not insignificant, however. It owned a range of industries, including coal mines, railroads, public utilities and maritime shipping. The number of state-owned enterprises totalled 169 in 1939, accounted for 8–9 per cent of industrial production, and 15 per cent if cooperatives are included (Lampe 1986, 100–110). The role of foreign capital declined in this period, though it still accounted for some 40 per cent of corporate capital, being especially prevalent in power generation, food, tobacco, metal, and chemical and mining activities (Hoffman 1972, 54; Lamer 1938, 503–506).

Though import substitution led to a rise in the consumption of Bulgarian-produced goods, from 61 to 88 per cent of total consumption, the country's industrial structure changed very little. Textiles, foodstuffs and construction materials still accounted for the major share of industrial output, though there was some increase in the shares of metals and chemicals. In general industrial production was dominated by small firms. The highly protected market tended to breed inefficiency and also restricted the spatial dispersion of industry. The concentration in and around Sofia continued to prevail, which accounted for around a third of industrial production in the later 1930s (Hoffman 1972, 55; Lampe 1986, 97).

Yugoslavia

Yugoslavia was an anomaly from its very inception and remained so down to its disintegration in 1992. This new state, formally proclaimed the Kingdom of the Serbs, Croats and Slovenes (and from 1929 officially known as Yugoslavia) by Prince Alexander, Regent of Serbia, on 1 December 1918, consisted of a motley collection of territories and an even more motley collection of peoples. Much of it had been put together in the grab for territory in the closing stages of the war and was reluctantly sanctioned by the Paris peacemakers and formally confirmed in the peace treaties with Austria, Hungary and Bulgaria. By any stretch of the imagination it could scarcely be said to have historical legitimacy on its side. It consisted of the former independent kingdoms of Serbia and Montenegro, and incorporated respectively Croatia-Slavonia, part of Banat and other bits of territory from Hungary; the province of Dalmatia, Carniola and the mainly Slovene-speaking areas of Styria and Carinthia and part of Istria from Austria; Bosnia-Hercegovina from Austro-Hungary; and small bits of territory from Albania and Bulgaria (Singleton and Carter 1982, 59). The final result was a country three times the size of the original Serbia (population 12 million in 1921), whose peoples 'had little in common except language' and could never conceivably agree 'on a common interpretation of what the country meant' (MacMillan 2003, 133). As was to be expected, scarcely a single frontier of the new republic went undisputed in the interwar years and Yugoslavia had border squabbles over peoples and territory with nearly all its neighbours, Austria, Italy, Hungary, Albania and Bulgaria.

An 'ethnic soufflé' would be a good description of the new state since Yugoslavia had more nationalities and religions than almost any other country in Europe. In fact it was even more diverse ethnically than the Czech Republic, with 57 per cent of its population being classed as minorities, though at least the bulk of the population was of Slavic origin while the non-Slavic minorities were divided and weak (Pearson

1983, 156). There were 43 per cent Serbs, 23 per cent Croatians, 8.5 per cent Slovenes, 6 per cent Bosnian Muslims, 5 per cent Macedonian Slavs, 3.6 per cent Albanians, 3.6 per cent Germans, 3.4 per cent Magyars, with the remaining 3.9 per cent made up of Jews, Romanians, Gypsies, Vlachs, Italians and Turks (Jelavich 1983, 151). None of these peoples regarded themselves as belonging to one nation and so a distinct national Yugoslav identity failed to materialise. From the inception of the new state the minority Serbs, who were weaker than their Czech brethren and economically inferior to the Croats and Slovenes, sought to dominate the regime by imposing centralised control and for the most part disregarding the interests of many of the smaller minority groups. The Croats and other minority groups, on the other hand, attempted to resist the rule of the Serbs and struggled to gain greater autonomy and power. While apologists have sought to play down the charge of Serbian domination and exploitation, the fact remains that ethnic conflict was a serious source of weakness from the foundation of the new kingdom (Dragnich 1983, 135–51). The most bitter rivalry occurred between the two largest groups, the Serbs and Croats, which at times paralysed the nation and left it vulnerable to external predators (Jelavich 1983, 151).

Given the clash of interests it is not surprising that political life was turbulent and that democracy had a tenuous hold on the country, which soon gave way to dictatorship. An official report of 1941 described the events as follows:

> During the years 1919–29 advanced democracy in a country where more than half the population was illiterate and the ruling class of Serbs was more conspicuous for heroic conduct in war than for humdrum efficiency in peace, brought disastrous results. The absolutism of the State in all walks of life, supported by a large army and police force, made political strife so continuous and so confused that between 1921 and 1929 there were twenty-five ministries and at times twenty-one parties. The complex problem of legal and agrarian reform and many other urgent tasks had to wait while politicians manoeuvred for personal power and enriched themselves by hidden methods. As a result, and in conjunction with the economic crisis, since 1929 Yugoslavia has been under a dictatorship, royal or non-royal, camouflaged or non-camouflaged.
> (Foreign Office 1941, 304)

War losses and devastation were severe, especially in Serbia. Yovanovich (1930, 302) described war losses in Serbia as 'overwhelming' and by far the worst of any other country. As far as the human factor is concerned this was certainly the case. No other country mobilised so extensively; virtually the whole of the male population between the ages of 18 and 55 were drafted into the forces (822,000 in total) and approximately half of them perished. If we add to this the civilian deaths due to war-related causes such as occupation, deportation, disease and famine, the total loss is probably nearer one million, or one quarter of the prewar population. Taking account also of wartime birth deficits – that is, estimates of children not born because of enforced mobilisation of male citizens – then the final tally is well over one million, or some 31 per cent of the peacetime population (Notestein et al. 1944, 75). In addition, some 250,000 were wounded or incapacitated in one way or another. In relative terms human losses in other countries pale into insignificance. Romania, with the second highest casualty list, suffered a population deficit of 14 per cent, Austro-Hungary 9.5 per cent and Bulgaria 9.2 per cent, while proportions for the Western belligerents were even lower: France 7.7 per cent, Belgium 5.4 per cent, Germany 8 per cent and the UK 3.9 per cent (Notestein et al. 1944, 75).

Material and physical losses were equally devastating. Estimates suggest that about one half of the prewar wealth was destroyed or three times the current income (Yovanovich 1930, 302). Following the Austro-Hungarian retreat nearly all the factories and industrial establishments were found to be in a useless condition. Many of them had been totally wrecked, while farms had been stripped of most of their livestock and implements. In total, about one half of the livestock was destroyed. Some of the damage done to the land was almost beyond repair and so food production at the end of the war was only 30–40 per cent of peacetime levels, and consumption was little better. The railways were rendered unworkable and in some districts houses had been gutted of fixtures and fittings (Berend 1985, 151; Yovanovich 1930, 298; Temperley 1920, 147). Losses in former Habsburg lands were less severe but many troops died or were taken prisoner on the Italian and Russian fronts, while about one fifth of the prewar wealth was destroyed (Lampe 1980, 139; 1996, 107).

Thus when it came to reconstruction and unification the tasks facing Yugoslavia were probably greater than those of any other country in Europe. Apart from the ethnic issue, there was little that was uniform throughout the whole country. In nearly every respect there was fragmentation and diversity in institutional structures, legal and business codes, fiscal and monetary systems, customs duties and so on. There were six customs areas, five currencies, five railway systems, 12 separate tax systems, three divergent banking systems, and a variety of legal and business codes (Lampe 1980, 139; Bicanic and Skreb 1994, 148). Even the agrarian sector was riddled with different land tenure systems left over from previous empires. There were also considerable differences in income levels between different parts of the country (Hocevar 1965, 114–15).

It took a decade or more to unify the economic system of the country. For political and social reasons it was the issue of land reform that received early attention. One of the first declarations of the new regime was the promise of land reform – that is, the abolition of feudal rights and the break-up of large estates. There was a variety of agricultural systems and land tenure patterns: small peasant ownership in Serbia and Montenegro, a mixed system with large estates in former Habsburg territories, while feudal relics persisted in Bosnia and Macedonia, a legacy of Ottoman rule (Djordjevic 1992, 315).

The Land Reform Act of 1919 swept away feudal rights and made provision for extensive land redistribution. Because of bureaucratic mismanagement it took much of the interwar period to complete the reform. In the process most peasants could lay claim to some land though few had enough. Nearly 70 per cent of the total number of holdings in the 1930s had 5 hectares or less and 88 per cent 10 hectares or less. Only a very few large estates remained, accounting for some 10 per cent of the cultivated land (Moore 1945, 82).

The chief drawback was that land reform did not solve the agrarian problem. Many of the plots were too small to be viable. Those with dwarf holdings (under 2 hectares) even had to borrow money to buy food! (Singleton and Carter 1982, 82). As time went on the land hunger got worse since the total rural population rose from 9 to 11.5 million between 1921 and 1938. This kept agricultural productivity low as many peasants found it difficult to generate sufficient income to meet a heavy tax burden and service their debts, let alone invest in their farms (Dyker 1990, 5). One estimate suggests that some 7 million peasants were unable to secure an adequate standard of living (Berend 1985, 155), while the surplus agrarian population was the highest in Europe, at 65 per cent (Moore 1945, 208). The pressure on rural resources had unfortunate consequences in that it resulted in marginal land, including forests, being cleared for cultivation, which in turn led to soil erosion and increasing aridity in drier zones (Dyker 1990, 5).

Reform in other economic spheres was equally protracted. A uniform tax system was proposed in 1922 but not implemented until 1928. A uniform system of railway rates was introduced in 1925 but the proper integration and development of the railway network was slow and uneven, and by 1940 many regions were still without a unified system or even a basic network (Hoffman 1972, 65). A uniform tariff and common currency, the Serbian dinar, did not materialise until 1925, while a uniform budgetary accounting system was not complete until 1934 (Bicanic and Skreb 1994, 148–49).

The internal convertibility of the other currencies took place in 1925 when the dinar was stabilised *de facto*. The delay was occasioned by the fact that the trade balance was negative in the years 1919–22 with the exchange rate depreciating sharply until the beginning of 1923. In addition, budgetary problems of the new state led to a large rise in the money supply with a corresponding effect on prices. The note circulation increased from 812.6 to 5790.2 million dinars between 1 February 1920 and the end of 1923 (Calic 1994, 222). During 1923 there was a marked improvement in trade; imports were checked and the value of exports rose sharply owing to favourable prices for timber, eggs, pigs and maize. At the same time the National Bank was instructed to reduce the note issue. The exchange rate quickly appreciated, and as the export surplus lasted until the middle of 1925 the opportunity was taken to stabilise the currency at 56–57 dinars to the dollar, or 9.1 per cent of the prewar parity, the rate being finally adopted *de jure* in May 1931 with the aid of an international loan. This probably overvalued the currency and led to a temporary deflation (League of Nations 1946a, 126; Lampe 1996, 150). However, the inflationary episode gave a boost to company formation. New enterprises sprang up like mushrooms in the early postwar years, some 500 between 1918 and 1922. Of the total number of new factories or workshops established between 1919 and 1938 (2193), no less than 31 per cent (682) were formed in the first five years of the new state (Calic 1994, 222).

Despite the enormous problems facing the new state, Yugoslavia's economic performance in the 1920s was very creditable and better than that of Romania, which had started out with more factors in her favour. Agriculture certainly responded more positively. There was a significant increase in the output of crops and in crop yields compared with prewar levels (Berend 1985, 169; Janos 1989, 345). Trade expanded rapidly from the low levels recorded in the early 1920s. Between 1922 and 1929 export values nearly tripled, though imports were more restrained (Royal Institute of International Affairs 1936, 24). This expansion was accompanied by a significant shift in the composition of exports. Cereals became much less important, declining from 33.1 to 16.8 per cent of total exports between 1913 and 1926–30; by contrast there was a large rise in the share of forestry products, from 0.8 to 20.0 per cent, and also significant share gains for livestock, eggs, and fruit and other crops (Lampe and Jackson 1982, 369).

Industrial development proceeded apace under government encouragement, favoured by tax exemptions, subsidies and tariff protection, though the latter was not as severe as in other Balkan states. It was also assisted by the influx of foreign capital following stabilisation of the currency, the sectors most favoured being mining, electric power and chemicals. The rapid rise in new factories during the early 1920s was maintained later in the decade, though at a slightly slower pace, with nearly 600 new creations between 1924 and 1928 (Calic 1994, 224). Fixed assets in manufacturing, mining and electricity rose much more rapidly than in other sectors, by 83 per cent between 1910 and 1929, compared with 17 per cent in agriculture, only 7 per cent in transport and communications, and 19 per cent for total fixed assets in the economy. It is noteworthy, however, that even with this large increase industry's share of the total stock of fixed assets had only climbed to 6 per cent by 1929 as opposed to 4 per cent in 1910. Agriculture and transport still accounted for over 40 per cent of total assets, while the share of buildings (including houses) was nearly 50 per cent (Vinski 1955, 214–15).

It is difficult to calculate precise estimates for movements in industrial output because of the changes in territorial coverage and the absence of reliable statistical records, especially for earlier years. The work of Lampe and Jackson (1982, 406–409) would seem to indicate that the rate of growth averaged more than 3 per cent a year over the period 1913–29 with some acceleration in later years.

Yugoslavia was not quite as badly affected as Bulgaria and Romania by the adverse price movements during the depression. Nevertheless, there was no room for complacency as incomes fell sharply in the primary sector and budgetary and balance of payments problems loomed large. One third of rural households were heavily in debt and their total indebtedness was equal to 80–90 per cent of their cash incomes (Rothschild 1974, 271).

In an attempt to balance the budget and save the currency the government, following French thinking, adopted a severely deflationary policy and imposed exchange control in October 1931. However, Yugoslavia was one of the first Balkan countries to change course. Between 1933 and 1935 cheaper money, reflationary government spending and a relaxation of exchange control signalled an end to orthodox economic policy. In the summer of 1934 the government attempted to lower interest rates charged by the banks, while in the following year it issued a loan for spending on public works (Royal Institute of International Affairs 1936, 127–28).

The relaxation of exchange rate policy began even earlier. By the spring of 1933 the National Bank was purchasing at a premium the foreign currency obtained by exporters trading under clearing agreements. The premium was steadily increased to give a discount of some 23 per cent on the gold parity of the dinar, and by the later 1930s this discount was around one third. In effect this adjustment acknowledged that the dinar had been overvalued when finally stabilised in 1931. However, in order to protect the currency it did mean that Yugoslavia was forced to increase its dependence on clearing transactions, especially with Germany. By 1938 the share of Yugoslavia's trade conducted under clearing agreements had risen to 80 per cent. Schacht's bilateral clearing agreements offered an artificial exchange rate that paid prices 30 per cent above world levels. Trade with Germany therefore increased steadily: the share of exports going to Germany increased from 8.5 per cent in 1929 to 42.0 per cent in 1938, while the proportion of Yugoslavia's imports derived from that source rose from 15.6 to 39.4 per cent over the same period.

On balance Yugoslavia probably gained from her closer association with Germany even if it did sometimes result in the importation of unwanted products such as aspirins and cuckoo clocks. Increasing dependence on the German market did not lead to control of Yugoslavia's economy. On the other hand, trading relationships with Germany could be unpredictable. In September 1939, for example, Germany suddenly decided not to purchase Yugoslavia's bumper plum crop despite a previous contractual obligation to do so. The story did have a happy and somewhat amusing ending. The plums were turned into brandy on which the Bosnians got drunk, but at least it solved the problem of the aspirins, since according to Hoptner (1962, 103), the Bosnians 'were able to absorb on a mass scale the aspirin dumped on Yugoslavia by the Germans through clearing agreements'. Whether the Romanians found such a ready outlet for their even larger supply of German aspirins is unknown.

Some commentators have been highly critical of certain aspects of the state's policy, especially with regard to the distribution of public expenditure and the incidence of taxation. The chief contentions are that too much of state spending went on administration and later defence rather than on improving the infrastructure, which was in a very poor condition, and that regressive tax systems hit the peasantry. Between 28 and 35 per cent of budgetary expenditure went on military activities during the interwar years whereas direct spending on promoting economic activities and improving the social infrastructure was quite modest by comparison. This, argues Tomasevich (1955, 694–702), sapped economic and financial strength and retarded development.

The tax system was highly regressive and lacked both logic and equity. Tomasevitch (1955, 682, 688) was of the opinion that the administration of the system was designed more to suit the convenience of officials and that the principles of taxation involved those 'of charging its citizens as often as possible and as heavily as possible; taking the money where it could find it, and getting it from those who make the least outcry, rather than according to the principle of the ability to pay'.

In the early 1930s indirect taxation accounted for some three quarters of total state revenue, and though there was some reduction of this proportion in subsequent years, the incidence still bore heavily on the poor peasants. At times some 50 per cent of the cash income of the peasants went to pay taxes. By contrast better-off groups such as government officials, businessmen, rent-receivers and even urban workers escaped relatively lightly. The distortions and anomalies in the tax system are legendary. To give one glaring example: owners of urban housing paid very little tax on rental income as well as benefiting from subsidised interest rates, a practice which resulted in some 50–60 per cent of capital formation finding its way into residential property and government buildings at the expense of more productive investment in industry and social infrastructures (Tomasevitch 1955, 686–87). Fiscal systems in other Balkan countries had their distorting features but probably none more so than in Yugoslavia.

The government also implemented various relief measures to help the farming community in the 1930s. These included reduced taxation and the elimination of debts of some 654,000 small farmers (Berend 1985, 178). Along with export premia, the control of the export marketing of primary products and price support schemes were introduced to secure more favourable returns for farmers. In addition, there were also policies designed to encourage stockbreeding, the rotation of crops, the planting of more labour intensive crops, the cultivation of fodder and a shift from pasture to stable feeding (Royal Institute of International Affairs 1939, 145–46).

Yugoslavia was in something of a cleft stick between the wars. However rapidly it expanded it could not keep pace with the rise in numbers so that rural overpopulation got steadily worse. The number of industrial workers rose by about half a million between 1929 and 1937 but over the same period the total population increased by 1.8 million (Basch 1944, 241). The industrial sector expanded steadily during the 1920s and 1930s, and very rapidly, at over 10 per cent per annum, in the three years or so before the Second World War due to the influence of state defence spending. Industrial growth accounted for about two thirds of the rise in gross domestic output (Lampe 1996, 184). Measures taken to encourage industrial development did enlarge the industrial base. Initially, policies of import substitution were more successful in traditional sectors of activity such as textiles, leather and food processing, given the low level of purchasing power, shortages of capital and skilled manpower and limited technical capability. By the end of the 1930s many consumer goods could be produced domestically and a promising start had been made on the establishment of a capital goods industry, iron and steel, cement, metals and machinery, chemicals and construction materials (Lampe 1986, 96). By 1938 industry accounted for some 30 per cent of national income, though very much less in terms of employment. Indeed, the rural share of the population scarcely changed in the interwar years owing to the rapid growth in population (Lampe 1996, 185).

The heavy side of industry was of course increasingly dependent on both state spending on defence and foreign capital. By 1938 state enterprises and monopolies accounted for 15 per cent of industrial capital as well as providing one half of budgetary revenues (Lampe 1996, 180). Dependence on foreign capital increased during the 1930s and by the end of the decade about one half of modern industrial development was owned and controlled by foreigners. External control was especially high in mining, metallurgy, chemicals, oil, electric power and timber, and less important in the consumer goods trades (Hoffman 1972, 52). Tomasevich (1949, 193) felt that the extent of foreign influence gave the economy a semi-colonial character.

That industrial growth was not more rapid can be attributed to several factors: the dearth of capital and of skilled manpower and competent management; a lacking in technical expertise; limited effective demand because of low agrarian incomes and the burden of taxation; the skewed nature of investment and state spending; the distortions of the tax system; and the low infrastructure development, especially the deplorable state of transport which often inhibited the exploitation of some of the country's rich mineral resources (Hoffman 1972, 52–53).

By the end of the period Yugoslavia still remained a very backward country. The bulk of its population was rural-based and only a small proportion of its labour force worked in modern industry. Jackson and Lampe (1983, 408–409) were impressed by some of the structural shifts towards modern industry in the Balkans and by the pace of import substitution in consumer goods sectors such as textiles and food processing. But their conclusion on Yugoslavia appears somewhat optimistic: 'Modern mechanical production had ... become the predominant form of industrial activity by 1939 in a territory where little statistical significance had existed before the turn of the century.' As in the case of Bulgaria, much of this industry was spatially concentrated around urban centres, which led to a marked regional imbalance in levels of development (Singleton and Carter 1982, 75). In other respects the country still had an underdeveloped appearance. The pattern of foreign trade, for instance, reflected the low level of development and the limited diversification of economic activity. Exports consisted mainly of primary products with five commodities, timber, corn, wheat, iron and copper ores, accounting for over one half of total exports. Conversely, 80 per cent of imports were semi-finished or finished manufactures (Hoffman 1972, 52).

Romania

Romania was the only beneficiary of the peace settlement to have had a fully independent existence before 1914 and therefore could claim some rightful legitimacy. It was favoured because it fought on the Allied side, even if late in the war and without great distinction, and it was anti-Bolshevik, an attribute which was put to good use in 1919 in the defeat of Bela Kun's short-lived seizure of power in Hungary.

Romania grabbed territory from Austro-Hungary and Russia and the peacemakers were quite happy to confirm the country's determination to forge a 'Greater Romania' as a useful bulwark against communism even if this did lead to the wrath of her neighbours. It therefore emerged as the major beneficiary from the peacemaking exercise without too much effort. It more than doubled in size; population increased from 7.5 to 17.6 million between 1914 and 1921, while the area increased from 137,903 to 304,244 square kilometres. Its major acquisitions included Transylvania from Hungary, Bessarabia from Russia, Bukovina from Austria and the Dobrudja from Bulgaria.

Despite these large acquisitions, Romania was much more compact ethnically than Yugoslavia. There was a very strong national Romanian contingent, some 71 per cent of the population, while the only minority groups likely to pose a serious threat were the Hungarians (8.6 per cent) and the Germans (4.2 per cent). There was, it is true, a wide variety of nationalities contained in Romania's borders, including significant contingents of Jews, Ukrainians and Russians, along with sprinklings of Serbs, Croats, Slovenes, Bulgarians, Czechs, Slovaks, Ruthenes, Turks, Tartars, Gypsies and Gagauze, but none of them posed a serious threat to the new state (Crampton and Crampton 1996, 117). In any case, the dominant Romanians, as with their counterparts in Poland, were determined to enforce assimilation in their drive to achieve a homogeneous nation-state even if this did prejudice minority rights. 'What has been termed "integral nationalism", already discernible before 1914, dominated Romania in the inter-war period, to the permanent detriment of its many minorities' (Pearson 1983, 167).

Romania also had a good natural resource endowment, especially with the acquisition of additional territory. The resource base was greatly increased by the rich cereal lands of Banat-Crisana and Bessarabia, and the productive grazing lands of Bukovina, Maramures and Transylvania. There was also considerable mineral wealth in some of these new lands including coal, iron ore, natural gas and non-ferrous metals. She also had her important oil reserves which had been developed before 1914. Contemporary observers felt the country had a great future (Turnock 1986, 49).

Although not a major theatre of war, Romania nevertheless suffered extensive damage largely as a result of the German occupation. The Germans ransacked the country and exploited its resources. By the end of hostilities industrial production was running at one third the prewar level. Oil production fell by one half, some of it occasioned by the action of the Romanians themselves in an attempt to keep the Germans from gaining access to the fields. Much of the railway system was rendered inoperable due to a lack of maintenance and the destruction of bridges, installations and rolling stock. By the end of the war rolling stock levels were only a fraction of those of prewar: locomotives 24 per cent, passenger coaches 35 per cent and wagons 14 per cent (Teichova 1985, 225). Agriculture also suffered severely from enemy occupation, with the loss of many farm buildings, 30 per cent of agricultural equipment and up to one half of the livestock. Exports of agricultural products were decimated, to a mere 109,000 tons compared with 4.6 million before the war (Berend 1985, 152). Romania also had the second highest casualty list, with a population deficit of 14 per cent.

As in most other countries, land reform was high on the political agenda for obvious political and social reasons. There were considerable variations in land tenure partly because of newly acquired territories, with some large estates especially in the former Hungarian lands. The authorities were also keen to get rid of non-Romanian holders if possible.

Laws enacted in 1918 and 1921 provided for the expropriation and redistribution of large estates. Altogether 6.3 million hectares of land were expropriated, approximately one half of which was in the newly acquired territories of Transylvania and Bessarabia (Petrini 1931, 103). Of this total 3.8 million were distributed among 1.4 million peasant families, 1.2 million was earmarked for state reserves and the rest retained for further settlement. As a consequence some two thirds of large estates disappeared (Berend 1985, 156). The reform was not as radical as in Yugoslavia and Bulgaria. Though, numerically, smallholders (1–5 hectares) predominated, they owned only 28.1 per cent of agricultural land (1930); nearly 40 per cent was owned by undertakings (24.3 per cent) in the 5–50 hectare range; while a mere 0.7 per cent of the holdings accounted for nearly a third of the land, though only about 14 per cent of the tillage area (Moore 1945, 82). Moreover, many peasants who should have received land from the distributions did not do so and there were still some 700,000 peasants without land after the distributions were completed.

Compensation also proved a heavy burden on the new holders. Recipients had to pay at once 20 per cent of the value of the land, 35 per cent was assumed by the state, and the rest was to be paid in instalments over a 20 year period. Since the expropriated land was paid for by the state in the first instance the peasants effectively became debtors of the state (Berend 1985, 156).

The chief question is how far the land reform was the cause of the poor performance of agriculture in the interwar period. Romanian agriculture fared badly compared with other Balkan countries. The prewar level (1909–13) of output was surpassed in only five years in the interwar period and yields declined as did exports, despite an increase in the area under cultivation (see Table 4.1). Wheat yields were below that of any Balkan state apart from Albania and very low compared with best Western standards.

Table 4.1 Indices of Area, Yield and Production of Cereals in Romania

	1909–13	1920	1924	1926	1933–37
Area	100	84.4	101.2	102.8	114.3
Yield	100	86.7	60.0	99.2	81.7
Production	100	72.9	60.6	101.6	93.1

Source: Roberts 1951, 57.

It would be easy to conclude that agrarian reform was the reason for this poor showing. As Turnock (1986, 79, 85) points out, the main purpose of agrarian reform 'had been to distribute wealth rather than produce it' and 'peasant states could only become prosperous once they ceased being peasant states'. The reform certainly aggravated the situation. It burdened the peasants with large debts, it made no provision for consolidation of holdings, nor did it give any incentive for improvements in efficiency and better techniques of cultivation. The worst aspect was the fragmentation of holdings and the prevalence of strip farming. The reform aggravated both features since appropriated lands were often divided into very small holdings consisting of between one half- to 5-hectare plots often separated by some distance from each other. The average distance was between 4 and 7 kilometres and many strips were very long and narrow (Roberts 1951, 58–59). The problem of dwarf holdings became worse over time as particle inheritance led to further fragmentation with the result that:

> A holding of a few acres may consist of as many as forty small strips, separated from each other by several miles. Large areas of cultivated land were wasted in the form of paths enabling owners to walk from one strip to another. The strips are incapable of efficient production.
> (Seton-Watson 1946, 81)

Thus instead of viable units becoming the norm it was in fact the least viable units that predominated numerically. In 1941 over 58 per cent of properties were below 3 hectares, 'a perilous minimum for a self-sustaining cultivation' (Roberts 1951, 53). The average size holding of 3–5 hectares only accounted for just over 18 per cent of the total and even these proved a struggle for survival because of low productivity. Such holdings scarcely provided a decent living (Hitchins 1994, 341).

Yet however inefficient these smallholders may have been, they cannot be held solely responsible for the poor agricultural performance. After all, holdings of between 1 and 5 hectares only accounted for some 28 per cent of the agricultural land, while those between 5 and 50 hectares cultivated 40 per cent and the rest was held by units of over 50 hectares. Unless it can be assumed that all holdings were inefficient and unviable, a rather heroic assumption, we must look elsewhere for the causes of agricultural stagnation.

One major problem was the lack of adaptation in the crop structure. Romanian agriculture held tenaciously to producing cereals, which even by 1938 accounted for 82 per cent of the arable cultivation, with wheat and maize taking up two thirds of that total. The market for cereals was scarcely buoyant for much of the period yet little diversification was evident. Low productivity was caused by many factors, including the limited use of manures and fertilisers, primitive crop-rotation practices, the low quality of livestock, backward techniques of cultivation, shortage of implements and farm machinery – though many farms were no doubt too small to use equipment effectively – and of course the prevalence of strip farming. Shortage of capital and credit and the burden of taxation acted as further disincentives to improvement and modernisation. Thus for the most part Romanian agriculture remained backward and unyielding, and more than one half of the farming population could be classed as surplus to requirements when the productivity of agriculture is related to Western standards (Turnock 1986, 83; Moore 1945, 208).

Government policy did little, at least in the 1920s, to assist agriculture. If anything the reverse was the case since the major priorities were to encourage industry, integrate the country and balance the national accounts to enable currency reform to take place. In the immediate postwar years Romania was occupied with the task of absorbing the new lands, keeping the Bolshevik menace at bay and with land reform. However, a start was made on unification. By 1923 all the main railway lines had been converted to standard gauge and a single currency had been introduced. Currency stabilisation, however, was not achieved *de facto* until 1927. Though the government maintained a policy of fiscal retrenchment to bring about budgetary equilibrium, currency reform was also dependent on the improvement in the trade balance. This was very volatile in the postwar years depending on the state of the harvests and the vagaries of the international market for commodities. However, from early 1923 improvements in the trade balance and curtailment of the money supply improved the strength of the lei, which was kept stable for two or more years. A new depreciation set in after mid-1925 due to poor harvests but the following two years brought an improvement which enabled stabilisation to take place in mid-1927 at 160 lei to the dollar, or 3 per cent of prewar parity. Final stabilisation occurred in 1929 at a slight discount of 167 to the dollar, with the help of an international loan (League of Nations 1946a, 126–28).

In 1923 a new constitution was introduced which was strongly centralist with the aim of breaking down regional differences. Political life for much of the 1920s was dominated by the Liberal Party under the leadership of the Bratianu brothers (Ion and Vintile). The title was something of a misnomer since their government was anything but liberal. In economic terms it could best be described as neo-mercantilist since its aim was to foster industry by protection and subsidies, limit the influence of foreign capital and protect the currency. It was also corrupt. Corruption in fact was common in all the Balkan countries but none more so than in Romania where it was carried to extreme lengths. Bribery, corruption and dishonesty were prevalent in official, political and business circles. Hordes of politicians and officials waxed fat on the Treasury, as did the business intimates and friends of the Bratianu brothers, who dispensed largesse on a liberal scale to their supporters. As one contemporary observed, the state administration was 'annexed by the party bosses and the public budget has been confiscated for the benefit of the clients of these parties' (Logio 1932, 128). It was in fact rule by the elite for the elite, who had little interest in the welfare of the masses (Gilberg 1992, 278–83).

Romania provides a good example of the way in which new mercantilist doctrines were implemented to foster industrialisation at the expense of agriculture. Industry was favoured by many privileges and incentives, including tax reliefs, cheap factory sites, subsidised railway rates, a cap on fuel prices, exemptions from duties on imported raw materials and equipment used in manufacture, specific subsidies for certain sectors such as armaments, and of course high duties on competing imported goods. By 1927 Romania had one of the highest tariffs in Europe. A special Institute for Industrial Credits was established in the early 1920s, with 60 per cent of the capital contributed by the state, to encourage industrial development by the provision of cheap credits (Hoffman 1972, 53). A limit was imposed on foreign shareholdings in domestic concerns of 40 per cent of the total invested, while a majority of directors and employees had to be of Romanian origin (Crampton 1994, 111).

By contrast, the agrarian sector secured very little assistance. Indeed, industry's gains were agriculture's losses. Farmers faced high import duties on machinery and implements and on consumer products, there were taxes on the exports of agrarian products, and price controls on some agricultural commodities. Farmers also bore the main burden of indirect taxes. Peasant agriculture was neglected in favour of forced industrialisation with economic self-sufficiency the goal:

> All the weapons of the new mercantilism were utilised for the industrialization of the country, whilst agriculture was left without machinery or tools, cheap credits, selected seeds, or technical improvements, actually in the critical phase which inevitably followed the measures of expropriation and the handing over of the land to the peasants.
>
> (Madgearu 1930, vi; Hertz 1947, 102–103)

Despite all the help given to industry its performance was not particularly noteworthy in the 1920s. It is true that the number of enterprises rose rapidly, from 86,000 to 273,000 between 1918 and 1930, and that there were some impressive gains in metals, metallurgy and mining, with some quite modern works in and around Bucharest (Hitchins 1994, 359–60). But much of what seemed like spectacular growth represented a regaining of the prewar level of output after the big setback during the war, and the growth rate for the period 1913–29 was only 1.7 per cent a year. This was very much lower than had been achieved in the last prewar decade (Turnock 1986, 85–86). There had been some important additions to the industrial base, such as iron and steel, textiles, light industries and coal mines, arising from territorial acquisitions. But even with these the industrial base was still very small and the bulk of Romania's exports still consisted of commodities, agricultural products, oil and timber.

The most spectacular development was that of the Romanian oil industry. This had been opened up before the war largely by German capital, and when these interests were sequestered after the war other foreign enterprises stepped in. Though Romanian participation increased, its capital contribution remained small, and out of necessity Romania adopted a more liberal policy toward foreign influence in oil than its nostrification policy elsewhere. Oil production, which had halved during the war to 0.9 million metric tons, rose rapidly during the 1920s and early 1930s, to 5.6 million metric tons in 1930 and 8.4 million in 1935. By then Romania was the fourth largest oil producer in the world, after the United States, the USSR and Venezuela. The industry was an important addition to her industrial base since a large refining industry was created, mainly under foreign ownership. Some 70–80 per cent of the output was exported, which accounted for 30 per cent of total exports in the early postwar years rising to 52 per cent in 1934. In addition, nearly one third of the state's revenues were derived from various taxes on the industry (Royal Institute of International Affairs 1936, 16–17).

The recovery of the 1920s was cut short abruptly by the Great Depression. Agriculture fared the worst because of the massive fall in commodity prices. The index of agricultural wholesale prices fell from 100 in 1929 to a low of 44–45 in 1933–34, whereas that for industrial products consumed by the farmer declined much less steeply from 100 to 81–82 over the same period (Polonsky 1975, 180). The farming community in fact suffered from deteriorating terms of trade throughout most of the interwar years and by the early 1930s the Romanian peasant was one of the most heavily indebted in the Balkan region. Production in most branches of industry declined substantially and export receipts fell by no less than 73 per cent. Even oil exports declined quite significantly, but not by as much as other exports so that the share of oil in total exports rose to over 50 per cent (Pearton 1971, 200).

In the early 1930s policy was dominated by short-term rescue measures to deal with the most pressing concerns. Although the plight of the peasants was recognised as critical, especially by the National Peasant Party which was in power from 1928 to 1931, substantial relief could not be made until the budgetary situation improved. Retrenchment was necessary in expenditure as tax receipts declined and the collection of farm taxes became more difficult (Royal Institute of International Affairs 1936, 90–92). It was not until 1932 that significant relief could be made. In that year taxes were reduced, albeit modestly, while a government moratorium was imposed on farm debts following default by many peasants on their loans. Over the next two years there was a major debt conversion of peasant debt. The principal capital sums were halved and interest rates thereon reduced. Some 70 per cent of farm debtors derived benefit from these provisions which also included a modest programme of agricultural reconstruction (Lampe and Jackson 1982, 451; Seton-Watson 1946, 83; League of Nations 1939a, 15–16). Price support schemes for various agricultural commodities and exchange control premia also provided further relief to the agrarian community.

The large fall in export receipts, the increasing burden of foreign debt – the servicing cost of which rose sharply – and the drying up of international credits in the financial crisis of the early 1930s required action to deal with the external account. Restrictions were increased on imports and exchange control was imposed in May 1932. Subsequently Romania concluded a trading agreement with Germany to secure markets for her exports. In 1933 Germany agreed to take substantial quantities of cereals at prices of 10 per cent above world levels. Two years later further agreements were negotiated for oil exports to Germany, in return for Romanian orders for German industrial machinery, generating equipment and munitions. In 1939 collaboration between Germany and Romania was arranged for the development of key industries, chemicals, engineering, metallurgy and timber, with a guaranteed market for Romanian exports of food, minerals and oil (Turnock 1986, 59–60).

In the circumstances of the time it is probable that Romania secured the best deal available since Western markets were virtually closed to Romanian exports. Romania was less dependent on the German market than Bulgaria or Yugoslavia. By 1938 her share of exports to that market was slightly less than in 1929, though the import share rose from 24 to 40 per cent. There is no reason to believe that Romania was unduly exploited by Germany, though there is evidence of the infiltration of Nazi agents under the guise of commercial agents. One example is the establishment of a soya-bean factory employing 3000 commercial agents to spread the Nazi gospel (Jones 1937, 64, 82).

Although for a time the emphasis on industrialisation was modified under the rule of the National Peasant Party, it was soon realised by both parties that industrial development was crucial if Romania was to become a strong and independent country. The drive to industrialise therefore became a key feature of economic policy in the 1930s and from 1936 it had a distinctly strategic flavour. Government assistance was forthcoming in a variety of forms, including tax reliefs, a further increase in tariffs on imported manufactures except capital equipment, finance and credits, state purchasing and monopoly provisions for certain sectors. The investment programme begun in 1936 conferred two-year monopolies for the establishment of industries considered essential to the national welfare, while the state also contributed part of the capital cost of new arms factories and guaranteed to purchase the output on favourable terms (Royal Institute of International Affairs 1939, 129–30; Hauner 1986, 90–91). The state's direct role in the economy became quite extensive, especially in strategic sectors. By 1939 the capital invested in state-owned or state-controlled economic enterprises was said to be actually larger than that in private commercial and industrial undertakings, while 70 per cent of the metallurgical output was consumed by the state, mainly for defence purposes (Roberts 1951, 32, 69, 82).

Industry performed somewhat better in the 1930s than in the previous decade. Output expanded at 3.4 per cent a year, with faster expansion in the heavy sectors under the influence of defence expenditure. Nevertheless, food processing and light industries such as leather, textiles and paper accounted for about one half of industrial production and by the end of the decade Romania was fairly self-sufficient in such products. This was reflected in the decline in the share of manufactures in total imports and the rise in the shares of semi-manufactures and raw materials. On the other hand, most of the machinery and equipment had to be imported and even in agricultural equipment domestic producers could only satisfy 16 per cent of requirements.

While some progress had been made on the industrial front by the end of the period Romania still remained very much a backward agrarian country. The bulk of its population continued to rely on agriculture and rural pursuits for most of its income, even though the share of national income from non-agrarian activities had increased steadily. Industry was heavily protected and subsidised, without which it is doubtful if it could have survived. Exports consisted largely of primary commodities including the all-important oil. The poverty of the mass of the population set limits to the expansion of industry, which would have been much lower in the latter half of the 1930s in the absence of defence procurement. In fact, if the estimates reported by Hitchins are correct, namely that the real prices of industrial products purchased by the peasant community increased to three times those of agricultural produce between 1913 and 1940, then it is not surprising that the domestic market for manufactures was weak (Hitchins 1994, 354). There is even some evidence of spare capacity developing as capacity outstripped output requirements.

CHAPTER FIVE

The Baltic States

For centuries the small Baltic states of Estonia, Latvia and Lithuania were dominated by their stronger neighbours and so much of their culture and development was determined by Swedish, German, Polish and Russian influences. In the eighteenth century the three provinces were acquired by Russia under whose domain they remained until the First World War.

All three, along with Finland, took advantage of the collapse of the Russian and German Empires, and the turbulent conditions which followed in the aftermath, to proclaim their independence and set up republics with their own constitutions. Though years of hostilities and the struggle for liberation had hit these countries hard, with severe population losses and considerable economic devastation (Von Rauch 1974, 81), they did have several advantages in comparison with many East European countries.

The Baltic states were more highly developed both economically and culturally before 1914 than Eastern Europe and Russia and they had a strong sense of national identity compared with some Slavic countries – in many respects their frame of reference would be close to the Scandinavian countries and Finland. Educational standards and infrastructure development were also better. Having said that one should recognise that by Western standards they were still very backward and agriculture remained the mainstay of their economies.

Nevertheless, there had been some worthwhile industrial developments before 1914 largely thanks to the spur provided by the large Russian market, though sadly these received a severe setback in the subsequent conflict. Berend (1998, 18) points out that, ironically, the Baltic states benefited more from the modernisation of Russia than Russia itself. In fact the Baltic provinces were, from the late nineteenth century, probably the second most rapidly developing industrial region in Russia. Latvia took pride of place in this respect and is said to have produced one quarter of the metal goods of the Russian Empire before 1914 (Hinkkanen-Lievonen 1984, 248). Latvia's industrial expansion was rapid in the latter half of the nineteenth century and by the turn of the century 67 per cent of Latvian industrial production was absorbed by Russia. It was based on engineering, chemicals, textiles, glass, rubber, wood and processed metal. Latvia was far more industrialised than the Russian Empire with some 31 per cent of its occupied population being classed as industrial (Berend 1998, 19).

The demographic structure of these three states was also fairly benign in comparison with that of Slavic countries. Minority groups accounted for a fairly small proportion of the respective populations: native Estonians totalled 86 per cent (1934), with Germans and Russians accounting for most of the remainder; Latvians were 77 per cent of the population (1935), with contingents of Russians, Germans and Jews accounting for the rest; and in the case of Lithuania, 81 per cent belonged to the indigenous population and the rest consisted mainly of Russians, Germans and Poles. This did not mean that the Baltic states avoided the minority issue altogether, but it was a far less serious problem than in, say, the Balkan countries, and for the most part the governments of the respective countries had a more tolerant attitude towards their ethnic minorities than was the case in many other European countries. The major threat was obviously the contingents of Germans and Russians.

The populations of the three states were small and growing less rapidly than in some of the other peripheral countries. Estonia's population in 1939 was just over 1.2 million and it scarcely grew at all in the interwar period. Latvia and Lithuania had populations of nearly 2 million and 2.6 million respectively at the same date with growth averaging around 1 per cent a year (Kirk 1946, 10). The populations were also reasonably well-educated. By circa 1930 Estonia had almost wiped out illiteracy – a mere 4 per cent – while in Latvia it was only 13.5 per cent and in Lithuania 36 per cent. Baltic governments in the interwar period put great emphasis on educational provision and social welfare legislation, which was made possible by the fact that state budgets were little encumbered by national debt.

Another favourable feature was the fact that dependence on agrarian pursuits was less pronounced than in Eastern Europe – 55–56 per cent in the case of Estonia and Latvia and 70 per cent for Lithuania, though this situation changed for the worse as a result of wartime industrial losses. This and the more favourable population structure meant a better man–land ratio so that surplus agrarian population was never a real issue in these countries (Moore 1945, 63–64). For example, Estonia had 1.6 hectares of arable land per head of farm population in 1930 compared with 1.0 in Romania and 0.9 in Poland (Köll 1998, 210). The Baltic states capitalised on the situation by a drive towards intensive farming based on livestock and dairy products under cooperative production.

The second major objective was to restore industrial activity, which had suffered badly during the war and from the loss of the assured

Russian market. In many parts – especially in Riga, the major industrial centre of the region – there had been wholesale sabotage and destruction of industrial plant and machinery together with evacuation of the workforce, so that 'the Latvian government was faced with the problem of having on its hands little more than empty shells of former great industrial concerns, with neither the machinery nor the work-force to run them'. The same was true of Estonia though to a lesser extent, but Lithuania was much less affected in this respect because the country had very little large-scale heavy industry before 1914 (Hinkkanen-Lievonen 1984, 248–49).

But in the early postwar years (1919–22) the immediate priorities were to establish parliamentary systems, undertake land reform (to break up large estates which accounted for one half or more of agricultural land in the Baltic provinces), and to sort out financial and currency issues, after which a proper start could be made on serious industrial reconstruction. As Hinkkanen-Lievonen records: 'The Baltic governments were grappling with the major tasks of remoulding the national life of their countries, of instigating far-reaching social reforms and of repairing the economic fabric the war and secession from Russia had all but torn apart' (Hinkkanen-Lievonen 1984, 273).

Estonia

Following peace with the Bolsheviks earlier in the year Estonia adopted its new constitution in December 1920. It was a very liberal one with a wide franchise, proportional representation and secret voting. It was also one of the reasons for the subsequent party fragmentation and government instability. During the period 1919 to 1934 there were no less than 21 different administrations. The strongest group in parliament was the agrarian interest under Konstantin Päts, who assumed the office of president in January 1934 and with the support of the army became leader of an authoritarian regime (Crampton and Crampton 1996, 69; Kirby 1995, 324).

Political instability did not especially impede the progress of the new republic. The first task was to settle the land question. In 1918 some 58 per cent of all agricultural land was held in large estates and two thirds of the rural population was landless. Under an appropriation law of October 1919 nearly all estates (over 1000 in number) were expropriated with only minor compensation granted to former owners, many of whom were German. The redistributed land was given to small farmers and landless agrarian workers thereby creating an additional 56,000 smallholdings to add to the existing 51,000 then extant in

Estonia. If this policy created an egalitarian landowning citizenship, with very few landless workers (some 13 per cent in 1939), it was not necessarily the most efficient. In fact many of the holdings were too small to be viable; they were less than 20 hectares whereas the average size of prewar holdings had been 34 hectares (Von Rauch 1974, 87–89).

To compensate for this deficiency the state made long-term credits at low interest rates available to owners for farm equipment and materials. It also encouraged the setting up of cooperative societies to improve the viability of smallholdings by providing modern machinery and organising marketing and purchasing facilities. There were also retail and banking cooperatives. By 1928 two thirds of all Estonian farmers belonged to cooperative societies the number of which rose from 763 to 1909 between 1925 and 1930. The latter were instrumental in promoting the exports of many farm products, especially bacon and butter, which went mainly to the German and British markets (Hope 1994, 56–57). From being a food importer in the first decade or so after the war, Estonia had become a successful European exporter of farm products by the mid-1930s (Smith 1994, 56).

Currency stabilisation took somewhat longer to achieve than in the other two Baltic states. Although a Central Bank was established soon after the war and state recourse to the printing press for budgetary purposes ceased in 1922, it was not until 1924 that *de facto* stabilisation was established at 1.1 per cent of the prewar gold value. It was another three years before it was possible to convert this to a *de jure* basis when an international loan was issued under League of Nation auspices to aid the reconstruction of the bank of issue. A new gold unit of currency, the kroon, replaced the Estonian mark (League of Nations 1946a, 123).

Estonia made significant advances in the industrial sector in the interwar years. Before 1914 the country had a fairly well developed industrial base centred on textiles, metals and the timber industries. The Kreenholm cotton mills located at Narva were reputed to be the largest in Europe. Industry was not devastated as it was in Latvia during the period of hostilities since heavy industry responded to the Russian war effort by supplying battleships, cruisers and railway rolling stock, mainly from works based in Tallinn (formerly Reval). Thus it was not until peace was declared that much of Estonia's industry felt the loss of its main market when the industrial workforce contracted by nearly one half (Berend 1998, 254).

The industrial structure therefore had to be adapted to peacetime needs and more towards the national market. It was assisted by an influx of foreign capital, much of it British. By 1926 three quarters of all foreign capital invested in Estonia came from Britain and was concentrated in textiles, the wood and paper industries, and banking

(Hinkkanen-Lievonen 1983, 333). Estonia made strong progress in a range of other industries including cement, shale-oil, chemicals and metals, some of which became significant exporters. Of the three Baltic states Estonia was the most developed industrially with the proportion of the labour force employed in manufacturing at over 17 per cent as against 13.5 per cent in Latvia and 6 per cent in Lithuania (Munting and Holderness 1991, 200). Between 1929 and 1938 industrial output rose by 45 per cent (Crampton 1994, 103). Industry was no longer dependent on the Russian market, which by 1930 accounted for only a small proportion of its output.

Latvia

Latvia was ravaged by the war; economically the country was devastated and the transfer of works and factories to the interior of Russia led to significant depopulation. By 1920 the population was down to just over 1.5 million as against 2.5 million in 1914, with a large imbalance between males and females (Spekke 1951, 361).

The egalitarian nature of both parliamentary constitutions and land reform in Latvia, as well as in Estonia and Lithuania, did not in fact lead to political stability. The Latvian parliamentary system spawned a plethora of parties and cabinets. The constitution of December 1920 was very liberal, with universal suffrage and proportional representation. This gave rise to excessive party splintering, along the lines of the ill-fated Weimar Republic in Germany. In fact at one point there was one party for every 45,000 citizens so there was no shortage of choice. In 1925, 26 parties were represented in parliament and between 1919 and 1934 there were no less than 18 governments (Crampton 1994, 100). It is not surprising therefore that there was steady pressure from right wing groups for greater stability, and in the *coup d'état* orchestrated by President Karlis Ulmanis in May 1934 parliamentary democracy was effectively terminated.

Despite political instability Latvia was remarkably successful in securing two important reforms – currency and land reform – in the early years of the new republic.

The currency reform was a model of its kind and an example to many countries who took much longer to sort out their financial and currency affairs and call a halt to the inflation which plagued much of Europe in the first half of the 1920s. Lacking her own currency and faced with a large reconstruction task at a time of severe inflationary conditions, Latvia managed to deal successfully with the problem in the summer of 1921. Even more impressive was the fact that the authorities were able to accomplish the task of stabilisation without resort to external aid. From the inception of the new republic a rigorous fiscal policy was enforced which checked the incipient hyperinflation of the early months of 1921. In May of that year legal provision was made for the collection of all taxes in terms of a new unit of currency, the lat, equivalent to one gold franc, or 0.8 per cent of the prewar gold value. This was in fact the first example of 'tax valorisation' in the history of postwar inflation control. By July 1921 state recourse to the printing press for budgetary purposes had ceased. In the latter half of the year prices stabilised and the exchange rate of the new currency appreciated. By early 1922 the dollar rate was comparatively stable (League of Nations 1946a, 121–23).

The land reform of 1920 swept away the feudal peasantry and landlords and created a nation of smallholders. The former landowners were only allowed to retain a maximum of 50 hectares of land and they received no compensation for their disposed estates. Some 1300 estates were broken up out of which emerged a quarter of a million new holdings with a maximum of 25 hectares. By 1930 there were very few large estates left and landless labourers were down to 23 per cent of the agrarian workforce compared with 61 per cent in 1897. Land reform provided the basis for the farming changes of the interwar period which were based on intensive production for export using cooperative methods which had their origin in the prewar period.

The land reform did not, as in some countries, lead to a setback for agriculture. This was partly because the government's economic policy gave priority initially to agriculture and supported the commercial and export-orientated nature of the newly established smallholders. The area under crops rose sharply – wheat, for example, from 32,000 to 140,000 hectares between 1914 and 1935 and potatoes from 80,000 to 127,000 – while several new crops such as sugar beet were introduced. There was also a marked rise in yields. By the 1930s Latvia was fairly self-sufficient in grain crops and there was even a surplus for export, while forest products accounted for over a third of total exports (Spekke 1951, 365).

Stock farming was particularly prominent in the agricultural transformation, with an emphasis on dairy farming and bacon production with an eye on the export market. The production of dairy products expanded rapidly once the stock herd had been restored in 1925 and by 1935 butter exports were nearly 17,000 tons, a level exceeded only by a few other countries (Denmark, the Netherlands and Ireland). A network of cooperative dairies and creameries, some 268 by 1937, supported the growing enterprise (Spekke 1951, 366; Hope 1994, 58). The production and export of bacon also increased but not on the same scale as dairy products. Some 70 per cent of Latvian farmers were members of cooperative organisations.

Agriculture remained the basis of economic life in Latvia though the population dependent on the land steadily diminished during the interwar period. Much of the success for the revival of agriculture and its important place in trade has been attributed to the favourable conditions established by the land reform. 'By creating a state of social stability and by fortifying the stimulus to individual farming ... the Land Reform greatly contributed to a rapid improvement in post-war conditions' (Spekke 1951, 366).

Latvian industry took longer to revive following the devastation in 1918 – especially in Riga – and the loss of the Russian market. The war in fact almost completely destroyed the industrial development that had taken place in the last decades of the Tsarist regime and which consequently had to be rebuilt from scratch (Spekke 1951, 369). This reconstruction depended very much on foreign capital, British and German, which in 1925 accounted for 50 per cent of the entire capital stock of the country. In some sectors foreign influence was overwhelming: for example, 80.5 per cent of the shares in the textile industry and over 70 per cent of banking capital were owned by foreigners (Hinkkanen-Lievonen 1983, 335). The main industrial advance came in the 1930s, and by the end of the decade approaching 100,000 workers were employed in a range of industries including metals, timber, food, textiles, clothing and shoes, chemicals and building. The exploitation of natural resources is reflected by the success of the timber industry, which eventually accounted for 40 per cent of exports (Smith 1994, 58). By the later 1930s two thirds of industrial output was consumed at home whereas before 1914 much of it had gone to the Russian market (Spekke 1951, 369). Estimates vary as to the extent of Latvia's industrial regeneration. While industrial output suffered some setback in 1931–32 it rose strongly thereafter and, according to one source, it was 58 per cent above that of 1913 by 1938 (League of Nations 1945, 137). However, the Royal Institute of International Affairs (1938, 188) reckoned that the strong industrial advance of the 1930s was not sufficient to bring output back to the prewar level because of the magnitude of the losses in the intervening period of 1914–20.

Lithuania

Lithuania was the least developed of the Baltic states before the war and suffered more from the period of hostilities and its aftermath. For three years the country was a huge battlefield and in the subsequent fight for independence it was not free of foreign troops until the spring of 1920.

By that time the country was more or less completely devastated as a result of the wartime fighting, the German occupation, and the Russian evacuation of resources and equipment. Many towns and farms were ruined, and some 42,000 buildings were destroyed.

Political instability was just as evident in the new republic as it was in the other two Baltic states even though party fragmentation was less pervasive. This was partly due to the predominance of the Christian Democratic Party, an agrarian-based group in which the Church had a significant influence. Nevertheless, between November 1918 and December 1926 no fewer than 11 cabinets held office (Von Rauch 1974, 97; Crampton 1994, 102).

Parliamentary democracy was short-lived in Lithuania. It came to an abrupt end in 1926 when a group of right-wing forces and army officers occupied the parliament building and forced the Populist-Social Democratic Coalition government to resign. Antanas Smetona, a key figure in the independence movement, was installed as president. He proceeded to increase the powers of the presidential office and in the autumn of 1929 he assumed personal rule (Kirby 1995, 325; Von Rauch 1974, 97).

As in Latvia, reconstruction was begun by currency stabilisation and reorganising the distribution of land. Initially Lithuania had no currency of her own and had to rely on foreign currencies such as the ost-mark and US dollar notes. Stabilisation took place in 1922 when a new national currency, the lit, replaced the foreign ones, being equivalent to one tenth of a dollar. The newly established Central Bank had exclusive note issue rights and its notes gradually replaced the foreign currencies in circulation. The total note circulation of the Bank was completely covered by its gold and foreign exchange holdings, which ensured confidence in the new currency (League of Nations 1946a, 123).

Lithuania's land reform was less liberal than in the case of either Estonia or Latvia. Under the law of 1922 holdings of up to 150 hectares were permitted and moderate compensation was paid to former landowners other than Russian (Kirby 1995, 299). Even so, many new small farms were created from former estates and estimates suggest that the arable land owned by farmers in the 5–30 hectare range accounted for some 63 per cent of the country's total farming land. Under the new law the traditional village communes were broken up (Zilinskas 1946, 176).

The large estates were replaced by progressive cooperative organisations of small producers the leaders of which soon recognised that the peasantry would be condemned to mere subsistence farming if old practices were not to change. Under their guidance and with state support Lithuania, within a decade, like Denmark before her, had shifted from cereals to dairy and livestock products which could be sold abroad at excellent prices (Alpert 1951, 114). Again cooperative organisations were encouraged by the state and were an important factor in the success of the shift in production structure. From modest beginnings there was a large increase in the export of bacon, butter, eggs and meat products over the period 1926–39. Yields increased steadily, as did the quality of output, which was considered to match that of the Danish (Zilinskas 1946, 177). Agricultural improvement benefited from the positive agrarian policy of the government. Over the entire interwar period some 470,000 hectares of fallow land were converted to productive use.

Industrial reconstruction took somewhat longer partly because of the extreme devastation wrought by hostilities. But in any case, industrial development prior to the war had been somewhat more limited than in Estonia and Latvia, and it principally served the Russian rather than the home market. Leather and metal industries predominated alongside a few trades that were closely connected with agriculture or forestry products. Since most of it was subsequently destroyed or ravaged during the period of hostilities, Lithuania had to rebuild more or less from scratch and adapt industrial developments to suit the needs of an agrarian-based society: that is, to serve domestic market requirements for textiles, metals and chemical products; and to utilise raw materials for processed goods which could be exported, for example timber and forest products, leather goods and of course food products. Table 5.1 shows a quite remarkable growth in the number of concerns and employees in a wide range of industries between 1927 and 1938. In value terms the three most important industries in 1938 were food and luxury goods, textiles and timber (Simutis 1942, 70).

It is worth noting that Lithuania's industrial production continued to expand in the Great Depression of 1929–32 when in most other countries it fell substantially. Data derived from League of Nations sources indicate a large rise in industrial output from an index value of 100 in 1929 to 354.2 in 1939, which was much stronger than the growth in world industrial production during the same period (Simutis 1942, 70). This increase appears somewhat excessive though the data on industrial employment given in Table 5.1 would seem to indicate a strong expansion in this sector. While Lithuania still remained very much an agrarian country at the end of the period, this was quite a remarkable achievement given the very slender industrial base at the start of the period.

Table 5.1 Industrial Establishments and Employment in Lithuania 1927/38

	1927		1938	
	Establishments	Employees	Establishments	Employees
Peat-cutting	7	603	16	1086
Stone, clay products	94	1357	130	3566
Metals and machinery	97	1895	120	3327
Chemicals	49	885	48	1583
Leather and fur	40	657	58	1022
Textiles	55	1403	81	7019
Timber	185	3446	264	4852
Paper and printing	52	2115	84	2615
Foodstuffs	253	3786	394	6150
Clothing and footwear	139	1607	183	3056
Electricity and gas works	29	648	33	590
Total	1000	18402	1411	34866

Source: Simutis 1942, 69.

The Baltic states in perspective

The Baltic countries made a better showing in the period than countries further east. Agriculture in the Balkan states still remained a barrier to progress rather than an engine of growth because of half-hearted land reforms, a shortage of land for peasants, general poverty, and lack of capital and education, so that a transition away from traditional farming based on grain to more intensive livestock farming proved more difficult to accomplish.

The Baltic states were able to avoid being locked into a traditional low productivity agrarian structure. Lower man–land ratios, more efficient land reforms and more enlightened government policy towards the agrarian sector contributed to the transformation. In contrast to the situation in parts of Eastern Europe, the Baltic states seem to have been more perceptive in the matter of land reform. They addressed the issues of viability and land shortage by creating middle-sized holdings – over 90 per cent of holdings fell into this category circa 1930 – rather than excessive fragmentation even though this meant leaving a residue of the peasant population landless. Furthermore, Baltic governments encouraged export-orientated farm activities, and supported the extensive spread of cooperative organisations which proved to be an important force in the shift towards market-orientated production in dairy and meat products with an eye on the export market. There was a steady rise in agrarian productivity though it still remained below that of the Nordic countries (Köll 1998, 212–13, 226).

Though industrial activities still played a relatively small part in these economies, there were nevertheless some important advances in this period, especially in Estonia and Latvia, which is all the more striking given the setbacks in 1914–19 and the need to re-establish and re-adapt the manufacturing base. The limited indices that are available indicate strong growth for most of the interwar period, though some sources doubt whether it was sufficient to restore the prewar volume of industrial output given the damage incurred during the years of hostilities and the loss of the captive Russian market (Royal Institute of International Affairs 1938, 188–89). Tariff protection helped in this regard but it was not essential for industrial survival. There were also very important advances in education and social infrastructure facilities during the interwar period which no doubt helped to produce a better equipped and motivated workforce.

Even more remarkable is how well the three Baltic states adjusted to the virtual loss of the Russian market. These countries obviously had, by virtue of their political subjection, very close ties with the Russian market before 1914 but after the war the Soviet share of Baltic exports shrank to a few per cent. The Baltic states found replacement markets in Germany and Britain, and these two Western countries dominated the export and import trade of the Baltic countries in the 1920s (see Tables 5.2 and 5.3). They regularly accounted for one half or more of the trade of the Baltic provinces and as much as three quarters in the case of Lithuania. Britain and Germany vied for economic supremacy in the Baltic lands even though Britain regarded the states as political lightweights.

Table 5.2 Percentage Shares of Britain and Germany in the Imports of the Baltic States (1920s)

	Estonia		Latvia		Lithuania	
	Britain	Germany	Britain	Germany	Britain	Germany
1921	27.9	40.2	14.3	48.1	0.9	70.7
1923	19.7	51.0	17.0	45.2	5.3	80.9
1925	12.3	29.4	13.8	41.5	8.3	56.6
1927	14.3	26.4	10.6	40.6	6.8	53.2

Source: Hinkkanen-Lievonen 1984, 283.

Table 5.3 Percentage Shares of Britain and Germany in the Exports of the Baltic States (1920s)

	Estonia		Latvia		Lithuania	
	Britain	Germany	Britain	Germany	Britain	Germany
1921	39.6	3.9	35.6	17.9	27.1	51.3
1923	34.1	10.8	46.3	7.6	26.9	43.3
1925	25.0	31.2	34.6	22.6	24.2	50.7
1927	31.4	29.8	34.0	26.4	24.8	51.5

Source: Hinkkanen-Lievonen 1984, 282.

If anything the geographical distribution of Baltic trade became even more concentrated in the 1930s when exports to the Soviet Union dwindled still further. At the end of the decade Germany and Britain accounted for nearly two thirds of the exports of Estonia and Lithuania and almost three quarters of those of Latvia (Szlaffer 1990, 237). By this time Germany's political intentions in the region were even more transparent than they had been in the 1920s, whereas Britain still retained a benign political stance.

Though aggregate income statistics for the Baltic countries are very patchy and fragile, it is probably correct to say that the level of income per head in these states was higher than in Eastern Europe, and that there was a modest advance on the levels prevailing before the war. Structurally they were better adapted to sustained growth than most other European countries along the periphery. In fact given the enormous setbacks suffered in the period 1914–20 it is remarkable how well they adapted to the challenging conditions of the interwar period.

CHAPTER SIX

Poland and Hungary

There are contrasts and similarities between the two Central-East European countries. Both suffered very badly in the war and its aftermath and both experienced a spell of hyperinflation in the 1920s. Yet by the standards of the rest of the European periphery they were somewhat more developed industrially before 1914. By contrast, the postwar settlement dealt a different hand to the two countries. Hungary, as an ex-enemy country, was cut down to size and shorn of some of its vital assets, whereas Poland reappeared on the map as a nation in its own right, having been partitioned among the Russian, Austrian and German Empires since the late eighteenth century. Needless to say, neither country was especially happy with the new boundaries prescribed by the peace treaty settlements.

Poland

It would be difficult to exaggerate the enormity of the task facing the newly reconstituted state of Poland. The country had been literally ravaged by warfare, there were continuing border disputes with neighbours after 1918, there was the problem of trying to weld together what were virtually three separate entities, there were massive social problems, and then there was a bout of hyperinflation. Hence it is not surprising that Poland's reconstruction took the best part of a decade.

Few countries except for Serbia and northern France had suffered so much damage and devastation as a result of the wartime conflict. Some 90 per cent of Polish territory was the scene of war operations at one time or another, either during the main conflict itself or in the postwar border disputes, most notably the Russo-Polish War of 1919–21 (peace signed at Riga March 1921). The country was literally ransacked by the three occupying powers – Austria-Hungary, Germany and Russia – who destroyed or pillaged all they could lay their hands on. Total losses have been put at around 11 per cent of prewar national capital, which does not take account of the further losses incurred in the postwar border conflicts (Roszkowski 1989, 106). But judging on the basis of some of the information on material damage done this estimate would appear somewhat on the low side. Damage to property and infrastructure was very severe indeed. One half or more of bridges, station buildings, machinery workshops and locomotives were destroyed, while upwards of 1.7 million houses, including three quarters of farm buildings, were destroyed by fire or wilful destruction. Damage to the land and its resources was also very extensive. Many villages, especially in the eastern provinces, were levelled to the ground, while 4.45 million hectares of agricultural land were rendered useless, 2.43 million hectares of forest were destroyed and 215 million cubic metres of timber were removed by the occupying forces. Apart from the large tracts of agricultural land laid waste, 60 per cent of the livestock disappeared and agriculture suffered acute shortages of manpower and horsepower, both of which were pressed into military service (Roszkowski 1986, 287–89; Berend and Ranki 1985, 151). Thus by the end of the war crop levels were well down on prewar ones, possibly by 50 per cent or more.

As for industrial activity, this was almost at a standstill in the immediate aftermath of hostilities. At the beginning of 1919 industrial output was probably no better than 15 per cent of the prewar level – very similar in fact to that in the war-torn Soviet Union – and even by 1920–21 it was still only a third of the 1913 level (Teichova 1985, 224; Roszkowski 1986, 288). The metallurgical industry was completely immobilised and industry in and around Warsaw was severely crippled. The area worst affected was the former kingdom of Poland, part of the Russian zone which was evacuated in 1915 and thereafter occupied by the Germans (Roszkowski 1986, 288; Wynot 1983, 57; Rose 1939, 110; Kitchen 1988, 106).

Thus in the early postwar period Poland was destitute and starving. Everything, and especially food, was in short supply, unemployment was high, exacerbated by returning soldiers, and malnutrition and disease were widespread which led to a sharp increase in mortality. For some time too the country was on the verge of civil war. The conditions of life were described graphically by the British Director of Relief:

> The country ... had undergone four or five occupations by different armies, each of which combed the land for supplies. Most of the villages had been burnt down by the Russians in their retreat (of 1915); land had been uncultivated for four years and had been cleared of cattle, grain, horses and agricultural machinery by both Germans and Bolsheviks. The population here was living upon roots, grass, acorns and heather. The only bread obtainable was composed of those ingredients, with perhaps about 5 per cent of rye flour. Their clothes were in the last stages of dilapidation; the majority were without boots and shoes and had reached the lowest depths of misery and degradation. The distribution of food in the towns was very unequal. It was possible to buy almost anything in

> the restaurants at a price, and cafés and cake shops were well supplied, but in other parts of the same towns it was impossible to obtain food.
>
> (quoted in Clough, Moodie and Moodie 1969, 100)

The economic setback cannot be attributed solely to war damage and devastation. An additional problem was the greatly reduced export opportunities and the need to adjust production to new markets. Before the war Polish trade had been heavily dependent on the markets of the partitioning powers which absorbed some 80 per cent of her exports. These links were broken after 1918. The Russian market was virtually closed for obvious reasons and high tariffs of the successor states together with transport dislocation rendered trade difficult. Moreover, Poland lacked a deep water port until Danzig was declared a free city in 1920 (Leslie 1980, 139; Korbonski 1992, 241).

Poland's difficulties at this time were severely compounded by the fragmented nature of the country as a result of the original partition. There was no unified economic and administrative system. The new republic started out with a variety of legal, commercial, customs, fiscal and currency systems and different educational and military traditions, as well as different transport systems. As one observer noted:

> On the day of their political unification the three parts of Poland did not constitute a single economic unit. They had different systems of civil, commercial, and fiscal legislation. They belonged to differing customs units, to differing money and credit systems. Nor did they constitute a unity in the sense that they had developed after an organised pattern by constant and mutual testing. On the contrary some parts were over- and some under-developed.
>
> (Zweig 1944, 13)

The process of unification was a slow and difficult one not helped by the fact that there was a shortage of administrative expertise, weak administrations and an unstable political system. There were no fewer than 92 political parties by 1923 operating under a proportional representation system which in effect meant that coalition governments were the norm and rarely did they last for more than a few months. Not until General Pilsudski's *coup d'état* of May 1926 was a more stable authoritarian regime imposed (Crampton and Crampton 1996, 103).

By that time some progress had been made on the integration front. Despite the political instability Landau (1992, 144–55) believes that the economic unification and integration of the constituent parts of the new Poland were more complex and took longer to achieve than political assimilation. Each of the former occupied zones had different economic legislation and different legal, fiscal, monetary and currency systems, as well as contrasting commercial laws and practices relating to the establishment and operation of business undertakings. The wide variety of practices in use is well illustrated by the railways where it was difficult to keep things moving throughout the country because of the multiplicity of practices: 66 different types of rail in use, 165 types of locomotives and 32 different passenger vehicles.

The task of unification was complicated by the fact that the level of development and the extent of war damage varied considerably from region to region and separatist economic tendencies emerged in the more favoured provinces. In many cases it was several years before complete integration could be realised. Fiscal unification, for example, took three to four years to accomplish and even then it was not fully comprehensive, while in the case of currency reform the Polish mark only became the official medium of exchange throughout the country in November 1923 when it was finally applied to Upper Silesia. It was not in fact until the middle of the decade that economic unification was achieved over a fairly wide area, including transportation, legal and monetary systems, and in the development of uniform markets in capital, labour, and internal trade and price levels. Even then many regional differences remained but at least the main task of economic integration was nearing completion.

The financial problems of the new state were the ones that took the longest to solve. At the end of the war Poland had six different currencies and nine different fiscal systems in force. A single currency was issued in 1920 to replace the foreign ones in use though it was not until 1923 that it was in general use throughout the country. On the fiscal front the Treasury did not gain full control over taxation and fiscal matters over the whole of Poland until 1922 but even then things were far from plain sailing. War damage and the postwar chaos together with an inefficient bureaucracy rendered it difficult to collect taxes regularly. Consequently, with burgeoning expenditure demands – for military, reconstruction and welfare relief payments purposes – on a limited revenue base budget deficits spiralled. These were covered by the issue of money, which laid the basis of hyperinflation. Between 1918 and 1922 money in circulation rose from 1024 to 793,437 milliard Polish marks (Roszkowski 1989, 107). Initially the government was little inclined to check the process of money creation since it was felt, as in other countries (Austria, Hungary and Germany) which followed a similar path, that in difficult times money creation and price inflation provided a relatively painless way of financing reconstruction (see below). And so the value of the currency plunged and prices shot up to stellar magnitudes (for details see League of Nations 1946a, 106–11).

Given Poland's desperate plight at the end of the war it is scarcely surprising that monetary chaos ensued. Large budgetary deficits were financed by money creation which drove up prices and weakened the currency. The process of stabilisation was a long and protracted affair. Until 1921 little was done to check inflation since the executive machinery was too weak to impose effective fiscal control, while political administrations were short-lived and the country was still engaged in border conflicts. In any case, as in other countries with severe inflation, it was seen as a useful reconstruction strategy.

Several abortive attempts were made to bring inflation under control and stabilise the currency. The first two occurred between 1921 and 1923 but after temporary relief they failed, largely because the fiscal effort was relaxed too soon (Jack 1927, 181–84). Another attempt was made in 1924 following the surge in prices at the end of the previous year. In April 1924 a new Central Bank, with strict limits on the amount of credit that it could extend to the government, was set up, and a new currency based on gold – the zloty, equivalent to the gold franc – was introduced. Strict fiscal measures, including valorisation of taxes on a gold basis in line with the recommendations of Hilton Young's report on Polish financial conditions, were also imposed. For a time these new measures met with a degree of success; price inflation was checked and the new currency was stabilised. Unfortunately the success was short-lived. At the end of July there was a renewed depreciation of the currency which rekindled fears of another bout of hyperinflation, though as it turned out the price rise was relatively moderate compared with what had gone before.

Several factors contributed to this failure. Again the fiscal stance was relaxed too soon giving rise to renewed monetary growth, while a sharp rise in imports, partly due to harvest failure in 1924, and a decline in exports put pressure on the exchanges (League of Nations 1946a, 108). A tariff war with Germany and a virtual absence of any financial aid from abroad to bolster confidence in the new currency did not help matters (Smith 1936, 148–57; Mlynarski 1926, 27).

Success was finally achieved in 1926–27 after a further bout of inflation and currency depreciation. Improved trade and budgetary accounts were important in this regard, as was the negotiation of an international loan in the autumn of 1927. But the crucial factor, as in the case of the French franc under Poincaré, was the emergence of a strong government under Pilsudski (May 1926), who introduced a harsh package of fiscal and monetary reforms designed to bring a halt once and for all to Poland's financial disorders. Confidence in the currency was restored and the new exchange rate legalised in the autumn of 1927 with the help of the stabilisation loan (Yeager 1981, 53–54; Horsman 1988, 101–103).

There has been much debate on the question as to how far severe inflation was an aid to reconstruction in European countries in the first half of the 1920s. The evidence is somewhat mixed. Certainly it got the government out of a tight spot and for a time it provided a stimulus to enterprise as long as firms could keep one step ahead of their costs in pricing policy. Of course, one should recall that given the very low level of industrial activity at the end of and in the immediate aftermath of war, inflation and currency depreciation could scarcely fail to provide a boost to economic activity. There was a big rise in the number of factories established and in employment and industrial production in the years 1919–23, though manufacturing output still remained some 30 per cent below the prewar level (Ranki 1983b, 481; Landau 1983, 514; League of Nations 1945, 136). Currency depreciation also helped to insulate the domestic market from imports while it also made it easier to penetrate markets of countries with more stable currencies. The inflation tax (represented by the price rise) provided the government with much needed income, accounting for some two thirds of budgetary revenue between 1918 and 1923. Some of the proceeds were distributed in subsidies and credits to business and the propertied classes who gained at the expense of the rest of the population. The impact on the peasant community was mixed; they gained through diminished tax and debt burdens, but incurred losses on savings and from the deterioration in the terms of trade (Landau 1983, 514–18; Zweig 1944, 32).

The final tally is difficult to assess precisely, but on balance the majority of the population paid a price for the temporary and somewhat artificial boost to activity and employment. Wage and salary earners, as well as those living on fixed incomes and savings, found it difficult to protect themselves from the ravages of inflation since their incomes tended to lag one step or more behind the rise in prices. The working classes bore a large share of the inflation tax (40–50 per cent), while real wages fell sharply after 1921, to around one half of prewar values in 1923, as against 98 per cent in the first half of 1921, though it should be noted that for much of 1919 they were as low as 30 per cent (Landau 1983, 517–18). If the amount of social unrest in Poland later in 1923 is anything to go by, then one may assume that the working classes were not faring very well.

There is also a further aspect to consider, namely that the final move to stabilisation brought renewed stagnation and rising unemployment. Manufacturing output languished between 1924 and 1926 at less than 60 per cent of the prewar level, and even by the end of the decade it was still barely 86 per cent of that level, the worst performance of any East European country (Aldcroft and Morewood 1995, 44; League of Nations 1945, 136). Unemployment rose to 350,000 in early 1926, compared with only 52,000 at the peak of inflation in October 1923, which was worse than that recorded in the early postwar period (Jack 1927, 187; Landau 1983, 518).

Poland had barely completed her main reconstruction when she suffered another severe setback from the Great Depression. With heavy debt burdens and a sharp drop in commodity prices from the late 1920s the prospects of further progress were bleak. A good part of the country's reconstruction in the 1920s was dependent on imported capital and when commodity prices declined the servicing burden of the debt was enhanced. A third or more of the capital stock of joint stock companies was foreign-owned, and as much as one half in some sectors (Rose 1939, 194). Capital inflows were also required to finance a surplus of goods and services and to meet the servicing costs of past debt. Between 1929 and 1933 the index of wholesale prices of farm products fell by 57.4 per cent and by 61.3 per cent between 1929 and 1936, whereas the products bought by farmers fell by only 27.4 and 35.4 per cent respectively (Zweig 1944, 56). This price scissors movement left many farmers in difficult straits, with mounting debts as their incomes declined. It has been estimated that in 1935 peasants had to sell about double the quantity of produce to buy the same volume of consumer goods as in 1929 (Leslie 1980, 178). It also put severe pressure on government budgets and the external account. Poland's debt servicing costs as a percentage of export earnings rose from 11.3 per cent in 1928 to 27.0 per cent in 1931–32 (Nötel 1986, 223; Drabek 1985, 425). On the other hand, real wages in industry tended to rise during the depression, which put pressure on industrial costs.

Despite the severity of the depression the government's policy strategy was a classical deflationary one. Determined to maintain financial probity and solvency at all costs, and also maintain the value of the zloty and avoid exchange control, there was but little alternative. Thus when many countries left the gold standard and devalued their currencies in the early 1930s, Poland joined the small band of countries which clung to the gold standard. Belgium, France, Holland, Italy, Luxembourg and Switzerland along with Poland became members of what was known as the 'gold bloc'. This meant that their exchange rate structure became internationally uncompetitive and so they were forced to drive down domestic costs. And without the benefit of exchange control (Poland being the only East European country to eschew it) this meant the implementation of harsh fiscal and monetary policies, as well as stringent controls on trade by tariffs and quantitative restrictions on imports and subsidies for exports. In the years 1930–34 total budgetary expenditure was reduced by no less than a third, partly out of necessity from falling tax yields, while the commercial banks enforced severe credit contraction by reducing their bill portfolios by two thirds and their advances by one third (Taylor 1952, 43; Gorecki 1935, 109; Landau 1984, 130). The approach very much mirrored that of contemporary France, and for that matter that of the other gold bloc countries, where the authorities were similarly forced to adjust the whole cost and price structure downwards to offset their overvalued currencies (Smith 1936, 168–78; Zweig 1944, 54–56).

The strategy succeeded in so far as it achieved the declared objectives of maintaining the value of the currency, turning round the balance of payments, containing the budget deficits and avoiding financial collapse – there were no banking crises in Poland in the early 1930s – but all at a cost to the real economy. The deflationary policy did much to intensify and prolong the depression in Poland and it was not until early 1936 that a marked shift in direction occurred. By then the gold bloc was disintegrating. Belgium, Luxembourg and Italy had already left it and Poland ceased to be a member in April of the same year when she introduced exchange control. The rump of the gold bloc collapsed in the following September.

The abandonment of the gold policy left Poland with more room to manoeuvre on the domestic front. In keeping with the drive to industrialise in other East European countries, Poland embarked on a major state planning exercise with the launching of a four-year Investment Plan (1936–40) of 1800 million zloty to be concentrated on industrial enterprises and transport infrastructure, and a six-year Defence Expansion Plan (1936–42) of 6000 million zloty for military equipment, new armament plants, airfields and communications. The terms and conditions of both plans were revised in later years but the first one was completed ahead of schedule (Hauner 1986, 101–102). In conjunction with these projects there was a strategy of developing the central industrial district of Poland (the area bounded by Warsaw, Cracow and Lwow) as a major industrial region where much of heavy industry and military equipment would be concentrated away from the state's vulnerable frontiers (Taylor 1952, 86–88; Landau and Tomaszewski 1985, 118–19).

Given the country's poor financial resources and its low level of development the Polish defence strategy has been described as 'desperate but remarkable'. Estimates suggest that defence expenditure accounted for almost 50 per cent of the government budget and between 9 and 11 per cent of national income in the years 1936–39. The focus on defence needs is understandable since Poland was one of the most friendless and disliked of the new states and was very conscious of the potential threat from Russia and Germany, both of which had scores to settle with her relating to their prewar frontiers. Poland was therefore determined to become an effective military power whatever the cost to the welfare of the people. However, in view of subsequent events it is questionable whether it was all worthwhile since the gap between German and Polish defence build-up actually widened (Hauner 1986, 105). It is also to be debated whether the defence activity was actually beneficial to the Polish economy. Overy (1989, 4–5) is somewhat sceptical on this point, arguing that the quest for military strength weakened an already fragile economy and gave rise to permanent financial insecurity, low living standards and social unrest. This was one reason no doubt why the death of Pilsudski in 1935 was followed by what amounted to military control under the banner of a front organisation, the Camp of National Unity.

Though much of the new development involved a partnership between the state and private enterprise, the state itself did become a much more important direct force in the economy. It owned and operated around 100 large enterprises with more than 1000 separate establishments; the arms industry was almost completely state-owned as were most rail, shipping and aviation services. Around one half of the metallurgy industry was in public hands and 80 per cent of the chemical industry. The state also ran five monopolies in alcohol, matches, tobacco, salt and the lottery (Taylor 1952, 90–94).

Despite a sustained industrial recovery in the later 1930s, industry or manufacturing production barely surpassed prewar levels by the end of the decade. However, Alice Teichova (1985, 232) sounds a note of caution on the reliability of the existing indices of industrial activity for Poland given the changes in industrial structure. Taylor (1952, 150) suggests that industry and mining accounted for 50 per cent of total net output of the economy by 1939 compared with only 32 per cent in 1929. This appears rather a remarkable transformation given the stagnation in the first half of the 1930s, but then agriculture was losing ground throughout the decade.

The agrarian sector continued to cast a shadow over Poland's development during the interwar years. Not only did it have to contend with the reconstruction of a war ravaged landscape and the catastrophe of the Great Depression, but also there remained the underlying problem of the whole structure of landholdings and accommodation to cater for a rapidly rising population. Furthermore, much of agriculture remained undercapitalised and inefficient apart from some of the larger estates.

At the start of the period large estates of over 100 hectares remained an important feature accounting for some 47 per cent of all arable land. At the other end of the scale there were a large number of tiny holdings – less than 5 hectares – many of which were not self-supporting. In time these holdings tended to fragment further as they were divided up among successors to take account of population pressure, while often they were not composed of one compact plot (Ponikowski 1930, 291). At the same time about one third of the population had no land at all (Berend 1985, 157). Land reform provided some relief, but it was less extensive than in other East European countries apart from Hungary. Land reform acts of 1919 and 1925 provided for the partial break-up of larger estates and the redistribution of land to existing smallholders or to those without land. Over the whole of the interwar period 133,000 hectares were redistributed annually or a total of 2.65 million hectares, which amounted to just over 10 per cent of the agricultural land of Poland. These, together with other land transfers, reduced large estates to about 20 per cent of arable land (Berend 1985, 157).

The reforms did not really solve the agrarian problem. The annual redistributions of land fell short of the annual increase in the agrarian population, which meant that dwarf holdings became even more fragmented. Farms of reasonable or viable economic size (20–30 hectares) accounted for no more than 10 per cent of the arable land. But even more radical reforms could not have solved the land hunger completely given the pressure of rising population and the already large numbers without land. One contemporary study of the late 1930s estimated that the total area of land required to ensure that 'redundant' peasants were made economically viable or self-sufficient was of the order of 7.7 million hectares, but that the total cropland available from a complete parcelling out of all private and public large estates was only 4.7 million hectares (Roszkowski 1986, 292).

Apart from the land hunger problem the majority of peasants who owned land were barely self-sufficing because their holdings were too small. They lacked the capital to modernise or the incentive to combine holdings into large units to allow the use of improved techniques. This was especially true after the calamity of the great price fall in the early 1930s, which resulted in a large decline in farm incomes and a rise in debt burdens. Real incomes of peasant households in 1932–33 were only 66 per cent of the 1913 level and a good part of this diminished income was swallowed up in debt service and amortisation charges (Berend 1985, 173).

Thus agriculture could not act as an engine of growth for the economy of Poland. Indeed, as Roszkowski (1986, 292) observes, the backwardness of Polish agriculture was a serious impediment to economic progress. Crop structures and yields remained fairly static, farming techniques were backward and farms were undercapitalised, and labour productivity levels were low by Western standards. In fact the input of labour into Polish farming was so large relative to the supply of land and capital that the marginal productivity of labour was probably close to zero (Korbonski 1992, 239). This is confirmed by estimates of the large surplus labour in Polish agriculture (Moore 1945, 64–65). Unfortunately, this large pool of surplus labour had nowhere else to go.

Despite some advances on the industrial front, especially in the latter half of the 1930s, Poland remained a poor country by the end of the period. Per capita income levels were little better than those of Spain, Portugal or the Balkan countries, while industrial production barely recovered to the prewar level. Social infrastructure facilities, such as housing, health, transport, education and water supply, were still very primitive by Western standards and they were indicative of a low level of development (Wellisz 1938, 254; Ehrlich 1985, 326).

Hungary

Hungary's situation at the end of the war was probably only marginally better than that of Poland even though physical destruction and devastation through conflict were less intense. By the autumn of 1918 Hungary, along with the whole of the Austro-Hungarian Empire was on the brink of collapse. Agricultural and industrial production were but a fraction of prewar levels and so it was almost impossible to feed and clothe either the civilian population or the troops in battle. Mounting inflation and large budgetary deficits coupled with loss of markets and resources left the country's economy in ruins.

The biggest blow to Hungary, however, came when the peace terms were announced in the Treaty of Trianon of 4 June 1920. This dismembered Hungary largely on grounds of its racial diversity so that she lost over two thirds of her former territory and 58 per cent of her population. The new Hungary bore little resemblance to any Hungary of the past millennium. The detached territories and peoples were distributed among the successor states, Poland, Romania, Yugoslavia, Czechoslovakia and also Italy. This meant that over three million Magyars – or nearly every third Hungarian national – found themselves under foreign rule, mainly on the borderlands of the new states. The irony of the settlement was that in the process of reducing the multinational character of Hungary it increased the racial minority component of the successor states (Halasz 1928, 28, 39; Kiraly, Pastor and Sanders 1982, 73–74).

It is true that most of the displaced Hungarians remained in their new locations, though some half a million eventually made their way back to their homeland. Hungarians were committed to a revision of the frontier changes to rectify what they regarded as a gross injustice, but the successor states rejected any proposed revisions which they saw as a threat to their hard-won security. Hence there was bitterness on all sides and 'The resulting cool relations between Hungary and its neighbours weakened them all, increased their isolation, and prepared the way for domination of the entire region by a great power' (Mocsy 1983, 195). Throughout the postwar period, as one official source noted, 'The integral revision of the Treaty of Trianon ... became almost the exclusive object of Hungarian foreign policy ...' (Foreign Office 1941, 300). It was the strong commitment of all the country's politicians to the revision of the 1920 frontiers that led Hungary to cooperate with Hitler and Mussolini and which resulted in increasingly authoritarian domestic policies (Polonsky 1975, 60).

The territorial changes had a marked impact on the economic structure of the new Hungary. She lost many of her raw material supplies for manufacturing industry, but retained proportionately more of industrial capacity. Some 84 per cent of forest resources were relinquished and a similar proportion of iron ore, all copper, most non-ferrous metals and salt, 90 per cent of water power, 30 per cent of lignite as well as between one quarter and one half of the livestock. There were also substantial losses of industrial capacity but overall she was left with a relatively greater share of industrial undertakings, so that the country was somewhat more industrialised than before the war (Macartney 1937, 461–62). This had the effect of producing an even greater concentration of manufacturing industry in and around Budapest. In 1920 just over 65 per cent of the gainfully occupied population in manufacturing were to be found in the Greater Budapest region as against only one quarter before the war. Such excessive geographic concentration tended to restrict industrialisation of more backward areas in the interwar years (Bencze and Tajti 1972, 19–20, 28).

The postwar territorial adjustments complicated the task of reconstruction. The large internal market of the former Austro-Hungarian Empire disappeared and so new economic links and trading relationships had to be forged by the successor states. The old empire, whatever its political and social defects, had a certain economic coherence and recent research has shown that it made substantial economic progress in the half century or so before 1914 (see Good 1984 and Komlos 1983). It is true that Hungary was the less industrialised part of the Dual Monarchy but at least it had a ready market for its agrarian products and semi-processed goods in the customs-free area of the union. All this disappeared after the war as new states rose out of the ruins of the empire and as a consequence new custom units proliferated. Twelve additional independent units came into existence, making a total of 38 in Europe, seven of which emerged from the territory of the former Habsburg Empire. Transport and communications were also affected adversely by the territorial fragmentation. For example, the Treaty of Trianon destroyed Hungary's integrated transport system, especially the river and waterway network, the major part of the management of which was transferred to Prague, Bucharest and Belgrade (Halasz 1928, 26).

Many commentators, and not only Hungarian, deemed the treaty terms to be unduly harsh. They caused, as with the Germans' peace terms, much anger and resentment among Hungarians everywhere which helped to fan the forces of nationalism and revisionism in the interwar years and by so doing exacerbated the political tensions throughout Europe. The terms were scarcely designed to foster postwar reconstruction and recovery though no doubt they were never framed with that intention in mind. That apart, Hungary's reconstruction was delayed by internal divisions within the country and the mounting financial and currency problems in the early 1920s.

Hungary's inflation was greater than that of Austria but considerably less than Poland's or Germany's. Although financing the war effort by printing money had resulted in rising prices and a fall in the value of the currency, by 1919–20 the situation was by no means completely out of control. The value of the Hungarian crown was only 15 per cent of its prewar par value but this was no worse than the situation in Finland, Bulgaria, Romania and Yugoslavia, all of which managed to avoid hyperinflation (League of Nations 1943a, 42). Nor were budgetary and balance of payments deficits of unmanageable proportions.

The turning point seems to have come in the summer of 1921 following a failed attempt to stabilise the currency and check inflation. Opposition to the proposed capital level was the main stumbling block. According to Berend and Ranki (1974b, 103), it was then that it changed from a spontaneous phenomenon to a conscious policy designed to finance the reconstruction and recovery of the economy following its virtual collapse in the aftermath of war. The amount of currency in circulation grew by leaps and bounds, from 17 billion in the summer of 1921 to 2.5 trillion in May 1924, by which time the currency had become worthless (Nötel 1986, 178, 182).

Politically the prospects for monetary stabilisation should have been propitious from 1920 onwards for, in the counter-revolution following the Red Terror and the Romanian invasion of the country, Hungary emerged with a strong right-wing regime under Count István Bethlen (Prime Minister 1921–31) and Admiral Miklós Horthy (Regent of Hungary 1920–44). Unfortunately the initial attempt at stabilisation was defeated by opposition from the propertied classes to a capital levy on their assets (Ranki 1983b, 526), by which time the government had come to the conclusion that there were some merits in letting inflation continue. Moreover, there were also concerns about the implications of a counter-inflationary policy in the wake of postwar unrest and the recent defeat of the short-lived Soviet-style republic under Bela Kun in 1919. Dornbusch (1992, 410–13) reckons that it was not until the big explosion of prices in 1923 that the political conditions were ripe for reform, by which time the inflationary benefits had turned distinctly negative for most groups.

Much of the credit for the success of monetary and currency stabilisation is attributable to a firm resolve by the government to bring inflation under control, together with the intervention of the League of Nations and the raising of a loan to facilitate the process. By mid-1924 the inflationary spiral had been brought to a halt and the exchange rate of the crown stabilised by linking it to the pound sterling. In the following year monetary reform was completed when a new unit of currency, the pengö, was introduced. Once the currency was secured fiscal equilibrium was soon restored and only one quarter of the international loan was needed for the purpose (Horsman 1988, 61–62; Yeager 1981, 52–55; League of Nations 1926, 37–39). In retrospect, it is a pity that the League did not step in at an earlier date and then perhaps Hungary would have avoided the traumas of hyperinflation.

As in the case of Poland, inflation was initially beneficial to Hungary, at least for certain sectors of the economy. Economic activity and trade were stimulated though the extent and depth of the boom are sometimes exaggerated. Most industrial sectors, apart from clothing, recorded an expansion in capacity and employment and many new enterprises were founded. Inflation reduced production costs considerably in real terms largely because of the big fall in real wages, by over one half between 1914 and mid-1924, and cheap loans (Ranki 1983b, 527; Pasvolsky 1928, 159–60, 350–52). The steel, metal and coal industries were specially favoured. The property-owning classes also reaped considerable gains, especially large landowners who received substantial loans from the state which they repaid in depreciated currency, as well as being able to liquidate their prewar debts by the same token (Held 1980, 212).

However, the main stimulus to the economy appears to have been concentrated mainly in one year, 1922, when manufacturing output rose by just over one quarter, though still some 20 per cent down on the 1913 level. Thereafter it collapsed again, and even with some recovery in 1924 and 1925 it was still 23 per cent below the prewar level, and between the years 1921 and 1924 it remained almost static (League of Nations 1945, 137; Boross 1994, 129). In fact industrial performance was better and more sustained in the post-stabilisation period through to 1929, which underlines the rather artificial and temporary stimulus imparted by inflation. Real wages remained depressed throughout the inflationary years, while unemployment rose sharply following monetary reform. Estimates vary somewhat but Wicker suggests that unemployment among trade unionists more or less doubled between March 1924 and March 1925, from 4.6 to 8.7 per cent on the best scenario and from 7.7 to 14.5 per cent on the worst, while it did not return to earlier levels until late in 1926 (Wicker 1986, 396–97).

Thus while there was undoubtedly some fillip to economic activity the effects were short-lived, and as the value of the currency declined very rapidly in the final throes of inflation capital tended to move away from the productive sector of the economy and into fixed assets of any sort including speculative transactions on the stock exchange, as well as abroad. The major beneficiaries were undoubtedly the propertied classes and those with large debts, but wage earners and those on fixed incomes fared very badly indeed. In the longer term inflation did little to solve the capital shortage in Hungary, one reason why foreign borrowing became significant in the later 1920s, with severe consequences during the depression (see below). Finally, the stabilisation recession was quite severe and so readjustment to the new boundaries was delayed.

After the stabilisation setback economic activity in Hungary recovered in the latter half of the 1920s. Bethlen's policies to encourage manufacturing industry were partly responsible though much of the upswing could be ascribed to the low level of output recorded in the early 1920s. The main policy stimulus came with the Tariff Act of 1924 which covered 2000 items compared with only 100 before. Protective duties were also much higher than previously, up to 50 per cent *ad valorem* for light industrial products and consumer goods, but the state also placed high duties on finished goods used in farming which were detrimental to the primary sector – even more so because the revenue collected was used to subsidise industrial enterprises (Janos 1982, 219–20). Between 1923 and 1929 manufacturing production doubled, but even by the latter date it was still only about 12 per cent above the prewar level. The agrarian sector fared less well. Output continued to trail behind the prewar level, peasant indebtedness increased once again and wages of farm workers were well behind those in manufacturing (Gati 1974, 61; Janos 1982, 240).

The depression cut short Hungary's recovery. The disaster hit the country especially hard though the origins of the problems can be located in the 1920s. During the latter half of that decade Hungary had come to rely heavily on foreign capital not all of which was put to good use. By 1930 Hungary was the most heavily indebted country in Europe on a per capita basis, with a total debt of some 4300 million pengös. This included postwar loans, prewar debts and accumulated interest. Only a small proportion of foreign capital went directly into productive investments (about 20 per cent). The larger part of the inflows was swallowed up in service charges (40 per cent), while most of the rest was absorbed by landed property and social and infrastructure projects in cities and towns (Rothschild 1974, 168–69). Over the years 1924–29 foreign capital inflows (both long- and short-term) were approximately equal to the volume of domestic accumulation. Rothschild (1974, 168–69) accuses Hungary's rulers of soliciting credits that were too large relative to the current capacity of the economy to deal with them. It would be more accurate to say that too few of them found their way into activities that would generate exchange earnings to help service their costs. The crunch came when these credits dried up at the end of the decade and commodity prices collapsed thus reducing export earnings. Debt service payments, which absorbed almost 18 per cent of export earnings in 1928, more than doubled to 48 per cent in 1931–32, while foreign credits, which had barely matched debt service charges in 1929, had all but disappeared (Nötel 1974, 84–85). Thus the seeds of the crisis were already sown before the depression struck and even without that calamity Hungary's debt situation would eventually have become untenable.

The massive fall in commodity prices and with it export earnings hastened the day of judgment. Hungary's exports consisted mainly of agricultural commodities (75 per cent) and they were heavily concentrated in grain products, which experienced some of the sharpest price falls. On average Hungarian export prices fell by about 60 per cent between 1929 and 1933, while import prices fell less steeply so that the terms of trade deteriorated. This meant that Hungary received 15–20 per cent less imports for the same volume of exports. At the same time export volumes also declined as increasing self-sufficiency and tariff protection in Hungary's main markets took effect. The overall effect of price and volume changes reduced Hungary's agricultural exports by nearly 70 per cent between 1929 and the trough in the early 1930s (Drabek 1985, 433). Industrial production declined by 25 per cent and employment by 30 per cent between 1929 and 1932, and as foreign capital inflows soon dried up the government was forced to take drastic action (Eddie 1994, 112).

The price collapse was of course disastrous as far as the farming community was concerned. Many farmers were on the verge of famine and became even more heavily indebted as their incomes plummeted. The decline in commodity prices also undermined state finances, the balance of payments and the market for industrial goods. The final crunch came with the international financial crisis of 1931, when many financial institutions were on the verge of insolvency, short-term credits dried up and capital flight took place on a grand scale – 5 billion pengös were converted into foreign currencies. At this point emergency measures became essential: exchange control was imposed in July 1931, a moratorium on debt service payments in December of that same year, while tariffs and quota restrictions on imports and export subsidies became widespread (Ellis 1941, 96–97).

External protection was accompanied by orthodox monetary and fiscal policies which involved a rigid deflationary policy to balance the budget and so demonstrate to the world that Hungary was a safe haven for inward investment (Polonsky 1975, 56–57). This strategy obviously delayed recovery but there was some relaxation by the middle of the decade as the government sought to foster industrialisation at the expense of agriculture.

Protection and exchange control helped to insulate the domestic market for home producers, while export subsidies and the use of multiple exchange rates assisted exporters. But Ellis doubts whether these, along with other devices to assist farmers, were sufficient to offset the high pengö rate under exchange control (Ellis 1941, 113–14). On the trade front, commercial policy was influenced by the affinity with other exchange control countries in Europe (East/Central Europe excluding Poland) which led to the spread of clearing agreements among members. These entailed the bilateral balancing of claims between exchange control countries, thereby eliminating the need to use free foreign exchange. Towards the end of the decade more than half the trade of Hungary and the Balkans was passed through clearing, and as much as 80 per cent in the case of Nazi Germany (League of Nations 1942). The dominant partner was of course Germany, which increased its penetration into Eastern Europe. It was difficult to resist this encroachment since Germany was one of the few countries offering a ready market for agrarian products and raw materials at reasonable prices, in exchange for much needed capital equipment and armaments. There has been considerable debate as to who gained the most from this strategy and whether Germany exploited its position. It would seem that the smaller countries did not do too badly, and the charge of economic exploitation by Germany's foreign trade and exchange policies is still an open question (Ritschl 2001, 324–45). Hungary of course had a closer political affinity with Germany and one would expect greater accord, though Friedman's conclusion as to the effects of German bilateral trade with Hungary is scarcely positive (Friedman 1976, 113–25; Aldcroft and Oliver 1998, 76–77). Be that as it may, Hungary's trade with Germany increased in importance throughout the decade. In 1929 only 11.7 per cent of Hungary's exports went to Germany but this had increased to 40 per cent by 1938; imports from Germany over the same period increased from 20.0 to 40.9 per cent of the total (Hiden 1977, 173; Kaiser 1980, 325–26).

State intervention became increasingly apparent in the 1930s as foreign and bank sources of capital dried up. However, state ownership was not as extensive as in other East European countries, accounting for only about 5 per cent of industrial investment. The role of the state was also influenced by the spread of cartels, which eventually became an instrument of government policy. By the later 1930s they accounted for some 40 per cent of industrial production (Spulber 1959, 276).

Towards the end of the 1930s defence requirements became an increasing influence on state policy. In March 1938 a four-year rearmament programme of 1000 million pengös was announced, 60 per cent to be devoted to military purposes and the rest for public works. By the following year the plan had been revised to a two-year time scale and then later increased in value. Defence spending rose very rapidly in these years, from 137.9 million pengös in 1937–38 to 618.9 million in 1938–39 and 1845.7 million a year later, by which time it accounted for nearly 20 per cent of national income (Hauner 1986, 96–97).

Overall there was substantial progress in industrial production between 1929 and 1938, though estimates vary somewhat, ranging from 15 to over 35 per cent (Ellis 1941, 101–103; Berend and Ranki 1985, 92). But compared with some European countries Hungary's performance was not very impressive over the whole of the interwar period. Apart from Spain, Austria and Poland, most European countries had stronger industrial growth. In fact Berend and Ranki (1974b, 132–42) are rather disparaging in general about Hungary's industrial record. Though industry became a more important sector of the economy and there were some signs of improvement in terms of efficiency and international competitiveness, the sector still remained weak overall. There were some bright spots in newer sectors of activity, notably in the electrical industry, pharmaceuticals and engineering. Radios and light bulbs made in Hungary were famous throughout the world (Hanák 1992, 190). But it was in some of the traditional sectors (textiles, food processing, clothing, construction), which accounted for a large share of total industrial output, that the fastest growth occurred. In textiles, for example, the number of workers increased five times and output sixfold. This sector had absorbed one third of all industrial investment in the 1920s.

Structurally, manufacturing industry remained weak. Hungary retained a dual industrial structure, consisting of many small-scale inefficient firms alongside a few modern large-scale enterprises. Small-scale industry employed nearly one half the industrial labour force. Small businesses remained viable for a variety of reasons, including protection from imports, the weakness of big business, the abundance of cheap labour and the predominance of more traditional sectors of activity in which small-scale enterprises tended to flourish. Large-scale concerns were not technically dynamic and they failed to make much headway in modern production and management methods. Western-style mass-production methods were something of a rarity, and in some industries, notably engineering and iron and steel, the typical large company was little more than a 'general store' whose plants supplied a multiplicity of products in small batches to limited markets.

For agriculture it is a sadder tale. Throughout the interwar period agriculture languished and the output of the sector failed to regain the prewar level. Perhaps this is not altogether surprising given the problems it faced: weak prices, institutional rigidities, the structure of output, lack of credit and capital, and limited technical progress.

In the 1920s, when farm prices were firmer for a time, the agrarian sector did not do too badly, even though the debts of small farmers were increasing following stabilisation of the currency, while output failed to recover to the prewar level. But with the dramatic fall in world prices during the depression agriculture really suffered. The real value of agricultural purchasing power in 1932–33 was down to 53 per cent of the 1927–28 level and only slowly climbed to 73 per cent by 1938–39 (Berend and Ranki 1985, 109). Recovery from the slump was a slow and painful progress. Gross capital formation in agriculture was only half that of the 1920s.

Some writers have accused the government of neglecting the sector and of writing off the peasant proletariat in its quest for modernisation and industrial advance (Janos 1982, 323–33). This is not entirely correct. It is true that in the 1920s most of the assistance in the form of cheap loans and subsidies went to the large or medium-sized farm units, while the peasants received very little. This is one reason why peasant indebtedness increased in the later 1920s. Peasants also bore an unfair burden of tax. Land reform (see below) did little to improve the structure of landholdings. But in the 1930s there was a more concerted effort to rescue agriculture. The interest charges on agricultural indebtedness were significantly reduced, while a moratorium was placed on debt repayments to prevent foreclosure. These provisions covered 22 per cent of farms under 4 hectares and 62 per cent of holdings over 40 hectares (Berend 1985, 178). Measures were also taken to support prices and assist marketing. Price support schemes were introduced as early as 1930 and eventually covered grain, wool, milk, potatoes, oil and seeds, and other products. Some commodities, for example flour, also received subsidies to assist exports (Royal Institute of International Affairs 1939, 117–18). From 1934 the state also intervened on a significant scale in the marketing of agricultural produce, mainly to assist exporting. Through largely government-owned agencies – cooperatives and joint stock companies which had a monopoly in the buying and selling of certain agricultural products at guaranteed minimum prices – eventually some 80–85 per cent of foreign trade passed through semi-official channels. Such arrangements fitted in well with the trade agreements with Germany (Berend 1985, 179).

While these measures staved off a complete abandonment of the soil by the peasant, nevertheless they did little to improve materially the very low earnings of farmers or rural wage-earners compared with those outwith the agrarian sector. Nor did they do anything to improve the viability of tiny holdings. Land reform in Hungary was too limited to change significantly the still semi-feudal pattern of land tenure.

Of all the peripheral states, land reform was least in evidence in Hungary either before or after the Great War. Large estates were more predominant than in any other European country, side by side with a host of very small smallholdings. In the aftermath of the abortive Red Revolution of 1919 the landed classes regained the upper hand, consolidated their power and so put an end to any prospect of radical land reform. However, there was a token gesture of reform to forestall any further revolutionary activity. This was the Land Reform Act of 1920 which was a minimalist piece of legislation that did not envisage the wholesale break-up of large estates. In total approximately 6 per cent of the arable area was included in the reform and only about half of this came from large estates. Altogether 700,000 hectares were redistributed to roughly the same number of peasants, which meant they gained on average 1 hectare per head; 250,000 of the recipients were landless peasants, thus adding to the number of tiny and unviable holdings, while the rest went to owners of dwarf holdings. In addition, another one million hectares were distributed through public institutions to provide medium-sized holdings for ex-servicemen and supporters of the counter-revolution (Berend and Ranki 1985, 103–104).

The overall result was a minimal change in the structure of land ownership. Medium and large estates (over 100 hectares) continued to predominate, accounting for nearly 50 per cent of the cultivable land, not very much changed from the position at the end of the nineteenth century. The bulk of the farm population consisted of small farmers, those with dwarf holdings or tenancies, and landless workers, in roughly equal proportions (Kerék 1940, 477). Thus the act of 1920 did little more than consolidate the position of large landowners and increase yet further the number of uneconomic units. The only other attempt at reform was the Settlement Act of 1936 which ostensibly addressed the latter problem. It attempted to create more viable units by parcelling out a fixed amount of land from large estates, rather than distributing land to as many peasants as possible. But the legislation proved to be a dead letter since by 1940 there had been no appropriations of land, the only transaction being a small amount of land bought by the state.

Thus the fates conspired to undermine the agrarian sector in Hungary in the interwar period. The share of income generated by agriculture declined from 50 to 32 per cent, yet by the end of the interwar years half the labour force was still engaged on the land. As in several other European countries it was not the dynamic sector required for modern development. Even at the peak, output trailed the prewar levels and Hungarian agriculture had not adapted to the postwar conditions as successfully as, say, the Baltic countries had done. The continued heavy reliance on cereals and the antiquated pattern of landholdings bore testimony to the sector's problems. Far from being a prime mover in the economy it could be said that agriculture acted as a drag on the country's development (Berend and Ranki 1985, 112).

CHAPTER SEVEN

Spain and Portugal

In one important respect Spain and Portugal differ from the other countries studied in this volume. Though they were affected by the backwash of the First World War, they were not major participants in the conflict (Spain was neutral and Portugal did not join the Allied cause until March 1916); nor did they experience significant territorial or population changes as a result of the postwar peace settlement. In most other respects, however, they had much in common with the countries of the European periphery. A large proportion of the population was dependent on agriculture, illiteracy was fairly high, especially in Portugal, and by any measure of development they could be classed as backward, with income per head levels of less than one half those in the highly developed countries.

Spain

Britain's leading authority on the economic history of Spain refers to the country as 'a prime example of economic backwardness' on the eve of the First World War, a state that was 'overwhelmingly agrarian and underdeveloped ... with few signs of modern capitalist development' (Harrison 1985, 15).

Once a world power, Spain languished in the seventeenth and eighteenth centuries and by the mid-nineteenth century had fallen well behind the dynamic nations of North-west Europe. It is true that various estimates of national output by Spanish historians suggest a not unworthy performance after 1850, though one should bear in mind that development was taking place from a fairly low base. Real GDP per capita grew at around 1 per cent per annum in the period 1850 through to 1913, which more or less matched that of Britain and France and which was also close to the European average. Industrial development was also quite rapid in the years 1850–90, at a little over 3 per cent a year, falling to 1.5 per cent thereafter (Prados de la Escosura 1993, 30, 48, 58). However, what this means was that Spain was barely holding her own in the half century down to 1914 so that there was no convergence in her income levels with those of the more advanced countries of Europe. But the fact that Spain experienced reasonable growth in this period suggests that the initial lag had occurred before the mid-nineteenth century. In the first decade of the twentieth century income per capita levels were perhaps 40–50 per cent of the British, and, according to some scholars, similar in fact to the Italian. The main difference was that Italy had more depth in its structural transformation whereas Spain gave the impression of being steeped in traditional modes of behaviour which blocked dynamic change (Molinas and Prados de la Escosura 1989, 396–97).

All the circumstantial evidence points to the fact that Spain was well behind the advanced nations in industrial development. In fact Nadal (1987, 73) ranks Spain a failure as far as industrialisation is concerned. Spanish industry was certainly limited in comparison with that of Western Europe, being confined to a few islands of progress on the periphery of the country, in Catalonia, the Basque Country and Asturias. It tended to be dominated by textiles and foodstuffs, though there were important mineral deposits which were exploited by foreign firms in the latter half of the nineteenth century. Nadal (1987, 70–71) refers to Spain as a pawn in the process of the mining activities of overseas companies who set up development enclaves which generated plenty of money 'very little of which filtered down to Spanish society'. There were also the beginnings of an iron and steel industry in the 1880s centred around Bilbao, but it was not internationally competitive and it was dependent on government orders (Harrison and Corkill 2004, 71; Tipton and Aldrich 1987, 27). Bilbao however was one of the most highly developed cities after Madrid, with a range of industries and services including shipping and banking.

Nevertheless, one should not write off Spanish industry altogether. It may have been limited in scale and concentrated spatially, while not very competitive in world markets. But it had a consistently positive rate of growth in the century from 1830, at a compound rate of 2.85 per cent per annum, though from a relatively low base. However, this was insufficient for it to make up the leeway with the faster growing countries in Western Europe and North America (Carreras 1987, 76–85).

Agriculture remained extremely backward and inefficient throughout most of Spain, with levels of productivity far behind those of Britain and Denmark. It was dominated by the large estates which relied on cheap labour and tariff protection, and by small farms in the north and centre of the country. Innovation and technical change were very limited and the famine of 1904–1906 was indicative of the poor state of the agrarian sector. There was a heavy concentration on cereals and legume production which accounted for some three quarters of the cultivated land but which had a poor record in productivity and innovation. The bright spots were the more productive sectors such as olives, citrus fruits and wine production, but these only accounted for a small share of total output (Tortella 1987, 51–53). Agriculture could not therefore fulfil the crucial functions for the modernisation process, especially those of market demand and capital accumulation, to the same extent as in Western countries (see Tortella 1987, 55–58).

Many reasons have been put forward to account for Spain's backwardness. Tortella (1987, 43, 58–59; 1994, 1–21) points to unyielding agrarian structures, partly due to geographical factors, and low investment in human capital as the main reasons for retardation in both Spain and Portugal. Clara Núñez (1990, 135–36) also cites deficiency in human capital formation as an obstacle to economic modernisation, and stresses the big gender differences in literacy levels. Until the turn of the century literacy levels were very low in Spain – well under 50 per cent and among females one quarter or less.

But there is much more to Spain's lagging economy than these two factors. Harrison and Corkill (2004, 71) cite a list of causes including low levels of aggregate demand, shortage of cheap energy and misguided government policies. High taxation, not an uncommon feature of underdeveloped countries, impinged heavily on agriculture and especially on the peasantry, which deterred innovation and accumulation. Yet the tax revenue was not wisely used, much of it going on military activities and other unproductive employments (Tortella 1987, 57). One might also add cultural and religious factors – for example the Church's opposition to secular education – inefficient bureaucratic administration, costly colonial wars and the regional segmentation of the country.

As a neutral country Spain stood to benefit from wartime hostilities. Industry in particular was able to take advantage of the dislocation in the belligerent countries. There were growing opportunities for exports to countries engaged in war and to those markets formerly supplied by Britain, Germany and France, as well as the prospects for import substitution as foreign competition in the domestic market eased. The Basque metal and engineering industry and the Catalonian textile mills were the major beneficiaries of the industrial boom (Ranki 1985, 37). But a whole range of industries, including chemicals, coal, shipbuilding and electrical goods, was also stimulated at this time as a result of increasing import substitution. Coal production, for example, rose by no less than 50 per cent between 1913 and 1928 (League of Nations 1929, 6–9). The benefits were reflected in Spain's trading accounts. A balance of trade permanently in the red before the war was transformed into a substantial surplus in the years 1915–19 (Harrison 1985, 37).

But one can easily exaggerate the impact of the wartime boom. While industry obviously benefited, the construction industry languished, as did the service sector, so that the rise in total gross domestic product was quite modest. In fact the most buoyant sector was agriculture, which suggests that Spain became an important source of foodstuffs as supplies elsewhere were interrupted in wartime. It should be noted that some of the wartime developments could be classed as hot-house growth which withered or became stunted once conditions returned to normal and foreign supplies were resumed (Moulton 1923, 58). This was certainly the case in Spain and a number of other countries which had benefited from the artificial boom of the war years. By 1920 the wartime boom was over, the balance of trade again turned negative and the international recession of 1921–22 hit Spanish industry hard. Many textile and metal firms closed down or were forced to work at a much reduced rate.

Unfortunately Spain did not really capitalise on her good fortune. By all accounts both manufacturers and the farming sector made substantial profits during the period of hostilities, yet very little of these were used for modernising Spain's archaic industrial and agricultural structures. Spanish industry did not make the best use of its wartime profits bonanza by investing to provide a firm foundation both to serve newly-won export markets and to secure the domestic market. Instead 'the owners used their excess profits to swell their current accounts, to buy properties in the country and in the cities and in putting up new buildings' (Fontana and Nadal 1976, 470). All of which sounds very familiar. Government, too, lacked initiative and Harrison (1985, 43–50) refers to the failure of economic reconstruction. In fact, as in many other European countries at this time, the immediate postwar years were marked by mounting economic and financial crisis and social and political unrest which eventually put paid to embryonic reconstruction plans. There were rising budgetary deficits, resulting from a combination of factors, the main one being the cost of military operations in Morocco, while the revenue side did not respond adequately due to the antiquated tax system and the impact of recession on receipts. A doubling of the cost of living between 1914 and 1920 was an important factor causing increasing discontent among workers, both rural and urban, and leading to a wave of strikes – no doubt also sparked off by the contagion of the international revolutionary fervour of this period and aggravated by postwar recessionary conditions, rising unemployment and a string of bank failures. The government was unable to stabilise the peseta and there were fears that inflation would run out of control as it was doing in several Central and East European countries.

The deepening economic and financial crisis proved too much for the weak parties and administrations of the restoration monarchy, which was incapable of implementing a coherent programme of economic reconstruction. The worsening economic situation eventually undermined the political system of the restoration. On 13 September 1923 a *coup d'état* was launched by the army under the leadership of General Miguel Primo de Rivera, which was the prelude to a dictatorship lasting until January 1930 when Primo was ousted from power and a civil directory took over prior to the emergence of the Second Republic in April 1931.

It is difficult to classify the dictatorship of Primo de Rivera into any known category of regimes since its policies, especially on economic and social issues, were eclectic and pragmatic, aimed at restoring order and stability, stimulating the economy, while at the same time preserving established institutions and traditional orders. According to Fontana and Nadal (1976, 473), 'the regime never attempted a mobilisation of the masses of a fascist type. It was a regime of landowners, of order-loving people and small gentry, which would follow a policy of pure conservatism, varied with flashes of enlightened paternalism.'

There have been somewhat mixed views on the economic achievements of the dictatorship. Fontana and Nadal (1976, 474) believe that there were few if any signs of genuine economic growth and that the extensive public works programme made for an ever worsening budgetary deficit. Ranki (1985, 61–62) points to the dilemma over economic policy between export-led growth and import substitution which was never fully resolved. He also argues that the wartime trade advantages were to some extent sacrificed in the process, so that gains in industrial exports were not consolidated in the 1920s, while the pattern of agricultural exports tended to shift back towards traditional lines such as wines and oranges.

Other writers provide a more optimistic interpretation of Spain's achievements in the 1920s. The industrial sector enjoyed something of a boom according to Harrison and Corkill (2004, 72; see also Table 7.1), while GDP per capita is estimated to have risen by 22 per cent between 1921 and 1929 (Prados de la Escosura 1993, 86). Increasing urbanisation which resulted from this development also gave a fillip to housing construction. However, while most recent estimates indicate clear industrial expansion, it tended to be extensive rather than intensive development. There seems to have been very little underlying increase in productivity in the interwar years, simply a replication of nineteenth century development (Maluquer de Motes 1994, 64).

The achievements of the 1920s have been attributed to the following factors:

1. The *modernisation of agriculture* which improved incomes in the primary sector and led to a greater demand for manufactured goods.

Table 7.1 Annual Rates of Industrial Growth 1913–50

Years	Spain	Europe (14 countries)
1913–22	0.93	–1.72
1922–29	5.61	5.53
1929–35	–0.47	–0.19
1935–50	0.58	2.71

Sources: Carreras 1987, 86 and Harrison and Corkill 2004, 72.

There were certainly many improvements in the countryside including irrigation work, resettlement policies, improved yields and a better balanced output, with more livestock, and greater concentration on high value products such as citrus fruit and horticulture for the export market. But there was no radical reform of the archaic structure of landholdings and settlement. Large unproductive estates, owned by absentee landlords exploiting low paid workers, continued to predominate in southern and central Spain, while to the north there existed a multitude of tiny farms whose owners or tenants barely scratched a living. Such conditions were scarcely conducive to efficient and high yielding farming practices and the agrarian sector was dependent on protection for support. Modern techniques of farming were conspicuous by their absence while the use of machinery and fertilisers was limited. In some areas conditions were little advanced on medieval times. In a country of low rainfall there was surprisingly little use made of irrigation which could have allowed much more land to be brought into cultivation (Thomas 1961, 50–51). To make matters worse, in several product areas, especially cereals, prices were weakening so that margins were under pressure. Thus, while agricultural output increased modestly in the 1920s, one could scarcely argue that it was the engine of growth for the economy.

2. The ambitious *infrastructure programme* carried out under Primo de Rivera's regime, which included roads, reservoirs, railways, electricity supply and the like. Scepticism has been expressed as to the growth-promoting value of many projects and the propriety of them. The enormous costs placed a heavy burden on state finances and there was an alleged waste of resources on unfavourable contracts and corrupt concessions (Fontana and Nadal 1976, 474). This is perhaps an unduly harsh view. Spain's infrastructure was badly in need of renovation and one of the declared objectives of the regime was to provide a basis for sustained industrial development

(Harrison 1985, 62). Transport improvements were critical in a large country, especially road transport as the number of vehicles rose rapidly from 37,169 in 1923 to 201,249 in 1929. The same applies to electricity, a new and more efficient source of power and one that helped to free industry from dependence on coal imports and also made it more foot-loose locationally. In the period 1925–30 capacity increased by around one half and electricity output by 60 per cent (Harrison 1985, 62–63).

3. A *boom* in residential construction, urban development and services, especially in the major cities such as Madrid, Barcelona and Bilbao. Services were in fact the fastest growing sector in the 1920s, ahead of agriculture and industry. Again it should be noted that, as in the case of other peripheral countries, there was heavy spatial concentration of industrial activity in key locations.
4. *Technological advances* in a range of industries such as metallurgy, shipbuilding, chemicals, and railway materials. This involved to some extent a catch-up process towards best Western practice, but Spain still remained far behind in levels of productivity.
5. *Trading advantages* as a result of the protection of the domestic market and foreign trade benefits from a floating currency. The latter issue has been rather neglected by many historians. One of the factors that helped Spain in the 1920s was that, like Turkey, Spain did not return to the gold standard but retained a floating currency. This meant that the economy was not constrained by the strait-jacket of a fixed exchange rate regime at a time when the correct currency valuations were difficult to determine precisely. Many countries stabilised their currencies and returned to gold at inappropriate exchange rates which overvalued their currencies and left them at a trading disadvantage. Though there was speculation from time to time in anticipation that the Spanish authorities might make a move to stabilise the currency, in fact Spain maintained a free float into the depression. Just prior to the institution of exchange control in May 1931, the peseta had dropped to around 50 per cent of its 1868 parity, as a result of currency expansion prior to 1929 and then a deteriorating trade balance (League of Nations 1937, 30).

It has been argued that the floating exchange rate regime served to insulate Spain from the worst ravages of the depression (Temin 1993, 92; Choudhri and Kochin 1980, 569). This view requires some modification. It is true that Spain fared better than many of the major economies, with only a modest decline in total output. This was largely due to the stability of agriculture as a result of good harvests and to the buoyancy of the service sector. On the other hand, industrial production peaked late (1930) and then declined by 16.5 per cent to the trough in 1933, while trade volumes fell by one quarter (Prados de la Escosura 1993, 86; Ranki 1985, 63). In value terms the trade decline was much greater because of the fall in commodity prices. There were hefty losses in some key exports such as wines, oranges, almonds, olive oil and rice (Harrison 1978, 128–29). In any case, after 1931 the currency advantage disappeared as many countries left the gold standard and devalued, while Spain instituted exchange control which effectively tied her to the gold bloc countries whose currencies were overvalued (Harrison 1983, 316).

Recovery from the depression had scarcely begun to take hold when it was cut short by the protracted Civil War (July 1936 to April 1939) and the subsequent emergence of the Franco regime. The Second Republic no doubt set out with good intentions to reform some of the institutions of Spain and to foster economic development, but it ran up against strong vested interests and political discord within its own ranks. Nowhere was this more apparent than in the attempt to resolve the agrarian problem. It was not only the inefficient structure of agriculture that was at issue but also the fact that Spain, like Portugal, had many landless labourers, and unemployment among agrarian workers accounted for some 60 per cent of total unemployment in the first half of the 1930s (Harrison 1985, 93). Yet at the same time some 1 per cent of the population controlled just over half the land of the country. Several attempts at land reform ran foul of the vested interests of the large landowners, while implementing the measures that were passed proved more troublesome and time-consuming than originally anticipated so that peasant discontent was scarcely allayed. The failure to provide a solution to this intractable issue was to prove a catalyst in the internal upheaval which broke out in the summer of 1936 when the generals' *coup* challenged the legitimate government of the Republic (see Malefakis 1970).

The revolt against the proposed land and social reforms of the Popular Front government elected in February 1936 originated in Morocco and soon spread into mainland Spain. It was orchestrated primarily by General Francisco Franco, Chief of the Army General Staff since 1935, who promptly formed a rival government, based in Burgos, and proclaimed himself El Caudillo in the following year. The conflict split the country effectively into two halves with diametrically opposed ideologies: the secular and reformist interests of the republican supporters and the conservative, pro-clerical and nationalist leanings of the Falangists under Franco. The former drew their main support from dispossessed rural labourers especially in the regions of Andalusia,

Extremadura, New Castile and the Levante, the working classes of the industrial towns and the petty urban bourgeoisie. Behind the nationalists were many of the small peasant proprietors of northern Spain, the clergy, large landowners, monarchists and some of the major industrial and financial interests (Fontana and Nadal 1976, 503). Geographically the republicans' main stronghold, at the start of the conflict, was the South-eastern segment of the country running from Madrid down to Malaga round to Alicante and up to Barcelona, with a small centre in the extreme north based on Bilbao and Santander. The nationalists' major region of power was the north-west and north of the country (excluding the extreme north and north-east) from Corunna to just short of Madrid, together with a small centre in the south-west based on Seville and Cadiz (see map in Thomas 1961, 163).

In terms of resources the two sides were fairly evenly matched initially. Some 12.3 million people supported the nationalists while 12.7 million were reported to be on the republican side. The latter had control of much of the industrial activity as a result of their strength in the major cities and towns such as Madrid, Barcelona, Valencia and Bilbao, but they were short on food resources. By contrast the nationalists were weak on the industrial side but had strength in the production of foodstuffs.

The details of the war itself need not concern us here. Suffice to say that for nearly three years the republicans and the nationalists slugged it out with some assistance from abroad: idealists and sympathisers in the case of the former, and from the fascist powers, Italy and Nazi Germany, in support of the latter. The republicans gained financial assistance from the Soviet Union and active support from many young and idealistically-motivated people, and some rather less so, especially students, and including notable literati such as George Orwell and W. H. Auden, Hemingway and Spender. In fact it is probably true to say that Spain, or more specifically the republican cause, had more arty types than it knew what to do with. Not that the latter contributed much directly to the military cause except Orwell until he was injured: Auden had a very brief spell as a stretcher-bearer for an ambulance unit, while Spender and Hemingway possibly raised the morale of the injured and later wrote about their experience for the foreign press. 'Eventually over forty thousand young foreigners from over fifty nations went to fight [mostly on behalf of the republican cause] and many to die in a country about which most of them probably knew no more than what it looked like in a school atlas' (Hobsbawm 1994, 160).

Despite this support and the fact that the republicans initially controlled much of the country's industrial base, the republican campaign strategy and organisational effort could not match those of the nationalists. In contrast to the latter, the republican exercise was badly coordinated, there was a lack of central command and an absence of clear direction as to priorities, not helped by the fact that many of the republican supporters had their own ideals. Political fragmentation was no doubt inevitable given that the republican side was composed of many disparate elements, including socialists, communists, anarchists and a host of other leftist groupings all with their own idiosyncratic ideas on how to run the war. In fact the many different political factions on the republican side – all no doubt dedicated in one way or another to the cause of a free Spain – were constantly fighting against one another, at times almost as fiercely as they were fighting to save the Republic. It was a case of a war within a war. It was this internal disunity, coupled with the non-interventionist stance of Britain and France, that proved to be critical in the collapse of the republican forces. It was also difficult to integrate the many and varied volunteers from other countries who swept into Spain on a wave of enthusiasm for the republican cause but who had little experience in military combat and strategy. Shortages of food and military equipment and a tactical failure to employ guerrilla warfare to combat superior conventional forces also played a part in their downfall. Support for the Spanish fascist cause from Nazi Germany and Italy was also an important element in Franco's success. Hitler and Mussolini provided arms and men with some 100,000 German and Italian soldiers fighting alongside Spanish troops against the republicans.

Despite the nationalists' tactical advantages the Civil War proved a long and costly exercise for both sides and for Spain generally. But by a process of slow attrition Franco gradually extended his control over the country from his power base in the north. The progress of the nationalist forces can be followed from the excellent graphic maps in Thomas's book on the Civil War (Thomas 1961, 163, 202, 266, 400, 490, 543, 582). With the conquest of Catalonia early in 1939 the republican forces were left with only the south-east segment of the country extending north-westwards to Madrid. Their final defeat in the spring of 1939 was therefore no great surprise, whereupon Franco proceeded to set up a personal dictatorship which endured for three and a half decades.

Nearly three years of civil war led to a considerable loss of life and property and it devastated the economy, though it was by no means as ruinous as the Russian civil war. Estimates of the number of victims vary somewhat and we shall probably never know the exact tally. It is unlikely that they exceeded the million mark unless one takes into account the number of exiles and emigrants. In the third edition of Thomas's book on the Civil War the author reckons that loss of life from all causes was in the region of 500,000, but only 200,000, or 10 per cent of the total combatants, were the result of direct military action, with most of the rest being caused by murder and executions, both during and subsequent to the Civil War, and malnutrition. There was also a loss through permanent emigration of some 300,000 people, so that the total loss of population may be put at around 800,000 (Thomas 1977, 926–27). Many republicans were also taken prisoner by the nationalists. One estimate puts the number of persons passing through the prisons and concentration camps of nationalist Spain at some two million through to 1942, many of whom received lengthy prison sentences and some an even worse fate (Thomas 1961, 608). Other more fortunate individuals managed to flee the country and lived a precarious existence as refugees in France and elsewhere.

Damage to property and physical assets was considerable. Around 200 towns and cities were virtually obliterated with many of their buildings destroyed. The number of churches destroyed was 150 while as many as 4859 were damaged in some way; around a quarter of a million houses were so badly damaged that they were rendered unfit for habitation, while a similar number were partially damaged. Though many factories, especially around Barcelona and Bilbao, remained virtually unscathed, the damage to transportation facilities was considerable. There were heavy losses of railway rolling stock; 70 per cent of passenger carriages and about 40 per cent of locomotives and freight wagons were destroyed. The merchant marine also suffered a loss of about one third of its capacity. The roads were not too badly affected though transport vehicles remained in short supply (Thomas 1977, 928).

Possibly the worst affected sector was agriculture. Farm livestock was reduced by a third, 50 per cent in the case of pigs (1933–41), and much farm machinery was wrecked, while there was a certain amount of damage to agricultural land. There was also a big drop in the amount of land under cultivation; compared with 1935 the sown area of wheat in 1939 was down by nearly 30 per cent, while 37 per cent of the grape vines were lost in Gandesa (Thomas 1977, 928). Perhaps the most critical short-term problem was the shortage of food and the low stocks of raw materials towards the end of the war. The situation was worst in and around republican Madrid where many people were eking out a precarious existence on very limited rations in the winter of 1938–39 (Thomas 1961, 567, 588, 606–607; Harrison 1985, 117).

These losses, coupled with the diversion of resources to the military cause and the duplication of economic effort and institutions of the two sides, had a disastrous effect on economic activity overall. Having barely recovered from the depression years economic activity declined steadily after 1935 and through to 1939, with a drop of 21 per cent in agricultural production, 30 per cent in industrial production and around one quarter in GDP per head. Industrial production and GDP per head were even more depressed when compared with the previous cyclical peak of 1929 (Thomas 1977, 929; Prados de la Escosura 1993, 86). In fact by the end of the decade real GDP per head was slightly lower than it had been in 1913, and so Spain had lost all the gains made in the previous decade. This was a far worse performance than many other countries of the European periphery and compares unfavourably with her Iberian neighbour Portugal (see below). Added to this Spain had lost most of her gold reserves and was saddled with large debts to Germany and Italy. Though there was some recovery during the Second World War since Spain benefited from its neutral stance – it was not until the first half of the 1950s that the 1929 levels of economic activity and per capita income were regained (Payne 1968, 57; Lieberman 1995, 18; Prados de la Escosura 1993, 86).

Portugal

Portugal is something of an anomaly if we compare it with Spain. On circumstantial evidence it should have fared worse than the latter country since both before and after the war conditions in Portugal seemed less propitious for development than in Spain. Yet by the end of the interwar period Portugal finished in a stronger position relative to 1913 than her larger neighbour.

It is generally acknowledged that, before the First World War, the Portuguese economy and society were more backward than those of Spain. The majority of the population – some three quarters – were illiterate and were dependent on the land in one way or another for their livelihood. The land tenure system was reckoned to be one of the worst in Europe in that there were so many very small farms; there were 400,000 holdings of less than 1 hectare and another 238,000 with between 1 and 3 hectares (Ranki 1985, 60). Productivity levels, both per worker and per unit of land, were the lowest in Europe (always excepting Albania of course), while there was a large number of landless labourers. Exports consisted mainly of primary products such as wine, cork, sardines and fruit which were not especially competitive in world markets, but relied heavily on the British market. Wheat had to be imported since the country was not self-sufficient. Industrial development was more limited than in Spain, being mainly represented by textiles of low quality.

Economic progress in the nineteenth century was even slower than in Spain and, as in the case of the latter country, the main constraints to modernisation were the backward and unyielding nature of the agrarian sector and the low level of human capital formation. Portugal had the highest illiteracy rate in Western Europe and it was even worse than in some East European countries. Even as late as 1910 the literacy rate in Portugal was only 25 per cent (Tortella 1994, 8, 11, 14).

The postwar situation was even more daunting despite the fact that Portugal did not suffer material damage as a result of war. Siding with the Allies had cost the country dearly, resulting in the largest public debt in history and a large war debt owed to Britain. The state budget and the trade balance were in the red, while Portugal had one of the strongest inflations in Europe outside the hyperinflationary countries. This was largely due to the rapid rise in currency circulation during and after the war occasioned by the steady increase in government borrowing from the Central Bank to meet its obligations. Retail prices and the dollar rate of the currency moved in sympathy. By the end of 1920 prices were some nine times higher than in 1913 and by the end of 1923 more than 20 times higher than before the war. The escudo steadily depreciated to 31 per cent of its par value in 1920 and by 1923 it had sunk to 3.3 per cent of its original value (League of Nations 1943b, 42; League of Nations 1946a, 115).

Not surprisingly there was a sharp decline in real living standards for most workers and especially public servants. By 1921 real per capita income was less than 60 per cent of prewar levels and even in 1924 it fell short by nearly one quarter. Not until 1928 did real per capita income exceed the 1913 level (Nunes, Mata and Valério 1989). This occasioned a wave of strikes and labour unrest in the years 1919–25 as labour sought compensation in higher wages and social reform. Governments tried to assuage the situation by passing timid social reforms but they were limited in what they could do for two reasons. Falling tax receipts and budget deficits, not to mention a weak currency, meant that public expenditure had to be curbed. By 1923 it was running at one half of prewar levels so that the scope for social reform and infrastructure development was very limited.

The second problem was the extreme political instability. The constitutional monarchy which had been in existence since 1820 was overthrown in 1910 and replaced by a republic. But the new republican rule was never fully accepted by a large section of the population, including conservative forces such as the military and clergy. Political instability therefore ensued with constant upheavals and *coups*. Between December 1917 and January 1919 Portugal was ruled by a dictatorship, euphemistically called the 'New Republic', only to be replaced, after a brief civil war, by the restoration of the 'Old Republic' early in 1919. During the next few years coalition governments or one-party governments came and went with monotonous regularity. Between January 1919 and May 1926 there were no fewer than 28 different governments, and most of the prime ministers and many of the ministers were new to the job. Nearly half the cabinets were presided over by the military and since ministers revolved in rapid succession the administrations were weak and incompetent. A dozen or so parties were in existence at any one time which made for political fragmentation even though less than half were formally represented in parliament (de Oliveira Marques 1978, 90–95). Nevertheless, republican governments did recognise the need for improving human resource capabilities, and policy measures to improve primary and technical education were implemented accordingly.

Given the weakness and extreme fragmentation of democratic forces the upshot was that conservative interests and the military came to dominate the scene. Corruption and political violence were endemic with assassination of politicians and armed rebellions and right wing uprisings being regular events. The last of these, a military revolt in May 1926, proved successful and out of it emerged the figure of Antonio de Oliveira Salazar, a professor of economics at the University of Coimbra, who became minister of finance in 1928 and effectively dictator of Portugal from the early 1930s.

In point of fact economic and social conditions had begun to improve before the political *coup*. From the early 1920s living standards were improving, the budget deficit was being eliminated, the public debt was reduced and steps were taken to check the currency depreciation and halt inflation. Early in 1924 the government took a number of measures, including a reduction of borrowing and currency in circulation and the tightening of exchange control, in an effort to restore confidence in financial and currency markets. While these measures may have helped to precipitate a banking crisis in 1925, the policy of financial retrenchment did finally restore financial stability and paved the way for a sounder-based banking system, which had suffered several crises in the postwar years as inflation eroded the real asset base of the banks (Reis 1995, 483, 486). By the end of 1924 inflation had been checked and currency depreciation brought to a halt. The escudo remained fairly stable for the next three years and in 1929 *de facto* stabilisation was announced. However, it was not until June 1931 that Portugal formally went back on gold just as the gold standard was about to disintegrate.

That proved a blessing in disguise. The international depression of the early 1930s had relatively little impact on Portugal. In fact the country came through the crisis quite strongly with positive gains in both output and industrial production. After 1933, however, the economy remained rather flat and subsequently felt the backwash of the Spanish Civil War.

Industrial production charted an erratic course, falling slightly between 1932 and 1936 before rising strongly in 1937 and then falling back again. Total and per capita output were fairly static between 1932 and 1937 and then rose strongly in 1938 and 1939. Even so, through the cycle 1929–39 GDP per capita increased by as much as 21 per cent despite a strong rise in population (see Nunes, Mata and Valério 1989; Lains and Reis 1991).

It is somewhat difficult to explain readily why Portugal fared so well in the depression period. Most recent estimates suggest a 10 per cent rise in per capita output between 1929 and 1933. Corkill (1999, 11) explains the phenomenon in terms of the country's economic backwardness and its low exposure to external trade. Industrial development was still very limited and much of what there was consisted of small units of production serving local and regional markets. The agrarian sector was less vulnerable than many since it did not have a high dependence on products such as wheat, the price of which fell heavily in the depression. Some good harvests in the 1930s and government assistance through price support schemes and generous credits also bolstered the sector. Trade in primary products was concentrated in less price sensitive commodities such as wine, fruits and fish. Moreover, the special commercial relationship with Britain, a country which had a fairly mild depression, helped to insulate the Portuguese economy. Portugal also left the gold standard soon after Britain had abandoned it in September and became a member of the sterling area, which meant that she was not constrained by an overvalued exchange rate. The country had traditionally maintained large sterling balances in Britain so that any policy other than aligning her currency with sterling would have entailed a hefty capital loss (Aldcroft 2004; Drummond 1981, 7–8). Confidence in the stability of the currency as a result of its sterling link and in the economy in general helped to encourage the repatriation of capital, which compensated for losses in Brazil. This, together with growing receipts from tourism, led to balance of payments surpluses in the 1930s and a consequent accumulation of gold and foreign exchange reserves (Reis 1995, 490–91).

As in many other countries, the state assumed a much more interventionist role in the economy during the 1930s. Although the regime was increasingly authoritarian it could not be regarded as fascist. Unlike Italy and Germany, the Salazar regime was a low profile one which eschewed the demagogic tactics of the former countries. It was, however, intensely nationalistic and sought to strengthen Portugal's independence and position in the world. Salazar's background was that of a classical economics professor which meant that he believed ardently in balanced budgets, a sound currency and a restraint on public spending. However, he departed from other classical precepts in that he did not support laissez-faire principles or unbridled market mechanisms. He believed that Portugal had to develop from within by relying on its own resources even if at times this meant squeezing the rural sector to make way for industrialisation (Newitt 1981, 183).

The main objectives of the strategy were to maintain financial stability, to foster industrialisation through import substitution, and to improve the country's infrastructure. In the process most forms of economic activity were highly regulated by controls imposed by the bureaucracy under a corporatist structure. The system tended to protect existing interests, however inefficient, and repressed competitive forces, so that it is doubtful in the long run whether it was always in the best interests of the country. It certainly did little to increase international competitiveness or modernisation and technological improvement in industry. Nor was there much attempt to modernise agriculture. 'In the final analysis,' Corkill (1999, 16) writes, 'Portuguese corporatism was at best paternalistic and at worst stifling and repressive. State-dominated corporatist institutions created excessive bureaucratisation and encouraged favouritism and corruption.' Moreover, little was done to tackle the inefficient structure of the agrarian sector.

However, one should not be too negative about the *Estado Novo* regime's strategy since it did have some positive results. Industrial development was fostered through import substitution and direct government assistance to industry, as were infrastructure developments, even if perhaps a disproportionate amount of government spending went on defence in the later 1930s. Moreover, one should not underestimate the role of fiscal prudence and sound money in generating confidence among businessmen. And while fiscal policy did not allow for deficit financing, monetary policy was much more relaxed. Interest rates fell steadily during the 1930s while the money supply (M1) expanded at 6.7 per cent a year. The inflow of gold and foreign exchange reserves as a result of balance of payments surpluses was not automatically sterilised by the Bank of Portugal, but steadily pumped back into the economy through increases in the note issue (Reis 1995, 498).

Though estimates vary, there seems to be general agreement that Portugal performed better than Spain through the transwar period (1913–38). Whereas Spain recorded a small decline in per capita income in this period, Portugal achieved a rise of at least one fifth and possibly as much as a third. Thus in terms of the absolute level of per capita output the positions were reversed (Bairoch 1976; Nunes, Mata and Valério 1989).

Both countries, however, remained woefully backward by the end of the interwar period and both had failed to transform their agrarian sectors. There was at that time little prospect of either country maintaining sustained growth for any length of time had not war intervened to complicate the picture, since the foundations of modernisation had still to be put in place. Yet Spain at least was potentially a very rich country. Despite extremes of climate and land quality, it could grow all the major crops, while the country was rich in mineral and chemical resources, and in water power potential. The fact that all these were not exploited fully has been attributed to the reality that Spaniards had for the past four centuries turned the weight of their energies against each other, rather than against the elements of nature (Thomas 1961, 52). Nevertheless, despite its retarded development it would be unfair to class Spain as a Third World country. The Spanish economy prior to the Civil War may have been retarded and isolated with a backward agrarian sector and a low level of industrialisation, but, according to Molinas and Prados de la Escosura (1989), it had started on the path of modern economic growth.

CHAPTER EIGHT

Greece, Turkey and Albania

Greece

When Greece finally managed to gain independence in 1830 after centuries of being ruled as a peripheral province of the Ottoman Empire, it was a very small and very backward state of around three quarters of a million people that emerged. This was the problem. Since more Greeks lived outwith the new state than within it, scattered around the Balkans and in Turkish territory, the home nation harboured ambitions to incorporate all ethnically Greek nationals into a Greater Greece. The objective was known as the *Megali Idea* (Great Idea). It sought to incorporate the unredeemed Greeks into a greater Greek state largely at the expense of the Ottoman Empire. In fact, the Greek leaders became obsessed with the notion of an enlarged country that would include all Greek-inhabited territories and they pursued this objective with relentless vigour and at great cost. Domestic progress was neglected as a result and there was very little contact with the main European world. Until the Balkan Wars of 1912–13 Greece lacked a land frontier with Europe and it was only in 1920 that direct links between Paris and Athens were realised with the first Simplon-Orient Express service. The cost to the nation in terms of debts was extremely burdensome.

Greece's grandiose strategy was dependent upon the acquiescence of the Great Powers, and though she eventually achieved most of her ambition to unite Greek nationals, the policy sometimes met with setbacks and it was pursued at considerable cost to the nation in terms of lagged development and accumulated debts. As late as the 1870s only around one half of the potentially arable land was actually cultivated, while modern roads and railways scarcely existed before the turn of the century. Freris (1986, 32) states that during a period of more than sixty years prior to the First World War Greece's economy 'had changed very little if at all'. On the other hand, Psomiades (1965, 196) believes the economy had reached a level far above that of the Ottoman period, even though it was still very primitive by Western standards.

In fact there were some signs of change after the 1870s. The merchant marine expanded quite rapidly, from 1241 tons of steamships in 1875 to 893,650 tons in 1915, and Piraeus, the port of Athens, became one of the busiest ports in the Mediterranean. At the same time a skeletal railway network emerged totalling some 1600 kilometres by 1909, while more than 2500 kilometres of paved roads were constructed (Psomiades 1965, 196). Industrial progress was very slow and by 1913 most manufacturing activities were of the small workshop variety in enterprises of 1 to 5 workers. By 1913 there were only just over 100 factories with a labour force of over 25 workers apiece, mainly in such activities as food processing, shipbuilding and various repair activities (Hoffman 1972, 41). Some of this development had been assisted by foreign loans and emigrant remittances, though a large part of the funds derived from these sources went on costly foreign wars, in pursuit of the *Megali Idea*, as well as in meeting the expenses of corrupt and inefficient administrations.

However, the main source of economic activity, that is, agriculture, changed very little, nor did the overall structure of the economy. The bulk of the population were engaged in agriculture and the sectoral distribution of the economically active population did not change very much over a period of half a century or more (see Table 8.1). The efficient exploitation of the agrarian sector was held back by an archaic land tenure system and lack of capital, though it was not as backward as that of the Ottoman Empire. Nevertheless, because of the inefficient agrarian system one third of the grain consumed before the war had to be imported, along with some other basic foodstuffs.

Table 8.1 Distribution of Economically Active Population of Greece (%)

	1861	1925
Agriculture	74.0	70.0
Industry and handicraft	10.0	13.1
Commerce and transport	6.1	9.2
Public administration	4.4	2.0
Professional and other	5.5	4.8

Source: Freris 1986, 36.

The main reason for the slow progress in development before 1914 must surely be the draining of resources on costly wars and servicing public debt. From the inception of the new state Greece had been saddled with heavy debts, first to defray the cost of gaining independence, and then to meet the expenses involved in repeated conflicts in pursuit of aggrandisement, through to the final and disastrous war against Turkey in the early 1920s. In 1893 some 30 per cent of all public expenditure went on servicing internal and external debts and the share of the public budget devoted to defence rose continuously from just under 28 per cent in the years 1866–70 to 48.6 per cent between 1883 and 1895. In fact debt problems plagued Greece throughout the first century or so of her independent existence and by the end of the nineteenth century the country was declared bankrupt by the Western powers and international financial control was instituted down to 1913 (Freris 1986, 25–7). Other factors which militated against development were the lack of a good raw material and fuel base, the political instability of the country and the lack of a strong capitalist class of entrepreneurs. Ironically, there was a budding class of Greek merchants from the eighteenth century onwards in the Balkans and the Mediterranean Sea area, but they served more to promote European expansion and interests in the Ottoman Empire and elsewhere rather than development in the land of their origin (Evangelinides 1979, 179–80).

But at least one thing was finally achieved through the Asia Minor disaster, namely a unified and coherent nation incorporating most of the ethnic Greeks, which meant in theory that Greece could at last focus her attention on the internal development of her enlarged domain. Though accretions to the population had taken place during the nineteenth century bringing the total population to 2.6 million in 1907, the main change came in the period 1912–23 as a result of the Balkan Wars and the exchange of territory and populations with Turkey and Bulgaria following Greece's ultimately disastrous campaign in Asia Minor. In this period both territory and population approximately doubled: territory from 25,104 square miles to 50,146, and population from just under 2.7 million to over 5.5 million (Psomiades 1965, 197). For a time this vast increase in population over such a short period brought its own problems, but at least it was a fairly homogeneous population and Greece was now reasonably content in the knowledge that she had incorporated all the outlying nationals within one border.

As for the First World War, this brought with it mixed fortunes. The disruption of external trade was obviously advantageous to domestic production, especially in textiles, food processing and shipbuilding. On the other hand, it also led to inflationary pressures and enhanced debt problems which were to plague the country after the war. Politically the conflict split the nation. King Constantine, linked to Imperial Germany through marriage, was nominally neutral though backed by a vaguely pro-German government in Athens. In the opposing camp was Eleutherios Venizelos who, ousted as prime minister by the monarch, sided with the Allies and set up a provisional government in Salonika (Thessaloniki) which in 1917 became the legitimate government when the king was forced to flee the country. Greece therefore ended the war on the Allied side.

Venizelos was a flamboyant and colourful character who endeared himself to the leaders at the Paris Peace Conference in 1919 – at least, that is, until he presented his outrageous and unrealistic demands on behalf of Greece (MacMillan 2003, ch. 25). He had visions of enhancing the Greater Greece ideal at the expense of Albania and Turkey by claiming southern Albania, *all* of Thrace, a big chunk of Asia Minor and one or two other bits and pieces for good measure. Such extravagant claims were not to be entertained by the peacemakers. Greece was allowed to occupy Smyrna (Izmir) and it secured both western and eastern Thrace from Bulgaria and Turkey respectively, in dispositions made in 1920. Thus, as a result of involvement in both the Balkan Wars and the First World War, Greece had more than doubled its territory and population.

Unfortunately Venizelos' ambitions were not easily quenched. In the summer of 1920 he began his ill-fated campaign against Turkey by moving troops into Asia Minor in order to strengthen his claims on Turkish territory.[1] It was a disaster from the start. The Greeks were routed by the Kemalist Turks, who had been mobilising under their dynamic leader, Atatürk, in the interior.[2] Under the terms of the armistice of October 1922 Greece was forced to cede eastern Thrace to Turkey, which was confirmed by the revised treaty with Turkey (Treaty of Lausanne, July 1923). It was also excluded from coveted locations such as Constantinople and Smyrna. This second treaty, by overturning the original settlement under the Treaty of Sèvres (1920), which had favoured the Greeks and which the Turks had therefore rejected, thereby recognised Turkish independence. Fortunately from the Greek point of view, the Convention preparatory to the drawing up of the Treaty of Lausanne also provided for the compulsory exchange of minority populations between the two countries. Estimates of the numbers involved varies somewhat, but well over one million Greeks (possibly as high as one and a half million) were exchanged for some 400,000 Turks, while Bulgaria and Greece also exchanged some 54,000 Bulgarians for 46,000 Greeks (Hershlag 1968, 24; Pentzopoulos 1962, 18). In actual fact the official repatriation of Greeks from Turkey was quite small since most of them had already fled the country before the Lausanne provisions could be put into effect (Hirschon 2003, 14–15; Pearson 1983, 140–41; Keyder 2003, 43). Pentzopoulos (1962, 18) reckons that

---

1 Greek troops had already occupied Smyrna in the previous year and there was a token force in Constantinople to complement the Allied presence in the city.

2 Although Venizelos lost office in the election of November 1920 the Asia Minor campaign was continued under his successor with the return of King Constantine. The Allies refused to recognise Constantine and declined to make further payments on a promised loan to Greece, which meant that the latter could barely afford to maintain its forces in the field or restock their weaponry. This made it all the easier for the Turks to inflict defeat on the Greeks.

by the end of 1923 Greece was faced with the influx of some one and a half million Greeks – that is, an addition of over one quarter to its existing population.

Whether the unification of ethnic Greeks marked a new era for Greek society and the economy has been the subject of some debate. Judging by the performance of the economy over the interwar years, which was a good deal better than that of many European countries, one can only assume that at the very least it was a benign influence. Yet given the many problems that Greece faced during the period it is remarkable that the economy performed as well as it did. First we shall deal with the problems confronting the country in the reconstruction period.

The land issue was one of the most important and long-standing issues. By Western standards Greek agriculture was very inefficient. The other main problem was that Greece was short of good land. Though not an overpopulated country in absolute terms, when it came to arable land per head she was one of the most poorly endowed countries in Europe (Mazower 1991b, 46). The situation was further exacerbated by severe population pressure as a result of a high rate of natural increase and the influx of refugees. Greece in fact had one of the highest rates of population growth in Europe during the interwar period. Hence the pressure for land reform and land reclamation policies to contain peasant unrest and provide a solution to the refugee problem.

The main land reform legislation was passed during the war in 1917. Some 1684 estates were broken up and the land was redistributed to families numbering over one million persons in the 1920s. But this did not transform the agrarian sector. Some 50 per cent of agricultural land was still left in holdings of over 50 hectares, while in the case of smaller holders, uncertainty over ownership rights and high levels of debt hindered progress (Moore 1945, 82; Mazower 1991b, 79–81). Moreover, though Greece became numerically a country of small cultivators, many were too small and too poor to make much of their holdings. Even with a significant increase in the area under cultivation through land reclamation policies and irrigation projects funded by the government and international agencies, which increased the cultivated area by some 70 per cent, holdings remained minute and in any case much of the reclaimed land was of marginal quality and consisted of slope cultivation (Hoffman 1972, 50). Thus the cropland per person on Greek farms averaged around 1.31 acres, which was about the same as in India, while the average yield was 13.5 bushels of grain per acre – that is, one half to one third that of Western Europe. Frequent parcelisation of holdings, strip system cultivation, a low level of technology and lack of capital, as well as a reluctance to surrender traditional methods of cultivation, checked any major advance on the agrarian front

(Psomiades 1965, 197–98). The structure of farming output and exports remained fairly static though the influx of refugees did give a boost to the development of alternative crops. Nevertheless, four main products – tobacco, dried fruit, olives and olive oil – accounted for nearly three quarters of all exports. The backwardness of agriculture is also demonstrated by the fact that Greece had to import many essential foods, which made up over a third of all imports in the 1930s (Lykogiannis 1994, 346).

It is doubtful whether land reform was of any great benefit to agriculture generally since the 1920s proved to be a disappointing decade. Despite an increase in cereal production between 1922 and 1928, yields remained well below prewar levels. In fact domestic production could not keep pace with consumption so that over one half of wheat and flour needs had to be imported and between one sixth and one third in the case of other cereals (Kontogiorgi 2003, 68). Despite the contribution of refugees in some areas in improving crop output and diversifying the product mix, the small size and fragmentation of holdings were not conducive to efficient farming.

The assimilation of so many refugees, even if of common ethnicity, presented a major social problem. Adding as much as a quarter to the existing population, though less in net terms, involved an enormous settlement task in terms of housing, welfare and the like. Many refugees were obliged to make do with very poor living accommodation in slum conditions for many years. They were, moreover, not always accepted readily by the indigenous Greek inhabitants. On the other hand, on balance immigration was probably beneficial for the economy. It gave a boost to urbanisation and the construction industry, the enlarged labour force kept down real wages, and some of the newcomers added an enterprising element to both agriculture and industry. Many new but small business ventures were set up by refugees in a wide range of manufacturing industries, while they were also responsible for influencing the shift away from traditional crops in agriculture, such as currants, towards tobacco, grapes and garden vegetables. In Greek Macedonia and Thrace there were some promising reports of their beneficial influence on farming practices, especially with respect to tobacco cultivation (Kontogiorgi 2003, 67–68). However, Freris (1986, 52–53) reckons that while the overall benefit–cost ratio of immigration was positive, the refugees did no more than speed up existing trends or brought changes that did not involve radical shifts in the direction of the economy.

The costs of resettlement were substantial and virtually bankrupted the Greek state. International loans had to be raised for this purpose, and in several years through to the early 1930s around 40 per cent of the ordinary budget and a similar share of external borrowing were absorbed by resettling and supporting the refugees (Kontogiorgi 2003, 74).

Until the mid-1920s Greece, in common with many European countries, suffered from severe inflation and currency depreciation due largely to lax fiscal and monetary policies under a floating rate regime. The cost of living escalated from 100 in 1914 to 366 in 1918 and then rose erratically for much of the 1920s. Budgetary deficits largely associated with war conditions were partly responsible in the earlier years and a continuous increase in the note issue thereafter. The drakma followed a reciprocal depreciating course. Fortunately the authorities did not allow the process to get completely out of control, and with the establishment of the Bank of Greece in May 1927, a firm move was made to stabilise the currency. This was done during 1927–28 when the drakma was stabilised against sterling at one fifteenth of its prewar gold value. It was made fully convertible into foreign exchange and hence convertible indirectly into gold. The new Bank had to have a 40 per cent cover limit of gold and foreign currency against its note issue and in fact it started out with a cover of twice the stipulated figure (Freris 1986, 62). By this time inflation had fallen into single figures.

During the 1920s Greece had one of the fastest rates of growth in Europe, especially in industry. Between 1921 and 1927 industrial production surged ahead at 7.2 per cent per year. The fact that it started from a relatively small base obviously tends to magnify the values, and growth in the whole economy was somewhat lower because of the large weight of agriculture. The gains can be attributed to the short-term stimulus imparted by inflation and currency depreciation, and it is noticeable that industrial expansion tended to diminish in the later 1920s when the currency was stabilised. Industry also benefited from heavy tariff protection and a sharp fall in real wages after 1921 as a result of the depressing effect on wage levels of the large rise in the labour force due to immigration (Lazaretou 1996, 649–50, 664). However, despite the expansion of the labour force in industry from 60,000 workers in 1920 to 110,000 in 1930, this was not nearly enough to absorb the surplus rural labour.

Ironically, just as Greece had secured a more stable government and a sounder economic and financial position, the world crisis broke and upset the situation. The main impact was on the financial side of the economy rather than on the real economy since Greece was one of the few countries to record a positive expansion of output over the course of the depression. The main problem was the external situation. Greece was very dependent on foreign finance for its budgetary requirements and for purposes of closing the balance of payments deficits. The country had one of the highest per capita foreign debts in Eastern Europe and debt servicing absorbed around a third of export earnings on average for the years 1928–30 (Mazower 1991b, 112, 191). Budgetary revenues were declining while there was a big drop in export revenues, especially from tobacco, and a growing deficit on capital account. There was some compensation from the terms of trade as Greece was a large wheat importer, but not enough to ease the pressure on the external account which resulted in a drain on reserves. There were two options open to the government: severe internal compression to equate the accounts or tackling the position from the external side. Fortunately, Greece chose the latter and therefore avoided the extreme deflationary measures adopted by some countries in the early 1930s. The currency was devalued, exchange control was imposed and the servicing of foreign debt was suspended.

The currency history of the 1930s is a rather convoluted one. Greece did not follow sterling out of gold in September 1931 but switched to pegging against the dollar. Exchange control was introduced at the end of September 1931 which marked the beginning of *de facto* suspension of convertibility. In April–May of the following year convertibility was formally suspended and a moratorium imposed on interest and capital payments on outstanding foreign debt. Following the abandonment of gold there was a large depreciation in the drakma and by the middle of 1933 it was down to just over 40 per cent of its gold parity, at which level it remained for most of the decade. At that date Greece attached itself to the gold bloc countries and started to peg the drakma to the Swiss franc. When the gold bloc disintegrated in the autumn of 1936 the drakma joined the sterling area (Lazaretou 1996, 664–67; League of Nations 1937, 111–13).

These external operations were especially beneficial to Greece. She secured a competitive advantage since her currency depreciation was one of the largest of the countries leaving the gold standard. Moreover, as about one quarter of her reserves were held in sterling the British devaluation resulted in a substantial loss as long as Greece remained on gold. The debt moratorium was an immediate relief to the balance of payments. Indeed, had she not taken this course and had she remained on gold the burden would have been crippling on the economy. The government argued that default was imperative since almost 80 per cent of export earnings and 40 per cent of budgetary revenues would be taken up in servicing the external debt (Freris 1986, 81).

From this time the economy became even more inward-looking and state directed though it was never systematically planned as was the case in some Eastern European countries. The move to a more autarchic system was in part a response to the depression as controls on trade and payments became common in many countries. High tariffs, quantitative restrictions and the use of bilateral clearing agreements were extensively used and state involvement in economic affairs increased steadily during the 1930s, especially after General Metaxas established an authoritarian government under martial law in August 1936. On the whole there was not a great deal of coherence and consistency in policy strategy, the main aim being to achieve greater self-sufficiency based on the use of domestic resources where possible, and less reliance on the international economy.

Ostensibly the policy seems to have borne fruit, however, since Greece had a 'spectacular recovery', according to Mazower (1991a, 225), with one of the highest rates of growth in Europe. Depreciation of the currency, trade restrictions and a fall in real wages were the main forces at work. Import volumes fell sharply in the early 1930s and by the end of the decade they were no greater than in the late 1920s, whereas exports doubled between 1928 and 1938 (Mazower 1985, 373). A large part of Greece's trade was eventually conducted under bilateral clearing agreements; in 1936 some three quarters of all exports and over one half of her imports were subject to such arrangements (Freris 1986, 88). This involved a geographic shift in the structure of her trade towards totalitarian countries, especially Nazi Germany which became the dominant trading partner (Pelt 1998). By the end of the decade the League of Nations, in one of its reports, listed Greece as being part of the German economic bloc (League of Nations 1939b, 186). However, the structure of the trade did not change dramatically. In the late 1930s tobacco still accounted for nearly one half of all exports, while five or six products accounted for over 70 per cent of total exports (tobacco, currants, sultanas, olive oil, wine and skins).

The trend towards greater self-sufficiency was certainly evident in both industry and agriculture. The share of domestically produced manufactures in total domestic consumption rose from 58.6 per cent in 1928 to 81.6 per cent in 1939 (Freris 1986, 91). But again there was very little change in the structure of production. In 1938 four sectors, textiles, chemicals, food processing and tanning, accounted for nearly three quarters of industrial output. The main changes from the early postwar years were the decline of tanning and the rise of electricity generation which accounted for 8.5 per cent of industrial output (Freris 1986, 93). The structural mix of production probably changed more radically in the agrarian sector. Tobacco, wheat and cotton production all rose sharply during the interwar years, whereas the output of currants remained fairly stable. The success story was in wheat which was part of the government's policy to make Greece more self-sufficient in bread grains. This was achieved through the introduction of a price support scheme backed up by technical assistance, training schemes and favourable loans. Wheat production, which had been more or less static in the 1920s, rose more than threefold in the following decade and domestic production supplied more than 60 per cent of domestic consumption in the latter half of the 1930s compared with about half that share in the early 1920s (Freris 1986, 94–96).

Estimates of output vary considerably but all of them indicate that Greece grew very rapidly. Taking the late 1920s as a base, industrial production had by the late 1930s risen by more than 60 per cent, while agricultural production possibly more than doubled (see Freris 1986, 110 and Mazower 1991b, 307–11 for contrasting estimates). Lampe and Jackson's figures for growth rates in manufacturing industry and extractive industries in the Balkan countries during the years 1928–38 indicate that Greece was the top performer (see Table 8.2). The determination of the expansion of total output is less easy because of the difficulty of measuring the output of services, but it was probably of the order of 50 per cent or more.

Table 8.2 Growth Rates in Manufacturing and Extractive Industries in Greece and Other Balkan Countries 1928–38

	Manufacturing industry	Extractive industries
Bulgaria	4.8	2.8
Greece	5.7	6.1
Romania	3.4	1.6
Yugoslavia	2.6	11.3

Source: Lampe and Jackson 1982, 484.

Despite the impressive growth statistics it is doubtful if the Greek economy was based on very firm foundations by the end of the interwar period. Indeed, the governor of the Bank of Greece admitted in 1936 that the expansion of industry was built on sand and heavily dependent on stiff protection and depreciation of the drakma (Freris 1986, 91). Lykogiannis (1994, 347) maintains that the country's manufacturing industry was still one of general backwardness, with a proliferation of small, inefficient and family-owned businesses, wedded to old technologies with high production costs and relying on cheap labour. Employment in handicraft trades far outweighed that in modern factory operations. The relatively static structure of the economy and the foreign trade pattern was typical of an underdeveloped economy. The export trade was dominated by a handful of primary products; more than 80 per cent of the visible trade was made up of agricultural products with tobacco and currants accounting for the greater part (Koliopoulos and Veremis 2002, 171).

The structure of industry was likewise concentrated on a few products serving the domestic market and which were uncompetitive internationally. Moreover, the share of industry in total output did not increase significantly during the period. High protection tended to breed inefficiency and it also probably led to spatial concentration of industrial activity around Athens and to a lesser extent Salonika (Thessaloniki). In the late 1920s nearly one half of manufacturing industries were to be found in Athens and Piraeus (Hoffman 1972, 55, 63). Furthermore, despite the fact that Greece became much more self-sufficient in food production during the period, under a policy of government protection and assistance, agriculture could scarcely be described as a model of efficiency. There were far too many small units of production which were inefficient and unyielding to change, propped up by protection and price support schemes. Modern agricultural methods and equipment were conspicuous by their absence and animal husbandry was largely confined to sheep and goats. As for infrastructure facilities (roads, railways, education, health), these remained the most primitive in Europe, despite the programme of public works under the Metaxas regime, and probably only surpassed in inferiority by those of Albania and Turkey.

Overall, the Greek economy had by 1939 probably reached the limits of its development under a regime of high protection and support and unchanging production functions. As Kuznets once noted of underdeveloped societies, more could be squeezed out at the margin with existing technologies and traditional methods, but eventually a ceiling is reached and further progress is dependent on technical advance and shifts in production structures and methods. While progress along these frontiers was not completely static in Greece at this time, it is likely that the country was close to its production ceiling under existing technologies, and there were few signs that radical transformation was about to take place which would shift the supply curve outwards. The fact that reinvestment of industrial profits in modernisation and technical change was fairly limited in the 1930s – with funds often being channelled into speculative areas such as financial activities, residential construction and luxury consumption – suggests that entrepreneurs were not fully alive to the needs of a developing economy. Mazower (1991a, 228) sums up the situation as follows: 'impressive short-term growth rates masked an increasingly backward economic structure'.

Turkey

Strictly speaking, Turkey is predominantly a non-European Muslim country, but in view of its history and its past and current aspirations in Europe it seemed appropriate to include it in this volume. It also merits inclusion by dint of the fact of its long involvement in the affairs of the Balkan Peninsula, especially its stormy relationships with Greece. Moreover, along with Albania, it was the poorest and most backward of the countries covered in this study. Most of the population was dependent on agriculture of a subsistence type and illiteracy levels were the highest in Europe.

Turkey emerged out of the ruins of the Ottoman Empire. The latter, whose warriors had once reached the gates of Vienna, was by the nineteenth century an empire in terminal decline. It was a huge, rambling and crumbling empire which was prey to trading privileges extracted by the advanced West European powers on terms favourable to the latter, but which was never properly integrated into the Western economy in the nineteenth century. (Evangelinides 1979, 179). Bit by bit the Ottomans had been forced to surrender the bulk of their European possessions so that by 1914 they were left with only a toehold in Europe in the form of a small enclave in Thrace (MacMillan 2003, 382). The extent of the losses can be gauged from the fact that the area of the Ottoman Empire had been reduced to 1.3 million square kilometres by 1914 compared with three million in 1800, though the population remained roughly the same at both dates (Quataert 1994, 777). In the process Turkey had lost some of its best and most economically advanced regions.

However, one should not assume from this that the Ottoman Empire was completely static from an economic point of view during the nineteenth century. If anything, the Ottoman state was more responsive to the forces of modern development before 1914 than its arch-enemy Greece. Donald Quataert (1994), in his masterly survey of Ottoman economic affairs, has shown that much was going on in agriculture, industry and commerce in the years of territorial decline. There was a large increase in agricultural output based largely on extensive farming as much more land was brought into cultivation, an even bigger rise in the volume of international trade, and a nascent manufacturing industry in which one or two sectors, for example carpet-making, exported their wares to the West. Trade with Europe increased rapidly during the nineteenth century and by 1914 exports were more than 12 per cent of GNP and imports around 20 per cent (Pamuk 1994, 109; Pamuk 1987).

But when all is said and done, the rump of the Ottoman Empire remained a very poor and backward country on the eve of the Great War and resembled a modern day Third World country. The land was far and away the largest source of employment, and primary products, mainly of agrarian origin, accounted for over 90 per cent of all exports. Small landholding operations predominated which by Western standards were low in productivity and absent in modern methods and new technology. Modern factory works were thin on the ground and most manufactured products were made in handicraft and domestic establishments. One estimate suggests that in the whole of Ottoman Turkey by 1913 there were only 269 establishments working with machines and employing a total of 17,000 workers, over one half of which were in food processing and textiles (including carpets), while the remainder were in pottery, furniture, printing and paper, and tanning and chemical products (Hershlag 1968, 52). Quataert (1994, 898), however, gives a figure of 35,000 workers in large establishments of all kinds for the same date, while Pamuk (1994, 111) suggests that less than 5 per cent of the labour force was engaged in enterprises of all types. Most of the manufactured wares produced were destined for the home market although there was a flourishing export trade in lace and carpets. Infrastructure facilities were still very limited, especially railways, of which there were but 7500 kilometres of track by 1914, together with more than three times as many kilometres of roads, mostly of poor quality and badly maintained (Quataert 1994, 804–805, 818). For the size of the country this was very small beer indeed.

If in absolute terms there had been some progress, in relative terms the Ottoman Empire declined in importance in the century or so down to 1914. This was not simply because of the loss of the best parts of the empire but also due to the fact that progress was faster elsewhere, so that globally Turkey's position in the world economy was bound to diminish. By 1914 Turkey was poorer than in 1800 in comparative terms despite some expansion in the economy in the intervening period. Tentative estimates suggest that in the remains of the Ottoman Empire (effectively modern Turkey) per capita income was about one twentieth that of the British and one tenth that of the European average, and only one fifth of that in some of the successor states such as Serbia, Bulgaria and Romania (Quataert 1994, 705).

Turkey backed the wrong horse in the Great War when it chose the side of the Central Powers, though such an alliance is perhaps not altogether surprising since Imperial Germany had become the patron of the Ottoman Empire in the lead-up to the war. After valiant fighting Turkey eventually capitulated to Allied forces and awaited its fate at the hands of the victors. But peace was a long time in coming since there were so many interests involved. The Allied powers themselves were in disarray on the question of what should be done with Turkey. Indeed, for a time it seemed more than likely that the remains of the Ottoman Empire would be broken up and partitioned among interested parties. The Italians and Greeks were keen to gain footholds in Turkey; France and Britain, along with America for a time, were for establishing mandated territories for part of Turkey; while there were nationalist groups, the Kurds especially, who wanted to become independent. As for the Turks themselves, they were anxious to keep out the Greeks, retain a presence in Europe and hold on to Turkish speaking areas such as eastern Thrace and Anatolia.

The long and complicated proceedings before a final peace was concluded with Turkey in 1923 by the Treaty of Lausanne need not concern us in detail here. The first treaty with Turkey (Treaty of Sèvres 1920), which was signed by the weak government of the Sultanate, was not acknowledged by many of the people in Turkey because of its harsh terms and its concessions to Greek demands. It was tantamount to a break-up of the remains of the Ottoman Empire 'with Turkey serving as a mere rump of an inland state, encircled by a string of foreign states and spheres of interest' (Kinross 1976, 103). To substantiate their claims, the Greeks had been encouraged to send forces into Turkey, occupying first the prosperous commercial centre of Smyrna (Izmir), and then moving inland into Asia Minor to counter the threat of resurgent nationalist forces under Mustafa Kemal (or Atatürk). Atatürk, who had been undefeated in battle during the war, was to become the saviour of his homeland. He regrouped his troops in the interior of the country and set up a rival government in Ankara. His forces proved more than a match for the Greeks who were resoundingly defeated in battle in the summer of 1922. The victory confirmed Turkey's independence and Atatürk then proceeded to set up a Turkish Republic in October 1923 under his own presidency, assuming dictatorial powers. He remained in power until his death in 1938.

Atatürk's success meant that Turkey was now in a position to renegotiate more favourable peace terms. The Treaty of Lausanne of July 1923 swept away many of the offending clauses of the previous treaty. Turkey renounced all claims to territories with Arab majorities, but kept most of the Turkish-speaking territories. She retained a foothold in Europe by securing eastern Thrace from Greece, while keeping the latter out of strategic locations such as Constantinople (Istanbul) and Smyrna (Izmir), the Italians having lost interest in Turkey by this time (Parker 1969, 39). The economic clauses of the Treaty of Lausanne were less onerous than those contained in the abortive treaty of 1920. Turkey was not burdened by reparation payments, while she secured a reasonable deal on Ottoman debts, being responsible for £78 million. On the other hand, she had to retain concessions granted to foreign companies by the Ottoman regime and to hold tariff rates at the level of 1916 – apart from revisions to take account of the decline in the value of the Turkish lira – until 1929 (Hale 1981, 38–39).

On the eve of the formation of the new republic (October 1923) the Turkish economy was in a parlous state. 'After ten years of almost continuous warfare it was depopulated, impoverished and in ruins to a degree unparalleled in modern history' (Zürcher 1998, 170). The country was drained of resources, and left with a legacy of severe inflation, budgetary deficits, trade deficits and a weak currency. The most serious resource loss was a human one. The departure, flight or massacre of Armenians, Greeks and other foreign nationals – possibly amounting to several millions – meant the loss of some of the more skilled and commercially able people. Those who perished included 2.5 million Anatolian Muslims, possibly as many as 800,000 Armenians and around 300,000 Greeks. The population of Anatolia was reduced by 20 per cent as a result (Zürcher 1998, 171). In compensation Turkey received up to a million refugees, mostly from the Balkans, who were primarily of peasant stock (Mango 1968, 57).

This was a sacrifice the country could ill afford and the new Turkey was probably even shorter of skilled labour and entrepreneurial talent than the former Ottoman Empire had been. In total she probably lost over two million people of non-Muslim faith through slaughter and enforced exchange which left the population of postwar Turkey less than it had been before the war (Hirschon 2003, 15). Though she undoubtedly became a more homogeneous country from an ethnic point of view with a very small non-Muslim element compared with prewar times, the shifts in population arising from mortality and exchange were damaging to the economy. In contrast to Greece, it was the exodus of peoples, rather than the influx, that had the greater impact. 'The departure of Greeks and Armenians from Turkey meant that the most productive elements of the population, and a good deal of the entrepreneurial know-how, had left the country for good' (Aktar 2003, 79–81). Many of the Greeks and Armenians had played a vital role in the economy, in trade, finance and manufacturing activities, whereas the incoming flow of refugees was composed primarily of rural peasants of which Turkey had more than enough. The exchange of populations between Greece and Turkey following the Asia Minor confrontation was undoubtedly more beneficial to the former country than it was to the latter.

Yet an observer writing a decade later could claim that 'no country has undergone such drastic and fundamental changes as Turkey during the past ten years' (Wyatt 1934, 826). Such transformations were not limited to the economic field, for they also included those in education, public facilities and social mores. The latter were of especial significance since they sought to transform the basic religious ethos of society, which had so dominated lives in past centuries, by in effect substituting 'secular nationalism' for 'divine revelation' (Hale 1981, 34). Along with the end to the rule of the Sultanate and the Caliphate faith a whole host of changes were promulgated in ways of living, including the secularisation of education, the replacement of the Islamic civil and legal codes by Western Roman models, the adoption of the Latin alphabet in place of Arabic script, the emancipation of women and the abolition of polygamy, and the use of the Gregorian calendar and the metric system of weights and measures. Dress codes were also relaxed and recognition of the Islamic faith as the official religion was removed from the 1924 constitution (Wyatt 1934, 826; Hale 2000, 50–51).

These changes were accomplished relatively smoothly and without revolution and bloodshed, though only time could bring about fundamental shifts in traditional ways of living and worship. Nevertheless, they were made more palatable to society at large by the fact that they were backed by a strong man of vision who was determined to transform the institutional and cultural life of Turkey and to drag the country into the twentieth century. By the time Atatürk came to power Turkey had lost all her former possessions, was destitute after ten years of conflict, had little in the way of modern industry and was still partly in economic thrall to the Western powers. Atatürk pledged to modernise the country and make it economically and financially independent.

Not that there was any clearly laid out plan as to how this transformation was to take place. Policy is best summed up as being pragmatic and conservative with little ideological underpinning, though recognising the importance of economic development as a means of ensuring national sovereignty. The process would be a partnership of state and private enterprise with the state responsible for major infrastructure facilities and public services. Thus a large extension of the rail network was begun soon after 1923 together with the modernisation of ports and the construction of roads. The railway network was considerably expanded and a start was also made in buying out foreign-owned rail companies. By 1930, 3000 kilometres of track had been taken over by the state leaving 2400 in foreign control (Zürcher 1998, 204). The government also made significant advances in educational provision. By the early 1930s there were nearly three times as many schools and four times as many teachers as in 1913, while the education of women was made obligatory (Wyatt 1934, 827). But even these advances had only a marginal impact on the high rate of illiteracy. The state also had various monopolies in tobacco and liquor, matches, explosives, and the import of sugar and oil products.

Industrial development was left largely to private enterprise, though with some encouragement from the state. The Law for the Encouragement of Industry of 1927 extended the provisions of a similar one passed in 1913. They included various financial inducements including tax concessions, freedom of duties on imported materials and machinery, land grants and tariff protection. However, by international standards tariff protection was very low with an average weighted rate of 12.4 per cent in the 1920s (Keyder 1981, 79). This was due to the import tariff limitations imposed by the peace treaty terms; when they expired in October 1929 import duties were raised sharply except on products required for industrial development.

In the first decade of Atatürk's regime over 1000 new enterprises were established in a wide range of industries including sugar, flax, macaroni, wine, rubber goods, cement, leather goods, shoes, bags, perfumery, furniture, paints and wood products (Wyatt 1934, 833). The majority of these were small-scale and dependent on assistance of one form or another. There were few large-scale modern establishments except in textiles, carpets and cement, and very few trades could compete in international markets, the most successful in this respect being the carpet industry. Medium-sized or large firms employing mechanical power and using modern production methods were something of a rarity. Handicraft and artisan workshop production still predominated.

Despite increasing outlays on public works and industrial assistance the budgetary position improved during the 1920s. The massive deficits recorded under Ottoman rule and during wartime were brought under control so that by the late 1920s budgets were more or less in balance. This was mainly due to improvements on the revenue side through more efficient tax collection. At the same time a tight monetary policy prevailed which contained money supply growth. As a result the inflation of wartime was brought under control and stabilised by the mid-1920s (Hale 1981, 44–45).

What is perhaps surprising, given its importance in terms of income and employment and its role as the main source of foreign exchange earnings, is the relative neglect of agriculture. The latter's trade contribution was especially important at a time when Turkey depended so heavily on imports of machinery and equipment for industrial development. Though less than in prewar times, there was a persistent trade deficit throughout the 1920s (financed by capital inflows and a loss of reserves), despite a floating lira which depreciated almost continuously in the postwar years, by 32 per cent against the pound sterling between 1923 and 1929 (Keyder 1981, 85). In theory the free float should have worked to close the trade gap. However, the problem was the sharp deterioration in the terms of trade coupled with the fairly inelastic demand for Turkish exports. The trade terms declined by over 20 per cent between 1925 and 1929, due largely to a steady decline in export prices whereas import prices remained fairly stable. This meant that Turkey had to export some 20 per cent more simply to purchase the same quantity of imports as in 1925 (Keyder 1981, 82–83). Unfortunately, the price elasticity of demand for Turkey's exports was relatively inelastic so that the price declines did not generate increased sales abroad of tobacco, cotton, dried fruits and other primary products. The main drawback was the very heavy reliance on the export of primary commodities (accounting for 80–90 per cent of exports). Eight commodities (tobacco, raisins, cotton, figs, hazelnuts, wool, opium and eggs) constituted 60–70 per cent of total exports in the years 1924–29. The only manufactured or semi-processed exports of any importance were carpets (3–4 per cent of export earnings) and olive oil, which accounted for 5 per cent of exports in a good crop year (Keyder 1981, 74).

This all points to the unyielding nature of agriculture and the heavy export dependence on basic crops whose market potential was limited. In view of the weakness of primary product prices and the precipitous fall in the ensuing depression, one could argue that it might have been an unwise strategy to boost agricultural production unduly, which in any case would have required considerable investment in training, equipment and infrastructure facilities. On the other hand, structural diversification along the lines of some of the Baltic and Balkan countries could have paid off. In the event, the Turkish government plumped for a policy of encouraging industry so as to reduce the dependence on agriculture, though this was a strategy which would take many years to bear substantial fruit. In the meantime, agriculture remained a backward sector, with low productivity and low incomes, unable to generate a strong market for domestically-produced manufactures. As it transpired, agriculture performed quite creditably, with output more than doubling between 1923 and 1929 in real terms, though much of this increase simply recouped what had been lost in the years of conflict (Hale 1981, 46).

In the 1930s Turkey moved towards a more interventionist approach in the economy, especially in industry. This is usually described as the period of étatism, a term which defies precise definition. As in many other countries during this period, there was certainly greater state intervention in economic affairs with the implementation of a five-year planning exercise. In practice this was little more than a hybrid system of state and private enterprise with a sprinkling of joint ventures. Thornburg, while impressed with Turkey's industrial performance, refers to it as 'a poorly managed capitalist economy in which most of the capital happens to be supplied by the government' (Thornburg et al. 1949, 39).

The reasons for the shift in strategy are easy to enumerate. The impact of the Great Depression, and especially the big fall in primary product prices, hit Turkey hard and, as in many other countries at this time, state action was called upon to ease the situation. The examples of Soviet Russia and Nazi Germany in planning and state control also had some influence, though Turkey's was more a pragmatic response rather than an ideological one. It is worth noting, however, that a Soviet delegation had visited Turkey in 1932 to advise on industrial development and the Soviet Union made a gold loan of $8 million dollars for that purpose (Zürcher 1998, 206). The desire for greater self-sufficiency in industry and national defence motives were additional reasons for the change. In some respects too the strategy of the 1930s was merely building on earlier foundations under Ottoman rule and the postwar period. The Law for the Encouragement of Industry in 1927 aimed to foster industrial development through tax and other concessions, while two years earlier the government had appropriated several revenue concessions accorded to foreign nationals under the Ottoman Empire; these included tobacco, salt, explosives and alcoholic products which in 1932 were grouped under a single government agency (Kerwin 1959, 237, 246). An additional motive for intervention was the alleged shortage of indigenous entrepreneurs with the requisite capital to undertake large-scale industrial development.

The principles and objectives of étatism were enshrined in the first five-year plan, formulated in 1933 and implemented in January 1934. This was subsequently revised in 1936 by a second five-year plan and then reduced to four years in 1938. The chief aims were to utilise domestic raw materials and to produce goods that would reduce Turkey's dependence on imported manufactures. The main target areas for development were textiles (cotton, wool and hemp), ceramics, chemicals, iron and steel, paper and cellulose, sulphur and copper mining, glass, cement and the sponge industry. Apart from textiles most of these industries represented new lines of endeavour.

The mechanisms for implementing the planning exercise were two state agencies or holding companies, the Sümerbank and the Etibank, established in 1933 and 1935 respectively. They were charged with the task of building, financing and running the concerns in the industries listed. Eventually the two agencies ended up with a motley collection of enterprises in a range of industries which accounted for a good part of the new industrial development of the 1930s. The state also directly controlled a range of other activities in sugar, coal, forestry, defence factories, and infrastructure facilities such as railways, roads and ports, postal and telecommunications services and electric power (Kerwin 1959, 245). Defence operations became increasingly important in the later 1930s when budgetary expenditure devoted to the military sector rose to 44 per cent, assisted by armament credits from both Germany and Britain. Germany in fact had been both an important source of arms equipment prior to 1939 and Turkey's main trading partner. Nearly 50 per cent of Turkey's trade before the war was conducted with Germany or her allies under bilateral clearing arrangements (Hale 2000, 65; Zürcher 1998, 207).

By all accounts the state initiative was remarkable successful. Industrial growth was very rapid in the 1930s, especially after 1935, and most of the targeted areas were achieved except iron and steel. The state in one form or another became the largest single investor in industry, but this did not mean the extinction of private enterprise by any means. In fact by the end of the decade small-scale workshop or handicraft activities still bulked large, accounting for some 60 per cent of value added in manufacturing and around 80 per cent of total employment in that sector. Even in the state-controlled sectors of industry private enterprise continued to flourish and only in one or two sectors did the state have a near monopoly (for example paper and silk). Overall the private sector may have accounted for some 50 per cent or more of gross investment between 1933 and 1939 (Hale 1981, 59). But what is noticeable is that much of the large-scale modern industrial development was in the hands of the state and not private enterprise.

As might be expected, the planning experiment has had its detractors for it was by no means free of imperfections. There was no great coherence in the planning structure and it was certainly nowhere near as detailed and bureaucratic as that in Soviet Russia. It was probably more akin to the French indicative planning of the 1950s, with the driving aim of import substitution in industrial products. Large state investments, especially in industry, forced the government to extract resources from the rest of the economy which in practice meant high taxation for the impoverished agrarian sector. Though industrial expansion was certainly impressive in the 1930s, probably only surpassed by Japan, the Soviet Union and Greece, it tended to be high cost and inefficient. It was extensive rather than intensive development, utilising cheap labour but with stagnant productivity so that units costs were high. Other factors which added to costs were the lack of skilled labour and the difficulties of organising a large industrial labour force, low wages and salaries which encouraged corruption and inefficient management, expensive transport facilities, the high cost of fuel, and the poor planning and location of plants (Hershlag 1968, 329). Some enterprises were built for show or prestige purposes rather than efficient production and were dubbed 'Atatürk's minarets'. Much of the capital equipment for such enterprises had to be imported which put a strain on the balance of payments and the exchanges.

The problems of 'breaking-in' a workforce for modern industry were much greater than the state planners had originally envisaged. The Turks were not used to regular, disciplined work – they were first and foremost peasants, soldiers, civil servants and rulers, not capitalist workers in factories. The workforce was therefore highly unstable, with frequent turnover, high absenteeism and seasonal departure at harvest times. 'Seasonal and temporary labour in industry became a widespread practice in Turkey' (Hershlag 1954, 328). Pilfering was also rife. The problems encountered in setting up one of the largest state textile enterprises in Kayseri (in the heart of the country and once a caravan meeting point), which started production in September 1935 and mobilised a large workforce, were horrendous according to contemporary accounts (Linke 1937, 542–43).

The situation was little different in agriculture with regard to work practices, which were governed by long tradition and bitter experience. One contemporary observer was horrified by peasant inertia:

> The one place in the village which was always crowded was the coffee-house, where the men spent endless hours, leaving it to their women to scrape the food together as best they could. The sad experience of the past had led them to ask why they should slave merely to make the landowner and the tax collector rich. So often had they been called to arms that they did not quite believe that they could settle down at last to the work of peace, and they still had the air of men who enjoy the hours of sweet forgetfulness, since they might soon have to return to battle. Besides, had not Allah in his wisdom told them not to worry, not to hurry, but to take the days as they came, good-humouredly and in patience.
>
> (Linke 1937, 553–54)

Not surprisingly agricultural productivity did not change much. The expansion of output came from extension of the cultivated area rather than through greater efficiency, a strategy made possible by the fact that there was no great land shortage in Turkey. The man–land ratio was favourable though a good part of the land was rather infertile, at least given prevailing techniques of cultivation. But as with state-directed modernisation programmes in other countries, agriculture was relatively neglected. Hershlag (1968, 326) argues that the chief sin of the planning exercise was the failure to exploit the country's main asset, namely the agrarian resource base. The concentration on industrial development was at the expense of agriculture, which was starved of investment, lacked technical progress yet bore the burden of taxation. There was no clear conception of the changes required in occupational structures so that the release of labour from agriculture could take place. Hence the bulk of the population remained wedded to the land, quite detached from industrial developments elsewhere, isolated and in poverty, illiterate and culturally backward – in other words an obstacle to modern economic development.

Estimates of Turkey's overall performance in the interwar years vary quite considerably, but all suggest significant expansion. Georgieva (1998, 287) gives a rate of industrial growth of 8.6 per cent a year for the period 1923–40, with a high of 15.6 per cent for the years 1936–40, reflecting no doubt the influence of higher state investments in the planning era and the impact of the defence build-up.

The figures produced in Hale (1981, 46, 76) suggest more rapid growth in the 1920s overall, except in industry, with all sectors expanding rapidly (see Table 8.3). However, since there are no reliable estimates for the period 1913–23 it is difficult to say how far these high growth rates were influenced by recouping ground lost in the conflict years. After a decade of almost continuous warfare, aggregate output must have been well below the prewar level by the early 1920s so that much of the expansion after 1922 would represent recuperation from the setback. Total income estimates are even more puzzling. Hershlag's (1954, 336) estimates of national income per head indicate an increase of only 30 per cent between 1927 and 1939, which is less than half the 79.5 per cent given by Hale (1981, 46, 76). Pamuk (1994, 113), on the other hand, records stagnation in real wages and per capita incomes between 1914 and 1938, which does not quite square with other evidence. All of this only serves to demonstrate the fragility and conflicting nature of any estimates of income for this country.

Table 8.3 Growth Performance of the Turkish Economy by Sector 1923–39 (average annual growth rates)

	1923–30	1930–39
Agriculture	11.4	5.1
Industry	8.6	11.1
Services	7.7	5.9
GNP	9.6	6.2
GNP per head	7.3	4.0

Source: Hale 1981, 46, 76.

There is no question that Turkey made significant advances on the economic front during the interwar years, but at the end of the period the country was still a very backward one. The growth estimates appear impressive because they were from a relatively low base. Hershlag (1954, 337) states that there were two Turkeys, 'that of the aeroplane and that of the oxen-cart. The latter represented the actual living Turkey, while the former implied the potentialities.' Structurally there had been very little change. The bulk of the population was still land-based, culturally backward and living in poverty. The new industrial developments were little more than islands of capitalism in a sea of primitivism. The institutions of the country may have been given a more modern look but, as Mango (1968, 59) observed, 'the economy from which they drew their strength remained backward and the society around them desperately poor'.

Albania

Last – and in this case least! – we come to this member of Europe's periphery:

> Poor little Albania, with such powerful enemies and so few friends. And it had almost no industry, little trade, no railways at all and only about 200 miles of paved roads. It emerged out of obscurity just before the war, created out of four districts of the Ottoman empire. Few outsiders ever visited it; little was known about its history or its people. Only rarely had Albanians ... popped up in Europe's history. (MacMillan 2003, 368)

With a population of around a million, the majority of whom were Muslims, and an area of some 27,500 square kilometres, Albania was the smallest and also the poorest of the nations considered in this volume. It is also a country about which the least is known. Most of the people (80 per cent or more) were illiterate and scraped a precarious living from the land (Moore 1945, 26; Kirk 1946, 10).

Before 1914 there was very little that could be classed as modern economic development in Albania. The country had long been cut off from the rest of Europe and suppressed under Ottoman rule, from which it was finally released in 1912. The economy was essentially a primitive agrarian one where mountainous animal husbandry predominated (Berend 1985, 203). One of the few profitable exports was that of tortoises (Crampton 1994, 22). There was little in the way of manufacturing and any non-agrarian interests consisted of local handicrafts.

The First World War did little to improve matters. The northern part of the country was occupied by Austria, while Italian and French forces captured the southern part. At the conclusion of hostilities Albania was occupied and partitioned by troops of five countries (France, Britain,

Italy, Greece and Serbia), and a proper national government was not established until 1920 following the withdrawal of foreign troops. In fact for a time the Albanians lived in mortal fear that they might lose their recently-won independence and be partitioned, but they were saved from such ignominy by Britain and the United States. Even so, the postwar settlement left 44 per cent of Albanians (the highest of any country) outwith the new state, most of them in southern Yugoslavia and northern Greece (Pearson 1983, 177).

Political order and stability proved difficult to achieve in a country with no experience of parliamentary government and one in which clan and tribal loyalties and blood feuds counted for more than national interests. Consequently political stability proved elusive in the first few years, with no fewer than seven different governments holding power through to the end of 1922.

Fortunately at this time Ahmed Zogolli, leader of the Mati tribe in north-central Albania, was making his mark in politics, having returned from wartime exile in Vienna. He was determined to bring some sort of order and stability to his country so that modernisation could take place. From the end of 1922, when he became prime minister at the tender age of 27 and changed his name to Zogu, he dominated Albanian political life. Three years later, with the backing of conservative landlords and with help from Yugoslavia, he assumed presidential powers. He then secured, in exchange for mineral concessions, political and military support from Italy by treaties concluded in 1926 and 1927. A year later, in 1928, he proclaimed himself Monarch of the Albanians (under the title of King Zog) and ruled Albania with almost unlimited powers until the country was invaded by the Italians in 1939 (Hocevar 1987, 562). He has been described as an oriental potentate who exploited the masses and curtailed their political rights (Marmullaku 1975, 36–37).

Several measures were enacted from the mid-1920s in an attempt to modernise Albania. The first major reform was the establishment of the National Bank (1925), albeit based in Rome and effectively controlled by Italy, and the introduction of a national currency. Although Albania had never formally abandoned the gold standard, it did not have a currency of its own. Gold, silver and a motley collection of foreign currencies were used as the medium of exchange, though dependency on specie did ensure some measure of currency stability. In 1926 the Albanian franc was introduced which was convertible into gold and for which the National Bank held a gold and silver reserve of at least one third of the national note issue (Hocevar 1987, 563). These changes at least gave some measure of financial stability to the new kingdom.

The next set of reforms dealt with internal matters. Between 1929 and 1931 new civil, penal and commercial codes were instituted in an attempt to improve general law and order, reduce the forces of tribal custom, and regularise commercial and economic transactions. Land reform was also attempted at the same time. An Act of 1930 proposed to limit holdings to no more than 40 hectares of arable land in an effort to wrest the grip of large landowners. Unfortunately it proved largely ineffective with only a minute proportion of the land (1000 to 1200 hectares) having been redistributed by the end of the decade (Crampon and Crampon 1996, 45). Thus by 1939, 53 per cent of the peasants were still landless and large landowners owned more than 40 per cent of the cultivated land (Marmullaku 1975, 36). Feudalism still prevailed in some parts of the country, especially in the centre and south.

The next reform was in education which was reorganised and rationalised in 1933 in a drive to bring down the very high level of illiteracy. Again the impact was only marginal, partly because of a lack of funds for buildings and equipment and a shortage of good teachers. In addition, maintaining regular attendance levels in schools proved very difficult in a country where custom, habit and tribal rule had for so long prevailed. Thus by 1937 only about 37 per cent of the children of school age were receiving elementary education. There were only a handful of secondary schools and no universities and colleges, so that higher education had to be sought abroad. Thus the changes did little to bring down the level of illiteracy, which by the end of the period was still around 80 per cent.

Of all the Balkan states Albania changed the least structurally. It failed to enter the initial stages of industrialisation or show any real signs of sustained progress and modernisation (Georgieva 1998, 286). Industrial production accounted for less than 10 per cent of total output and in per capita terms it was easily the lowest in Europe. The industrial inventory at the end of the period consisted of a few concerns in textiles and food processing, several saw-mills, a few establishments making soap, cement, furniture, dolls and cigarettes, two olive-oil extracting plants and several handicraft trades. There were a few foreign concessions in minerals and oil extraction, though most were on a small scale and the bulk of the output was exported rather than used locally (Hoffman 1972, 56–57). The small domestic market, the lack of human skills and the shortage of capital all combined to limit progress in non-agrarian activities. Albania was not an attractive proposition for foreign capital. Virtually the only foreign creditor was Italy, whose financial assistance proved precarious and was no doubt the harbinger of ulterior motives for Mussolini's personal aggrandisement (Nötel 1986, 264). In April 1939 Italy occupied the country and ended the increasingly unpopular reign of King Zog.

Thus Albania remained a primitive agrarian-based society with an unchanged medieval technology and very little adjustment in land tenure. Modern machinery and implements were conspicuous by their absence. In 1938, for example, there were only 32 tractors in use. The semi-feudal type of farming meant that by Western standards output levels were extremely low and many peasants eked out a precarious existence on the mountain farms averaging about 2 hectares in size. Only a small proportion of the land was cultivated because much of it was not suitable for crop farming. In fact livestock breeding was more suited to much of the land and livestock and related products accounted for two thirds of the country's exports. The more fertile and productive land of the lowlands remained in the hands of feudal barons (Berend 1985, 204). So low was output that food had to be imported and about one quarter of the country's imports consisted of foodstuffs, especially grain. Most of the remainder of her imports consisted of industrial goods, while exports were made up of agricultural products and raw materials. Italy was by far her most important trading partner (Berend 1985, 204–205).

During the course of the interwar period Albania in fact became increasingly dependent on Italy for trade and finance, a semi-colonial dependence which suited Italy's own designs on the country. By 1938, 77 per cent of the foreign capital in Albania came from Italy and there was not one bank founded with domestic capital, including the Albanian National Bank, established in 1925, and the Agrarian Bank, founded in 1937, both of which were controlled by Italian interests. Credits provided by Italy were in the form of political concessions, used to build strategic roads which would serve Italian purposes later. The Albanian regime also allowed some of the fertile lowlands to pass into Italian hands (Marmullaku 1975, 37–38).

Although there are very few firm national statistics for this period, circumstantial evidence would suggest that Albania made very little economic progress between the wars. Data for 1927 indicate that the annual per capita income was not much more than half that of Yugoslavia and Romania and it is likely that this relative position deteriorated somewhat in the ensuing years (Marmullaku 1975, 37). Data on the value of economic transactions per head of population for 1928 suggest that the standard of living was extremely low even by comparison with other Balkan countries: it was only $2.42 for Albania as against just under $6.50 in Bulgaria and Romania, $7.89 in Yugoslavia and $10.9 in Greece (Marmullaku 1975, 37). Albania, like the Balkans only more so, remained so little industrialised that it was unable to generate sufficient savings to develop its non-agricultural sector without outside assistance. The per capita output of industrial goods was reckoned to be the lowest in Europe. The economy 'remained so locked in primitive patterns of agriculture and handicrafts that it barely achieved any economic progress during the interwar years' (Radice 1985, 63). Nor could one point to 'any decisive and effective economic decision to modernize traditional agriculture' (Berend 1985, 203). There was certainly no significant change in the overall economic structure of the country (Hoffman 1972, 57). There are very few figures for national income. There may have been a modest rise of 12 per cent in net national product between 1927 and 1938, as Lethbridge (1985, 596) suggests, but this was more than swamped out by the rapid rise in population of some 25 per cent over the same period, so that per capita income declined. Taking into consideration the difficult conditions pertaining during the war and early postwar years, it would seem more than likely therefore that Albania was worse off in per capita income terms by 1938 than it had been at the time of its liberation.

Albania faced many problems during this period and the possibilities for progress were distinctly inimical. Despite his wide powers King Zog could not remove the landed oligarchies, nor could he alter the traditional tribal way of life. Thus the agrarian sector remained poor and backward, still in the grip of a medieval technology, and acted as a drag on the economy rather than an engine of growth. Zog's regime was undoubtedly repressive and at times exploitative, yet he did bring some stability and order to the country and he did promulgate some worthwhile reforms. Unfortunately these had a very limited impact on transforming the country. But probably more than anything else Albania was defeated by her poor human resource endowment. By 1939 the bulk of the population was still illiterate and it was growing rapidly. This in turn reinforced the forces of custom and tradition which militated against improvement and modernisation. At the same time, social infrastructure facilities – health, education, social services and transport – were also extremely limited, largely due to the poverty of the national exchequer. Medical and health services were thin on the ground, with very few doctors, dentists or midwives, no medical schools and few good hospitals, while social services were almost unknown. Not surprisingly therefore the limited health and hygiene provision, the absence of preventive medicine and poor dietary conditions 'left the door open to the ravages of epidemics and disease, particularly malaria in the lowland and marshy areas' (Marmullaku 1975, 38). In many respects, then, Albania in this period had many similarities with African countries in the post-Second World War period. Perhaps this may answer Hobsbawm's conundrum when comparing Albania with Switzerland.

CHAPTER NINE

Development Stalled?

It is difficult to make broad generalisations about the performance of all the European peripheral countries as a group during the interwar period since their individual experiences were so disparate, while much of the aggregate data on incomes is fragile at best and subject to revision. Hence the question mark in the title to this chapter is justified on the grounds that we cannot say categorically that the period was a time of stalled development for all the peripheral countries. There were such cases of arrested development, but then again other countries managed to make quite reasonable progress. In fact, given the hostile economic climate, what is remarkable is that many countries did achieve some economic advance during the interwar period even measured against the base of 1913. However, the variations in performance are such that it is sensible to look first at each country in turn.

Kofman (1997, 202–205) believes that by the 1930s only three countries, Estonia, Latvia and surprisingly Poland, were either at the threshold or had already embarked on the take-off stage to modern economic growth. These countries, he says, saw 'the chance to extricate themselves quickly from economic underdevelopment, from the position described as the periphery (or even semi-periphery)'. His conclusion may, however, underestimate the potential of some of the other countries. But first to deal with the real laggards. Albania remained easily the most backward and illiterate country in Europe. It showed very few signs of real progress and modernisation and it is quite possible that income per capita was slightly lower at the end of the interwar period than it had been before 1913. Spain also falls into the stalled category. It showed promise in the 1920s but this was eventually cut short by the disastrous events of the Civil War. Turkey is a more difficult case. Superficially, it appears much like Albania, yet there were distinct signs of modernisation and development and the income data suggest that it did better than the former country (see below). Poland is a somewhat anomalous case. It was a country with potential but it never quite lived up to its prewar development expectations. On the industrial front there was a definite indication of stalling during the interwar years. By contrast, Greece and the Baltic states were probably the most promising performers of the peripheral nations and showed great resourcefulness in adapting to the setbacks caused by the First World War. The three main Balkan countries, Bulgaria, Romania and

Yugoslavia, did experience some progress, but their economies were still overwhelmingly agrarian at the end of the period and they remained very poor. In fact Berend (1984, 272) has argued that there was an increase in Balkan relative economic underdevelopment in the interwar years which could be classed as partial stalling, though one set of income data for Bulgaria is at odds with this conclusion (see below). Hungary made better progress than one might have expected given the losses of population and territory, and the fact that so many Hungarians now lived outwith the country. Finally, Portugal appears to have made some advance during these years.

The income per capita data produced in Tables 9.1 and 9.2 provide a general guide to the overall performance of the peripheral economies. However, the data should be treated with some caution since there are considerable margins of error in the estimates and one should not be surprised to find discrepancies among the different estimates. The most comprehensive for our purposes are those of Bairoch which are produced in Table 9.1, along with one or two tentative estimates of the present author. Table 9.2, on the other hand, includes various estimates by different authors of the growth in output or income per capita for a selection of countries. Broadly these estimates support our earlier conclusions. Albania and Spain were undoubtedly the worst two performers with their income per capita levels falling below those of 1913 by the end of thc 1930s. Had it not been for the Civil War Spain would no doubt have been in positive territory. As for Albania, this was a clear case of stagnation, with little significant structural change. True, there was an absolute increase in output but this was swamped out by the rapid rise in population, 1.5 per cent a year, the fastest in Europe except for Turkey. This was clearly a Malthusian situation. Turkey, on the other hand, managed to overcome the handicap of its burgeoning population, especially in the 1930s when all estimates indicate rapid advance in income per capita. However, it should be cautioned that the income estimates for Turkey are somewhat scrappy and not very reliable.

Poland and Romania were the other two really weak performers with very modest advances in per capita income. By contrast, Greece had the strongest growth, while the Baltic states also performed well. Unfortunately there are no separate estimates for each of the Baltic states, but non-quantitative evidence suggests that Estonia and Latvia did rather better than Lithuania. On Bairoch's estimates Bulgaria also showed a strong advance, though Maddison's data suggest otherwise, largely due to a poor showing between 1913 and 1929 according to that author. However, circumstantial evidence would appear to indicate that Maddison has probably underestimated the Bulgarian record in these

Table 9.1 Per Capita GNP (1960 US dollars)

	Level				Percentage Changes				
	1913	1929	1933	1938	1913–29	1929–33	1933–38	1929–38	1913–38
Albania	199	–	–	179	–	–	–	–	–10.1
Baltic countries	350	468	451	501	33.7	–3.6	11.1	7.1	43.1
Bulgaria	263	306	270	420	16.3	–11.8	55.6	37.3	59.7
Greece	322	390	506	590	21.1	29.7	16.6	51.3	83.2
Hungary	372	424	396	451	14.0	–6.6	13.9	6.4	21.2
Poland	340	350	332	372	2.9	–5.1	12.0	6.3	9.4
Portugal	292	320	398	351	9.6	24.4	–11.8	9.7	20.2
Romania	320	331	296	343	3.4	–10.6	15.9	3.6	7.2
Spain	367	455	403	337	24.0	–11.4	–16.4	–25.9	–8.2
Yugoslavia	284	341	292	339	20.1	–14.4	16.1	–0.6	19.4
France	695	982	846	936	41.3	–13.9	10.6	–4.7	34.7
Germany	757	770	716	1126	1.7	–7.0	57.3	46.2	48.8
Italy	441	517	492	327	17.2	–4.8	12.0	6.6	25.0
Sweden	680	897	816	1097	31.2	–9.0	34.4	22.3	61.3
Switzerland	963	1265	1223	1204	31.4	–3.3	–1.6	–4.8	25.0
United Kingdom	996	1038	995	1181	4.2	–4.1	18.7	13.8	18.6
Europe	534	571	543	671	6.9	–4.9	23.4	17.5	25.7

Sources: Bairoch 1976, 297 and author's estimates.

years. As for the remaining countries, Hungary achieved a reasonable advance in income per capita, as did Yugoslavia and Portugal, though there are some discrepancies in the magnitude of the changes between the different estimates. Maddison's estimates for Yugoslavia show a considerably stronger rise than Bairoch's, the main discrepancy being for the years 1913–29. In the case of Portugal the new estimates by Nunes, Mata and Valério suggest that Portugal performed above average in the interwar years.

Table 9.2 Alternative Estimates of GDP or Income Per Capita (% changes)

	1913–29	1929–33	1933–38	1929–38	1913–38
Bulgaria (Maddison)	–21.9	22.9	10.0	35.2	6.5
Greece (Freris)	–	8.9	20.4	31.1	–
Greece (Maddison)	47.2	2.2	11.8	14.3	68.2
Hungary (Maddison)	18.0	–4.1	11.8	7.2	26.5
Poland (Maddison)	–	–24.8	37.2	3.1	–
Portugal (Nunes, Mata and Valério)	19.1	10.2	4.9	15.5	37.6
Portugal (Maddison)	13.4	–	–	11.1	26.0
Romania (Maddison)	–	2.8	4.5	7.8	–
Spain (Prados)	31.2	–6.4	–20.9	–25.9	–2.7
Spain (Maddison)	30.7	–8.6	25.0	–31.4	–10.3
Turkey (Hale)	–	8.7	31.6	38.0	–
Turkey (Maddison)	–2.4	10.7	28.4	42.2	38.8
Turkey (Hershlag)	–	–	–	26.0	–
Yugoslavia (Maddison)	32.9	–14.5	16.3	–0.5	32.1

Sources: Freris 1986, 108 (based on GNP estimates of UN); Hale 1981, 46, 75–7; Hershlag 1954, 336; Maddison 1995, 198–200; Nunes, Mata and Valério 1989; Prados de la Escosura 1993, 108.

Thus, on balance, it was not a case of universal stalling by any means since most countries experienced some progress. Throughout the transwar period, 1913–38, only four countries, Spain, Albania, Poland and Romania, could be classed as outright laggards or stallers, while at least five or six countries, the three Baltic states, Bulgaria, Greece and possible Turkey, performed well, while the remainder, Hungary, Yugoslavia and Portugal, were close to the European average. It would be inappropriate, therefore, to liken the European peripheral countries to the dire state in which African countries found themselves during the latter part of the twentieth century (see Spulber 1966, 7–8, for this comparison). On the other hand, overall progress was not sufficient to make much difference to the relative ranking of the peripheral nations in the interwar period. Apart from one or two countries, for example Greece and the Baltic states, growth was not strong enough to change their performance ranking significantly. In fact just over half the peripheral countries grew less rapidly than Europe as a whole and so they were not making any headway in catching up with the West. Thus by the end of the period incomes per head still remained far behind those in Western Europe. Greece was one of the few countries that probably reduced the gap significantly, though even here income per head was still only half the UK level by 1938. The Baltic states managed to achieve just over 40 per cent of that level. But for the majority of countries per capita income remained at a third or less of the British level, while in the case of Albania and Turkey it was probably as low as 15–20 per cent.

In other words, though some progress was being made it was often slow and hesitant, and as far as industry was concerned it required heavy protection and state support in one form or another. There was a move towards manufacturing industry in most countries but the pace of structural change was scarcely dramatic. The share of industry in output and employment increased only marginally and levels of industrialisation, measured in per capita terms, remained only a fraction of those in Western countries (Bairoch 1982, 331). The low level of industrial development can be seen from key indicators such as the consumption of steel and the use of motor vehicles. Table 9.3 shows data for the consumption of steel per capita in six Western countries and eight peripheral ones. The average consumption in the peripheral countries was less than a quarter of the average in the Western countries in the 1920s and in all but one, Greece, consumption declined both absolutely and as a proportion of the Western level between the 1920s and 1930s. In the case of a new sector of activity, the use of motorised vehicles, the peripheral countries remained way behind the West. Thus the number of passenger cars per 1000 head of population in Eastern Europe in 1937 was less than 1 compared with 25.5 in Western Europe. Commercial vehicles were somewhat more in evidence at 0.68 per 1000 population as against 8.1 in the West. Needless to say, these figures appeared even more minuscule when set against the massive totals pertaining in the United States (Ehrlich 1985, 334–35).

Agriculture continued to be the mainstay of the peripheral economies and the major source of employment, with overpopulation on the land still widespread. In fact herein lay the main problem: the dominance of an antiquated and inefficient agrarian sector that produced low incomes and from which many would willingly have left, to the benefit of the sector, had they anywhere else to go. Past experience in Western

Table 9.3 Steel Consumption Per Capita (in kilograms)

	1922–29	% of Western average	1930–38	% of Western average
Denmark	108		139	
France	124		122	
Germany	150		152	
Norway	127		169	
Sweden	109		163	
UK	126		162	
Average of six countries	124		151	
Bulgaria	20	16.1	14	9.3
Greece	20	16.1	26	17.2
Hungary	38	30.7	32	21.2
Poland	33	26.6	22	14.6
Portugal	27	21.8	29	19.2
Romania	28	23.6	21	13.9
Spain	41	33.1	26	17.2
Yugoslavia	20	16.1	17	11.3
Average of eight countries	28.4	22.9	23.4	15.5

Source: Svennilson 1954, 311.

countries suggests that while agriculture may not necessarily have been the fastest growing sector of the economy in the transition to modern economic growth, it is vital that it responds in a way which facilitates modern economic development. Most writers on development would probably concur with the statement that 'The history of economic development shows that few countries have achieved sustained economic growth without first, or simultaneously, developing their agricultural sector ... Without an efficient agricultural sector, a country is severely constrained in its ability to feed itself or import foreign products for domestic consumption and development' (Birkhaeuser, Everson and Feder, 1991, 607).

In his analysis of Spanish agriculture Tortella (1987, 55) lists five main functions of the agrarian sector: the ability to produce enough to feed a growing population; to serve as a strong market for industrial goods; to generate savings which can be re-invested outwith the primary sector; to provide exchange earnings as a means of financing imports; and the importance of rising agrarian productivity which not only means higher incomes but which will help to release labour for industrial development.

Of these he particularly stresses the shallowness of the agrarian sector as a market for industrial products, which he sees as the worst failure of Spanish agriculture throughout the nineteenth century and beyond (Tortella 1987, 56–57). The same would no doubt be true in most of the other peripheral countries. In Hungary, for example, which was by no means the poorest of the bunch, the general poverty in the countryside provided little scope for a robust market for industrial goods. Even the wealthiest of the peasants, of which there were not that many, rarely exceeded the income of the lower orders of the city dwellers. But even more significantly, the poor peasants, who constituted about 40 per cent of the total population, had such low incomes that they scarcely featured on the domestic market for industrial goods. As Gunst (1994, 56) tellingly remarks: 'They had to think twice before deciding to buy even the most basic items, such as shoes or clothes. Food, clothing, and heating of their homes stagnated at the minimum level of subsistence.'

Moreover, as Crampton (1994) has noted in the context of peasant life in Eastern Europe, even if peasants did by some miracle have cash to spare they rarely used it for re-investment in agriculture or for the purchase of modern industrial goods. Force of custom and tradition meant that any surplus money went on family, religious or community festivals and wakes, rather than on conspicuous consumption.

Agriculture still played an important part in foreign trade, though because of the adverse international market conditions of the postwar years this was less significant than it had been before the war. On the other hand, the primary sector was definitely not an accumulator of capital for dispersion to other sectors of the economy. Indeed, most writers agree that agriculture did not play a significant role in capital accumulation and that the transfer of savings to other sectors 'was insignificant' (Berend 1985, 209). In fact, given the prevalence of high indebtedness in relation to assets and income, to which Moore (1945, 97) refers, it is probable that peasant agriculture was unable to service its own needs for capital let alone generate resources for other sectors. If anything, peasant agriculture was depleting its own assets. Thus the relationship between agriculture and industry which had been so important in transforming Western Europe in the nineteenth century did not exist in much of peripheral Europe. Agriculture did not provide a strong market for the products of industry nor did it generate savings for deployment in industry. Agriculture was therefore not only the weakest and most vulnerable sector of the economy but it also acted as a drag on economic growth in general in peripheral Europe. As Teichova (1989, 903–904) notes with regard to Central and South-eastern Europe, the vital relationship between agriculture and industry was caught up in a vicious circle and so no significant economic development was possible without breaking that circle.

A crucial factor here is the policy orientation of many peripheral countries. In many cases, especially in Eastern Europe, it was not simply a matter of the relative neglect of agriculture but also the blatant bias against the sector. Agriculture was burdened by high taxation (as it had been in the nineteenth century) in the belief that it should be squeezed for the benefit of industry, which was highly favoured and protected. This seems to have been a common feature of many poor countries, from East European, Russia and more recently African countries, which ultimately proved very costly. Yet past experience in the West and in the case of the newly industrialising countries of East Asia (for example South Korea, Singapore, Hong Kong and Taiwan) demonstrates that modern economic development is very dependent on transformation in the agrarian sector. In East Asia, in fact, modernisation first started with agricultural improvement, including land reform and investment in human rural resources and techniques, in order to raise productivity. These countries delayed labour transfer to non-agrarian activities until after the successful completion of agrarian development and until the expansion of non-farm income and employment opportunities existed to absorb labour from the land. This of course was a reversal of the Lewis model of development, which was based on the inducement to industrial development provided by unlimited supplies of labour coming forth at the ruling wage rate.

It is true that most of the European peripheral countries carried out land reforms and provided some assistance for agriculture. But the land reforms themselves were often mismanaged or inappropriate and there is doubt as to whether they did much to make agriculture more efficient, except perhaps in the Baltic states. More often than not they led to further fragmentation of peasant holdings and did little to change age-old farming practices. Peasant agriculture was short of capital, education and know-how and little was done to address these issues. Above all, it was highly taxed in the mistaken belief that this was the best way to accelerate development in non-agricultural activities. Consequently agriculture remained highly inefficient by Western standards, so much so that some peripheral countries were failing to produce enough to feed their growing populations and had to import foodstuffs. As Moore (1945, 95) wrote in reference to Eastern and Southern Europe: 'it is clear that the institutional framework, the economic organisation in productive enterprise, and the level of agrarian techniques provide a closely woven net of restrictions upon increased production in agriculture'.

The agrarian situation was not the only weakness of European peripheral countries, but it was certainly a distinct and major manifestation of their backwardness. Other notable shortcomings were the poor social infrastructure or limited social overhead capital, the low level of human capital formation and the deficiencies in statecraft or political institutions.

In some respects economic structures in general became less tuned to the needs of twentieth century development in the interwar period. Berend (1998, 272) has suggested that in an effort to avoid or alleviate the worst rigours of the Great Depression developments in infrastructures, technology and industry tended to preserve obsolete formats, whereas in the West the workout of cyclical forces brought with it creative capacity destruction, Schumpeterian-style, and so partly eradicated antiquated structures, while at the same time fostering new fields of endeavour. By contrast, in many peripheral countries the effect was to encourage the retention of 'the ballast of the obsolete' (Berend 1998, 272). The peripheral countries were forced to isolate themselves as far as possible from world markets not only by traditional protective measures but also, in Eastern Europe especially, by being drawn into a trading system which helped to preserve their traditional export structures. Thus many industries ended up as inefficient high cost producers with little prospect of competing on the world's free markets. According to Pollard (1981, 289), the constant protection and official support of these pampered industries generated massive corruption and 'placed an intolerable burden on the peasantry and on the state budget alike, and removed what little chance there had been of success as specialist primary producers'.

Their infrastructures were also sadly lacking. In fact their relative ranking in a survey of 28 countries showed very little change. The peripheral countries remained at the bottom of the league table with the Balkans, Turkey, Albania and Portugal the worst performers. Furthermore, in this period infrastructure development in Eastern Europe was actually falling behind the rate of economic development in general, with the most marked lag being in capital-intensive infrastructure facilities such as transport and communications (Ehrlich 1985, 325–30, 368–69). Education, on the other hand, which had been a major lagging area in 1920, showed some relative improvement. Even so, the low level of human capital development remained a serious problem in some countries, which served to hinder economic progress. It was not simply a question of a large number of illiterate people, for many who had been classed as literate in fact had only the most rudimentary qualifications, while at the apex there was a small elite with advanced qualifications who manipulated the levers of power.

It is perhaps not surprising that the infrastructures of the peripheral states were vastly inferior to those of the West since their fiscal systems in general were not designed for growth and development. As noted in Chapter 3, they were highly regressive and all too often they bore the hallmarks inherited from a bygone age. Budgetary spending was heavily skewed towards defence and administration. In Turkey, for instance, a third of budgetary expenditure in 1934 went on civil service salaries (Hershlag 1968, 68). In many other peripheral countries defence and civil administration along with debt service accounted for 60 per cent or more of public spending, leaving barely a third for economic and social services, including infrastructures, whereas in the case of contemporary Sweden these proportions were reversed (Political and Economic Planning 1945, 118–19, 164). Inevitably, therefore, key support services such as transport and communications, utilities, and medical and educational services were neglected. Moreover, given the highly regressive nature of taxation systems which bore heavily on the peasantry and small traders, together with gross tax anomalies, fiscal regimes in general did little to encourage enterprise and initiative except for those favoured by the political regimes.

Conveniently this brings us round to statecraft or the general governance of the peripheral countries and it is here that the educated elites, with the tacit support of the traditional ruling classes, were able to reign supreme. In this respect there is a striking analogy with post-Second World War African countries. In fact there seems to be some association between the degree of poverty and the political configuration of a country and its state capability. According to Janos (1989, 356), 'The further a society was located from the core, the poorer it was destined to remain, the more power its political classes accumulated, and the greater would be the scope of state authority.' Ethnic divisions and cultural and social forces may have played a part in this outcome, but economic explanations, he argues, are probably more powerful in determining the political configuration of peripheral societies.

As we know, most of the peripheral European states experimented with democratic and pluralistic forms of government in the early postwar years, but in time democracy broke down and was replaced by authoritarian regimes of one form or another. In the process 'positive sovereignty' was transformed into 'negative sovereignty' as the power elites captured control of the state organs of power and sought to impose their will on the masses. If the state apparatus falls into the hands of self-chosen elites it can often degenerate into 'negative sovereignty', that is, states in name only – inefficient, illegitimate, corrupt and frequently unstable, and therefore inimical to development.

The antithesis, 'positive sovereignty', is more likely to flourish under pluralistic democratic regimes, producing a social and institutional infrastructure more conducive to economic development (Jackson 1990, 1–21). It should be noted, however, that the rot had already set in before authoritarian regimes took root. The quasi-parliamentary regimes of the early postwar years were far from perfect. Elections were often a charade and the process by which the elites rigged the outcome is reminiscent of Third World practice. 'Governments mainly relied upon bribery, patronage, gerrymandering, electoral fraud, restriction of the franchise and (in the last resort) violence and intimidation to maintain themselves in office' (Bideleux and Jeffries 1998, 430).

In the case of Eastern Europe Seton-Watson explains the transformation in terms of the rise in influence of the intellectual and commercial bourgeoisie, who infiltrated the traditional ruling class structure and then sought to preserve their power by authoritarian means (Seton-Watson 1946, 125–29). By a process of divide and rule it was relatively easy to do this in countries fragmented by ethnic divisions and lacking any strong element of national identity or much experience with democratic pluralistic institutions. In the process public officials or bureaucrats paid homage to the ruling elites since their own well-being was dependent upon them.

What matters especially is the end result of this political configuration. While greater étatism need not necessarily lead to inefficient governance, in practice it did mean that the state was run more for the benefit of the ruling elites than in the interests of the masses or for developmental purposes. Peripheral states were noted for their corruption, extortionate tax drives and political engineering, to the detriment of the populace at large, as the ruling elites attempted to preserve their privileges and power. Peasants and workers were kept in their place by police terror and penal taxation. Taxes were often collected 'with ruthless brutality', especially later on in the period when governments needed all the revenue they could squeeze out of the population to meet the growing burden of military spending. According to Seton-Watson:

> If a peasant owed arrears of taxes, the gendarmes would come to his house when he was working in the fields – or when he and all adult males in his household were serving in the army. If the women could not pay, the gendarmes seized the few belongings of the household. If the wife and children objected, they were beaten. Outrages of this sort were often committed for the sake of a few pennies.
>
> (Seton-Watson 1946, 148)

Such practices were not in fact new since they had been going on before 1914, but Seton-Watson believes that oppression, robbery and general discontent were greater throughout Eastern Europe in 1939 than they had been at the end of the First World War. Stronger governments may have emerged from the ruins of parliamentary democracy but they were little more than 'greedy, corrupt and brutal class regimes, which did not feed but fed upon their peoples, and whose only strength lay in the bayonets of the gendarmes' (Seton-Watson 1946, 156). Moreover, unlike the regimes of Hitler and Mussolini the East European dictatorships had no basis of popular support. Not that their predecessors had been much better. Bribery, corruption, graft and dishonesty were prevalent in official, political and business circles even in the supposedly more liberal days of the 1920s, especially in the Balkans, though it should be stressed that nineteenth century experience was little different. In Romania, for example, hordes of politicians and officials waxed fat on the Treasury, as did the business intimates of the Bratianu brothers (leaders of the Liberal Party in the 1920s), who dispensed largesse liberally to their supporters. Once the land reform was out of the way the peasants were neglected except for purposes of raising revenue. One contemporary writer alleged that the Romanian state administration had been 'annexed by the party bosses and the public budget has been confiscated for the benefit of the clients of these parties' (Logio 1932, 128).

The similarity with many latter-day African countries is striking though perhaps not that surprising. Most of them are poor and divided and control has been captured by educated elites whose principal objective is to maintain power and prestige by authoritarian means to the detriment of the masses. Janos (1989, 356) argues that poor peripheral states are not necessarily born bad or profligate, but rather that they become so when the ruling classes and bureaucrats realise that the only way they can enjoy the trappings and life-style of Western civilisation is by controlling the levers of power for their own benefit, which enables them 'to convert private need into public policy'.

It is a sad tale and one that has been repeated many times in poorer countries. There is certainly evidence to suggest that the degeneration of the state was a characteristic of many European peripheral countries in the interwar years. It did not of course mean that economic development ground to a halt because of it since the evidence is to the contrary. On the other hand, it did mean that welfare of the masses was given short shrift and that balanced developmental policies were not in the best interests of the ruling elites.

Overall one may say that peripheral Europe did not do too badly in the interwar period taking account of the very disturbed economic and political conditions of the period. The interwar years were of course a difficult time for the advanced industrial countries as well as for the peripheral ones, the main difference being that the latter were so much poorer. And as Ranki points out, while there were some compensations in the West in the form of new cultural and recreational habits – as, for example, the introduction of the radio and motion pictures and new services such as regular visits to the hairdressers – in Eastern Europe 'such elements hardly existed, and for the most part life was truly miserable' (Ranki 1974, 314). Nevertheless, the peripheral European countries were by no means a lost cause, as seems to be the case with most sub-Saharan African countries today. Their subsequent performance in the post-Second World War period demonstrates that most of them already had sufficient latent potential to be able to profit from the sustained growth of the boom years of the international economy, when their incomes and economic achievements surpassed those of many Third World countries. Even so, by the end of the twentieth century their incomes still remained below those of the advanced nations of the West and only Spain seems likely to take its place at the Western league table.

References

Abramovitz, M. (1989), *Thinking About Growth*, Cambridge: Cambridge University Press.

Aktar, A. (2003), 'Homogenising the nation, Turkifying the economy: the Turkish experience of population exchange reconsidered', in R. Hirschon (ed.), *Crossing the Aegean: An Appraisal of the 1923 Compulsory Population Exchange Between Greece and Turkey*, Oxford: Berghahn Books.

Aldcroft, D. H. (1997), 'Depression and recovery in Europe in the 1930s', *Traverse, Zeitschrift für Geschichte*, **1**.

Aldcroft, D. H. (1998), 'Education and development: the experience of rich and poor nations', *History of Education*, **27**.

Aldcroft, D. H. (2001), 'The twentieth century international debt problem in historical perspective', *Journal of European Economic History*, **30**.

Aldcroft, D. H. (2004), 'The Sterling Area in the 1930s: a unique Monetary Arrangement?', *Journal of European Economic History*, **33**.

Aldcroft, D. H. and Morewood, S. (1995), *Economic Change in Eastern Europe Since 1918*, Aldershot: Edward Elgar.

Aldcroft, D. H. and Oliver, M. (1998), *Exchange Rate Regimes in the Twentieth Century*, Cheltenham: Edward Elgar.

Alpert, P. (1951), *Twentieth Century Economic History of Europe*, New York: Schuman.

Arrighi, G. (ed.) (1985), *Semiperipheral Development: the Politics of Southern Europe in the Twentieth Century*, Beverly Hills, Ca.: Sage Publications.

Artaud, D. (1973), *La reconstruction de l'Europe (1919–1929)*, Paris: Presses Universitaires de France.

Bairoch, P. (1976), 'Europe's gross national product: 1800–1975', *Journal of European Economic History*, **5**.

Bairoch, P. (1981), 'The main trends in national economic disparities since the industrial revolution', in P. Bairoch and M. Levy-Leboyer (eds), *Disparities in Economic Development Since the Industrial Revolution*, London: Macmillan.

Bairoch, P. (1982), 'International industrialization levels from 1750 to 1980', *Journal of European Economic History*, **11**.

Bairoch, P. (1989), 'Les trois révolutions agricoles du monde développé: rendements et productivité de 1800 à 1985', *Annales*, **44**.

Bairoch, P. (1991), 'How and not why: economic inequalities between 1800 and 1913: some background figures', in J. Batou (ed.), *Between Development and Underdevelopment: the Precocious Attempts at Industrialisation of the Periphery, 1800–70,* Geneva: Droz.

Bandera, V. N. (1964), *Foreign Capital as an Instrument of National Economic Policy: a Study Based on the Experience of East European Countries Between the Two World Wars*, The Hague: Nijhoff.

Bank for International Settlements (1935), *Fifth Annual Report, 1 April 1934–31 March 1935*, Basle: Bank for International Settlements.

Barro, R. (1991), 'Economic growth in a cross section of countries', *Quarterly Journal of Economics*, **106**.

Basch, A. (1944), *The Danube Basin and the German Economic Sphere*, London: Kegan Paul, Trench, Trubner.

Batou, J. (1990), *Cent ans de résistance au sous-développement: l'industrialisation de l'Amérique latine et du Moyen-orient au défi européen, 1700–1870*, Geneva: Droz.

Bell, J. D. (1977), *Peasants in Power: Alexander Stambolski and the Bulgarian Agrarian National Union, 1899–1923*, Princeton: Princeton University Press.

Bencze, I. and Tajti, E. V. (1972), *Budapest: an Industrial-geographical Approach*, Budapest: Akademiai Kiado.

Berend, I. T. (1974), 'Investment strategy in East-Central Europe', in H. Daems and H. van der Wee (eds), *The Rise of Managerial Capitalism*, The Hague: Nijhoff.

Berend, I. T. (1984), 'Balkan economic development', *Economic History Review*, **37**.

Berend, I. T. (1985), 'Agriculture', in M. C. Kaser and E. A. Radice (eds), *The Economic History of Eastern Europe 1919–1975*. Vol I. *Economic Structure and Performance Between the Wars*, Oxford: Oxford University Press.

Berend, I. T. (1998), *Decades of Crisis: Central and Eastern Europe Before World War II, Berkeley*, Ca.: University of California Press.

Berend, I. T. (2003), *History Derailed: Central and Eastern Europe in the Long Nineteenth Century*, Berkeley, Ca.: University of California Press.

Berend, I. T. and Ranki, G. (1974a), *Economic Development in East Central Europe in the 19th and 20th Centuries*, New York: Columbia University Press.

Berend, I. T. and Ranki, G. (1974b), *Hungary: A Century of Economic Development*, Newton Abbot: David & Charles.

Berend, I. T. and Ranki, G. (1982), *The European Periphery and Industrialization 1780–1914*, Cambridge: Cambridge University Press.

Berend, I. T. and Ranki, G. (1985), *The Hungarian Economy in the Twentieth Century*, London: Croom Helm.

Berov, L. (1983), 'Inflation and deflation policy in Bulgaria during the period between World War I and World War II', in N. Schmukler and E. Marcus (eds), *Inflation Through the Ages*, New York: Brooklyn College Press.

Beyen, J. W. (1951), *Money in Maelstrom*, London: Macmillan.

Bicanic, I. and Skreb, M. (1994), 'The Yugoslav economy from amalgamation to disintegration: failed efforts at molding a new economic space 1919–91', in D. F. Good (ed.), *Economic Transformations in East and Central Europe: Legacies from the Past and Policies for the Future*, London: Routledge.

Bideleux, R. and Jeffries, I. (1998), *A History of Eastern Europe: Crisis and Change*, London: Routledge.

Birkhaeuser, D., Everson, R. E. and Feder, G. (1991), 'The economic impact of agricultural extension: a review', *Economic Development and Cultural Change*, **39**.

Blum, J. (1978), *The End of the Old Order in Rural Europe*, Princeton: Princeton University Press.

Boross, E. A. (1994), *Inflation and Industry in Hungary 1918–1929*, Berlin: Haude & Spener.

Calic, M.-J. (1994), *Sozialgeschichte Serbiens 1815–1941: Der Aufhaltsame Fortschritt während der Industrialisierung*, Munich: R. Oldenbourg.

Carreras, A. (1987), 'An annual index of Spanish industrial output', in N. Sánchez-Albornoz (ed.), *The Economic Modernization of Spain, 1830–1930*, New York: New York University Press.

Chirot, D. (1976), *Social Change in a Peripheral Society: the Creation of a Balkan Economy*, New York: Academic Press.

Chirot, D. (1985), 'The rise of the west', *American Sociological Review*, **50**.

Chirot, D. (1989a), 'Causes and consequences of backwardness', in D. Chirot (ed.), *The Origins of Economic Backwardness in Eastern Europe*, Berkeley, Ca.: University of California Press.

Chirot, D. (ed.), (1989b), *The Origins of Economic Backwardness in Eastern Europe*, Berkeley, Ca.: University of California Press.

Choudhri, E. V. and Kochin, L. A. (1980), 'The exchange rate and the international transmission of business cycle disturbances: some evidence from the great depression', *Journal of Money, Credit and Banking*, **12**.

Cipolla, C. (1969), *Literacy and Development in the West*, Harmondsworth: Penguin Books.

Cipolla, C. (1981), *Before the Industrial Revolution: European Society and Economy 1000–1700*, London, Methuen.

Clough, S. B., Moodie, T. and Moodie, C. (eds) (1969), *Economic History of Europe: Twentieth Century*, London: Macmillan.

Cobban, A. (1944), *National Self-determination*, London: Oxford University Press.

Colman, D. and Nixson, F. (1994), *Economics of Change in Less Developed Countries*, Hemel Hempstead: Harvester Wheatsheaf.

Condliffe, J. B. (1941), *The Reconstruction of World Trade: A Survey of International Economic Relations*, London: Allen & Unwin.

Corkill, D. (1999), *The Development of the Portuguese Economy: A Case of Europeanization*, London: Routledge.

Crampton, R. J. (1987), *A Short History of Modern Bulgaria*, Cambridge: Cambridge University Press.

Crampton, R. J. (1994), *Eastern Europe in the Twentieth Century*, London: Routledge.

Crampton R. and Crampton, B. (1996), *Atlas of Eastern Europe in the Twentieth Century*, London: Routledge.

de Oliveira Marques, A. H. (1978), 'The Portuguese 1920s: a general survey', *Revista de Historica Economica e Social*, **1**.

Djordjevic, D. (1992), 'The Yugoslav Phenomenon', in J. Held, (ed.), *The Columbia History of Eastern Europe in the Twentieth Century*, New York: Columbia University Press.

Dornbusch, R. (1992), 'Monetary problems of post-communism: lessons from the end of the Austro-Hungarian Empire', *Weltwirtschaftliches Archiv*, **128**.

Drabek, Z. (1985) 'Foreign trade performance and policy', in M. C. Kaser and E. A. Radice (eds), *The Economic History of Eastern Europe 1919–1975*. Vol I. *Economic Structure and Performance Between the Wars*, Oxford: Oxford University Press.

Dragnich, A. N. (1983), *The First Yugoslavia: Search for a Viable Political System*, Stanford, Ca.: Hoover Institution Press.

Drummond, I. M. (1981), *The Floating Pound and the Sterling Area*, Cambridge: Cambridge University Press.

Dyker, D. A. (1990), *Yugoslavia: Socialism, Development and Debt*, London: Routledge.

Easterlin R. A. (1981), 'Why isn't the whole world developed', *Journal of Economic History*, **41**.

Eddie, S. M. (1994), 'The transition to market economies: a model for Central and Eastern Europe?', in D. F. Good (ed.), *Economic Transformations in East and Central Europe: Legacies from the Past and Policies for the Future*, London: Routledge.

Ehrlich, E. (1973), 'Infrastructure and an international comparison of relationships with indicators of development in Eastern Europe, 1920–1950', *Oxford Papers in East European Economics*, **33**.

Ehrlich, E. (1985), 'Infrastructure', in M. C. Kaser and E. A. Radice (eds), *The Economic History of Eastern Europe 1919–1975*. Vol. I. *Economic Structure and Performance Between the Wars*, Oxford: Oxford University Press.

Einzig, P. (1938), *Bloodless Invasion: German Economic Penetration into the Danubian States and the Balkans*, London: Duckworth.

Ellis, H. S. (1941), *Exchange Control in Central Europe*, Cambridge, Mass.: Harvard University Press.

Evangelinides, M. (1979), 'Core-periphery relations in the Greek case', in D. Seers, B. Schaffer and M.-L. Kiljunen (eds), *Underdeveloped Europe: Studies in Core-Periphery Relations*, Hassocks, Sussex: The Harvester Press.

Fischer-Galati, S. (1970), *Twentieth Century Romania*, New York: Columbia University Press

Fischer-Galati, S. (1992), 'Eastern Europe in the Twentieth Century: "Old Wine in New Bottles"', in J. Held (ed.), *The Columbia History of Eastern Europe in the Twentieth Century*, New York: Columbia University Press.

Fontana, J. and Nadal, J. (1976), 'Spain 1914–1970', in C. M. Cipolla (ed.), *The Fontana Economic History of Europe: Contemporary Economies Part Two*, London: Collins/Fontana.

Foreign Office (1941), 'Germany, the U.S.S.R. and South-eastern Europe', London: PRO/FO 371/29782.

Freris, A. F. (1986), *The Greek Economy in the Twentieth Century*, London: Croom Helm.

Friedman, P. (1974), *The Impact of Trade Destruction on National Incomes: a Study of Europe, 1924–1938*, Gainsville: University Presses of Florida.

Friedman, P. (1976), 'The welfare costs of bilateralism: German-Hungarian trade 1933–38', *Explorations in Economic History*, **13**.

Friedman, P. (1978), 'An econometric model of national income, commercial policy and the level of international trade: the open economies of Europe, 1924–1938', *Journal of Economic History*, **38**.

Gati, G. (1974), 'Hungary: the dynamics of revolutionary transformation', in G. Gati (ed.), *The Politics of Modernization in Eastern Europe*, New York: Praeger.

Georgieva, Maria (1998), 'Industry and protectionism in south-eastern Europe during the inter-war period: a path to modernization?', in J. Batou and T. David (eds), *Uneven Development in Europe: The Obstructed Growth of the Agricultural Countries, 1918–1939*, Geneva: Droz.

Gilberg, T. (1992), 'The multiple legacies of history: Romania in the year 1990', in J. Held, (ed.), *The Columbia History of Eastern Europe in the Twentieth Century*, New York: Columbia University Press.

Good, D. F. (1984), *The Economic Rise of the Habsburg Empire, 1750–1914*, Berkeley, Ca.: University of California Press.

Good, D. F. (1991), 'Austria-Hungary', in R. Sylla and G. Toniolo (eds), *Patterns of European Industrialization: The Nineteenth Century*, London: Routledge

Good, D. F. (1993), 'The economic lag of Central and Eastern Europe: evidence from the late nineteenth-century Habsburg Empire', *Working Papers in Austrian Studies*, 93–97. Center for Austrian Studies, University of Minnesota.

Goodman, J. and Honeyman, K. (1988), *Gainful Pursuits: the Making of Industrial Europe*, London: Edward Arnold.

Gorecki, R. (1935), *Poland and Her Economic Development*, London: Allen & Unwin.

Gunst, P. (1994), 'Living standards in Hungary between the first and second world wars', in V. Zamagni and P. Scholliers (eds), *Real Wages in the Nineteenth and Twentieth Centuries*, Milan: Università Bocconi.

Halasz, A. (1928), *New Central Europe in Economical maps*, Budapest: R. Gergely.

Hale, W. (1981), *The Political and Economic Development of Modern Turkey*, London: Croom Helm.

Hale, W. (2000), *Turkish Foreign Policy 1774–2000*, London: Frank Cass.

Hall, R. E. and Jones, C. I. (1999), 'Why do some countries produce so much more output per worker than others?', *Quarterly Journal of Economics*, **114**.

Hanák, P. (1992), 'Hungary 1918–1945', in J. Held (ed.), *The Columbia History of Eastern Europe in the Twentieth Century*, New York: Columbia University Press.

Hanson, J. R. II (1986), 'Export shares in the European periphery and the third world before world war I: questionable data, facile analogies', *Explorations in Economic History*, **23**.

Harris, S. E. (1936), *Exchange Depreciation: Its Theory and Its History 1931–35, with Some Consideration of Related Domestic Policies*, Cambridge, Mass.: Harvard University Press.

Harrison, J. (1978), *An Economic History of Modern Spain*, Manchester: Manchester University Press.

Harrison, J. (1983), 'The inter-war depression and the Spanish economy', *Journal of European Economic History*, **12**.

Harrison, J. (1985), *The Spanish Economy in the Twentieth Century*, London: Croom Helm.

Harrison, J. and Corkill, D. (2004), *Spain: A Modern European Economy*, Aldershot: Ashgate.

Hauner, M. (1985), 'Human Resources', in M. C. Kaser and E. A. Radice (eds), *The Economic History of Eastern Europe 1919–1975. Vol. I. Economic Structure and Performance Between the Wars*, Oxford: Oxford University Press.

Hauner, M. (1986), 'Military budgets and the armaments industry', in M. C. Kaser and E. A. Radice (eds), *The Economic History of Eastern Europe 1919–1975.* Vol. II. *Interwar Policy, the War and Reconstruction*, Oxford: Oxford University Press.

Held, J. (1980), *The Modernization of Agriculture: Rural Transformation in Hungary 1848–1975.* East European Monographs, 63, New York: Columbia University Press.

Henig, R. (1995), *Versailles and After 1919–1933*, London: Routledge.

Hershlag, Z. Y. (1954), 'Turkey: achievement and failures in the policy of economic development', *Kyklos*, **7**.

Hershlag, Z. Y. (1968), *Turkey: the Challenge of Growth*, Leiden: E. J. Brill.

Hertz, F. (1947), *The Economic Problem of the Danubian States. A Study in Economic Nationalism*, London: Gollancz.

Hiden, J. (1977), *Germany and Europe 1919–1939*, London: Longman.

Hinkkanen-Lievonen, M.-L. (1983), 'Exploited by Britain? The problems of British financial presence in the Baltic States after the First World War', *Journal of Baltic Studies*, **14**.

Hinkkanen-Lievonen, M.-L. (1984), *British Trade and Enterprise in the Baltic States, 1919–1925*, Helsinki: SHS.

Hirschon, R. (2003), 'The consequences of the Lausanne convention: an Overview', in R. Hirschon (ed.), *Crossing the Aegean: An Appraisal of the 1923 Compulsory Population Exchange Between Greece and Turkey*, Oxford: Berghahn Books.

Hitchins, K. (1994), *Rumania 1866–1947*, Oxford: Oxford University Press.

Hobsbawm, E. (1994), *Age of Extremes: The Short Twentieth Century 1914–1991*, London: Michael Joseph.

Hocevar, T. (1965),*The Structure of the Slovenian Economy 1848–1963*, New York: Studia Slovenica.

Hocevar, T. (1987), 'The Albanian economy 1912–1944: a survey', *Journal of European Economic History*, **16**.

Hoffman, G. W. (1972), *Regional Development Strategy in Southeast Europe: A Comparative Analysis of Albania, Bulgaria, Greece, Romania and Yugoslavia*, New York: Praeger Publishers.

Hope, N. (1994), 'Interwar statehood: symbol and reality', in G. Smith (ed.), *The Baltic States: The National Self-Determination of Estonia, Latvia and Lithuania*, Basingstoke: Macmillan.

Hoptner, J. B. (1962), *Yugoslavia in Crisis, 1934–1941*, New York: Columbia University Press.

Horsman, G. (1988), *Inflation in the Twentieth Century: Evidence from Europe and North America*, Hemel Hempstead: Harvester-Wheatsheaf.

Jack, D. T. (1927), *The Restoration of European Currencies*, London: P. S. King & Son.

Jackson, M. R. and Lampe, J. R. (1983), 'The evidence of industrial growth in South Eastern Europe before the Second World War', *East European Quarterly*, **16**.

Jackson, M. R. (1990), *Quasi-states: Sovereignty, International Relations and the Third World*, Cambridge: Cambridge University Press.

Janos, C. (1982), *The Politics of Backwardness in Hungary 1825–1945*, Princeton: Princeton University Press.

Janos, C. (1989), 'The politics of backwardness in continental Europe, 1780–1945', *World Politics*, **41**.

Jelavich, B. (1983), *History of the Balkans*, Vol. II. *Twentieth Century*, Cambridge: Cambridge University Press.

Jones, E. (1981), *The European Miracle*, Cambridge: Cambridge University Press.

Jones, F. E. (1937), *Hitler's Drive to the East*, London: Gollancz.

Kahn, H. (1979), *World Economic Development, 1979 and Beyond*, London: Croom Helm.

Kaiser, D. E. (1980), *Economic Diplomacy and the Origins of the Second World War: Germany, Britain, France and Eastern Europe, 1930–1939*, Princeton: Princeton University Press.

Kaser, M. C. (1985), 'Introduction', in M. C. Kaser and E. A. Radice (eds), *The Economic History of Eastern Europe 1919–1975*, Vol I, *Economic Structure and Performance Between the Wars*, Oxford: Oxford University Press.

Kaser, M. C. and Radice, E. A. (eds) (1985), *The Economic History of Eastern Europe 1919–1975*. Vol I. *Economic Structure and Performance Between the Wars*, Oxford: Oxford University Press.

Kaser, M. C. and Radice, E. A. (eds) (1986), *The Economic History of Eastern Europe 1919–1975*. Vol. II. *Interwar Policy, the War and Reconstruction*, Oxford: Oxford University Press.

Kerék, M. (1940), 'Agricultural land reform in Hungary', *Hungarian Quarterly*, **6**.

Kerwin, R. W. (1959), 'Etatism in Turkey, 1933–50', in H. G. J. Aitken (ed.), *The State and Economic Growth*, New York: Social Science Research Council.

Keyder, C. (1981), *The Definition of a Peripheral Economy: Turkey 1923–1929*, Cambridge: Cambridge University Press.

Keyder, C. (2003), The consequences of the exchange of populations for Turkey', in R. Hirschon (ed.), *Crossing the Aegean: An Appraisal of the 1923 Compulsory Population Exchange Between Greece and Turkey*, Oxford: Berghahn Books.

Keynes, J. M. (1919), *The Economic Consequences of the Peace*, London: Macmillan.

Kinross, Lord (1976), 'General Mustafa Kemel (Atatürk)', in M. Carver (ed.), *The War Lords*, London: Weidenfeld and Nicolson.

Kiraly, B. K., Pastor, P. and Sanders, I. (eds) (1982), *War and Society in East Central Europe*. Vol. VI. *Essays on World War I: Total War and Peacemaking, a Case Study of Trianon*, New York: Brooklyn College Press.

Kirby, D. (1995), *The Baltic World 1772–1993: Europe's Northern Periphery in an Age of Change*, London: Longman.

Kirk, D. (1946), *Europe's Population in the Interwar Years*, Geneva: League of Nations.

Kitchen, M. (1988), *Europe Between the Wars: a Political History*, London: Longman.

Kofman, J. (1997), *Economic Nationalism and Development: Central and Eastern Europe Between the Two World Wars*, Boulder, Colorado: Westview Press.

Koliopoulos, J. S. and Veremis, T. M. (2002), *Greece: The Modern Sequel from 1831 to the Present*, London: Hurst & Company.

Köll, A. M. (1998), 'The agrarian question in Eastern Europe: some answers from the Baltic region', in J. Batou and T. David (eds), *Uneven Development in Europe: The Obstructed Growth of the Agricultural Countries, 1918–1939*, Geneva: Droz.

Komlos, J. (1983), *The Habsburg Monarchy as a Customs Union*, Princeton, NJ: Princeton University Press.

Kontogiorgi, E. (2003), 'Economic consequences following refugee settlement in Greek Macedonia, 1923–1932', in R. Hirschon (ed.), *Crossing the Aegean: An Appraisal of the 1923 Compulsory Population Exchange Between Greece and Turkey*, Oxford: Berghahn Books.

Korbonski, A. (1992), 'Poland: 1918–1990', in J. Held (ed.), *The Columbia History of Eastern Europe in the Twentieth Century*, New York: Columbia University Press.

Kovatcheff, Y. G. (1934), 'Agrarian reform in Bulgaria', *International Review of Agriculture*, **25**.

Lains, P. and Reis, J. (1991), 'Portuguese economic growth, 1833–1985: some doubts', *Journal of European Economic History*, **20**.

Lamer, M. (1938), 'Die wandlungen der ausländischen kapitalanlagen auf dem Balkan', *Weltwirtschaftliches Archiv*, **48**.

Lampe, J. R. (1980), 'Unifying the Yugoslav economy 1918–1921: misery and early misunderstandings', in D. Djordjevic (ed.), *The Creation of Yugoslavia, 1914–18*, Santa Barbara, Ca.: Clio Books.

Lampe, J. R. (1986), *The Bulgarian Economy in the Twentieth Century*, London: Croom Helm.

Lampe, J. R. (1989), 'Imperial borderlands or capitalist periphery? Redefining Balkan backwardness, 1520–1914', in D. Chirot (ed.), *The Origins of Economic Backwardness in Eastern Europe*, Berkeley, Ca.: University of California Press.

Lampe, J. R. (1996), *Yugoslavia as History: Twice There Was a Nation*, Cambridge: Cambridge University Press.

Lampe, J. R. and Jackson, M. R. (1982), *Balkan Economic History, 1550–1950*, Bloomington: Indiana University Press.

Landau, Z. (1983), 'Inflation in Poland after World War I', in N. Schmukler and E. Marcus (eds), *Inflation Through the Ages*, New York: Brooklyn College Press.

Landau, Z. (1984), 'Poland's finance policy in the years of the Great Depression (1930–35)', *Acta Poloniae Historica*, **49**.

Landau, Z. (1992), 'The economic integration of Poland, 1918–23', in P. Latawski (ed.), *The Reconstruction of Poland, 1914–23*, Basingstoke: Macmillan.

Landau, Z. and Tomaszewski, J. (1985), *The Polish Economy in the Twentieth Century*, London: Croom Helm.

Landes, D. S. (1969), *The Unbound Prometheus: Technological Change and Industrial Development in Western Europe from 1750 to the Present*, Cambridge: Cambridge University Press.

Landes, D. S. (1990), 'Why are we so rich and they so poor?', *American Economic Review, Papers and Proceedings*, **80**.

Landes, D. S. (1999), *The Wealth and Poverty of Nations: Why Some Are So Rich and Some Are So Poor*, London: Abacus.

Lazaretou, S. (1996), 'Macroeconomic policies and nominal exchange rate regimes: Greece in the interwar period', *Journal of European Economic History*, **25**.

League of Nations (1926), *The Financial Reconstruction of Hungary*, Geneva: League of Nations.

League of Nations (1929), *The Problem of the Coal Industry: Interim Report on Its International Aspects*, Geneva: League of Nations.

League of Nations (1937), *Money and Banking 1936/37*. Vol. I. *Monetary Review*, Geneva: League of Nations.

League of Nations (1939a), *European Conference on Rural Life 1939: Population and Agriculture with Special Reference to Agricultural Overpopulation*, Geneva: League of Nations.

League of Nations (1939b), *World Economic Survey 1938/39*, Geneva: League of Nations.

League of Nations (1941), *Europe's Trade*, Geneva: League of Nations.

League of Nations (1942), *The Network of World Trade*, Geneva: League of Nations.

League of Nations (1943a), *Agricultural Production in Continental Europe During the 1914–18 War and the Reconstruction Period*, Geneva: League of Nations.

League of Nations (1943b), *Europe's Overseas Needs 1919–1920 and How They Were Met*, Geneva: League of Nations.

League of Nations (1943c), *Relief Deliveries and Relief Loans 1919–1923*, Geneva: League of Nations.

League of Nations (1945), *Industrialisation and Foreign Trade*, Geneva: League of Nations.

League of Nations (1946a), *The Course and Control of Inflation: A Review of Monetary Experience in Europe After the First World War*, Geneva: League of Nations.

League of Nations (1946b), *Raw Material Problems and Policies*, Geneva: League of Nations.

Lee, S. J. (1987), *The European Dictatorships 1918–1945*, London: Methuen.

Leslie, R. F. (ed.) (1980), *The History of Poland Since 1863*, Cambridge: Cambridge University Press.

Lethbridge, E. (1985), 'National income and product', in M. C. Kaser and E. A. Radice (eds), *The Economic History of Eastern Europe 1919–1975*. Vol. I. *Economic Structure and Performance Between the Wars*, Oxford: Oxford University Press.

Lieberman, S. (1995), *Growth and Crisis in the Spanish Economy: 1940–93*, London: Routledge.

Linke, L. (1937), 'Social changes in Turkey', *International Affairs*, **16**.

Logio, G. C. (1932), *Rumania: Its History, Politics and Economics*, Manchester, Sherratt and Hughes.

Logio, G. C. (1936), *Bulgaria: Past and Present*, Manchester: Sherratt and Hughes.

Loveday, A. (1931), *Britain and World Trade*, London: Longmans Green.

Lykogiannis, A. (1994), 'The early post-war Greek economy: from liberation to the Truman doctrine', *Journal of European Economic History*, **23**.

Macartney, C. A. (1937), *Hungary and Her Successors: The Treaty of Trianon and Its Consequences 1919–1937*, London: Oxford University Press.

Macartney, C. A. and Palmer, A. W. (1962), *Independent Eastern Europe*, London: Macmillan.

MacMillan, M. (2003), *Peacemakers: The Paris Conference of 1919 and its Attempt to End War*, London: John Murray.

Maddison, A. (1995), *Monitoring the World Economy 1820–1992*, Paris: OECD.

Madgearu, V. (1930), *Rumania's New Economic Policy*, London: P. S. King.

Malefakis, E. E. (1970), *Agrarian Reform and Peasant Revolution in Spain: Origins of the Civil War*, New Haven: Yale University Press.

Maluquer de Motes, J. (1994), 'El indice de la producción industrial de Cataluña. Una nueva estimación (1817–1935), *Historia Industrial*, 5.

Mango, A. (1968), *Turkey*, London: Thames and Hudson.

Marks, S. (1976), *The Illusion of Peace: International Relations in Europe 1918–1933*, London: Macmillan.

Marmullaku, R. (1975), *Albania and the Albanians*, London: C. Hurst & Company.

Mazower, M. (1985), 'L'economia greca durante la grande depressione dei primi anni '30', *Rivista di Storia Economica*, 2.

Mazower, M. (1991a), 'Banking and economic development in interwar Greece', in H. James, H. Lindgren and A. Teichova (eds), *The Role of Banks in the Interwar Economy*, Cambridge: Cambridge University Press.

Mazower, M. (1991b), *Greece and the Interwar Economic Crisis*, Oxford: Oxford University Press.

McNeill, W. H. (1963), *The Rise of the West*, Chicago: University of Chicago Press.

McNeill, W. H. (1979), *A World History*, Oxford: Oxford University Press.

Mehmet, O. (1995), *Westernizing the Third World*, London: Routledge.

Mendelsohn, E. (1983), *The Jews of East Central Europe between the World Wars*, Bloomington: Indiana University Press.

Mlynarski, F. (1926), *The International Significance of the Depreciation of the Zloty in 1925*, Warsaw: The Polish Economist.

Mocsy, I. I. (1983), *War and Society in East Central Europe*. Vol. XII. *The Effects of World War I. The Uprooted: Hungarian Refugees and Their Impact on Hungary's Domestic Politics, 1918–1921*, New York: Brooklyn College Press.

Molinas, C. and Prados de la Escosura, L. (1989), 'Was Spain different? Spanish historical backwardness revisited', *Explorations in Economic History*, **26**.

Moore, W. E. (1945), *Economic Demography in Eastern and Southern Europe*, Geneva: League of Nations.

Morewood, S. (2005), *The British Defence of Egypt 1935–1940: Conflict and Crisis in the Eastern Mediterranean*, London: Frank Cass.

Moulton, H. G. (1923), 'Economic conditions in Europe', *American Economic Review*, **13**.

Munting, R. and Holderness, B. A. (1991), *Crisis, Recovery and War: An Economic History of Continental Europe, 1918–1945*, Hemel Hempstead: Philip Allan.

Musgrave, P. (1999), *The Economy of Europe in the Early Modern Period*, Basingstoke: Macmillan.

Nadel, J. (1987), 'A century of industrialization in Spain, 1833–1930', in N. Sánchez-Albornoz (ed.), *The Economic Modernization of Spain, 1830–1930*, New York: New York University Press.

Newitt, M. (1981), *Portugal and Africa: The Last Hundred Years*, London: C. Hurst & Co.

Newman, K. J. (1970), *European Democracy Between the Wars*, London: Allen & Unwin.

Newman, W. J. (1968), *The Balance of Power in the Interwar Years, 1919–1939*, New York: Random House.

Nötel, R. (1974) 'International capital movements and finance in Eastern Europe, 1919–1949', *Vierteljahrschrift für Sozial-und Wirtschaftsgeschichte*, **61**.

Nötel, R. (1986), 'International credit and finance', in M. C. Kaser and E. A. Radice (eds), *The Economic History of Eastern Europe 1919–1975*. Vol. II. *Interwar Policy, the War and Reconstruction*, Oxford: Oxford University Press.

Notestein, F. W. et al. (1944), *The Future Population of Europe and the Soviet Union*, Geneva: League of Nations.

Nunes, A. B., Mata, E. and Valério, N. (1989), 'Portuguese economic growth 1833–1985', *Journal of European Economic History*, **18**.

Núñez, C.-E. (1990), 'Literacy and economic growth in Spain, 1860–1977', in G. Tortella (ed.), *Education and Economic Development Since the Industrial Revolution*, Valencia: Generalitat Valenciana.

Orde, A. (1990), *British Policy and European Reconstruction after the First World War*, Cambridge: Cambridge University Press.

Overy, R. (1989), *The Road to War*, London: Macmillan.

Overy, R. J. (1994), *The Inter-War Crisis 1919–1939*, London: Longman.

Palairet, M. (1997), *The Balkan Economies c.1800–1914. Evolution Without Development*, Cambridge: Cambridge University Press.

Pamuk, S. (1987), *The Ottoman Empire and European Capitalism (1820–1913). Trade, Investment and Production*, Cambridge: Cambridge University Press.

Pamuk, S. (1994), 'Long term trends in real wages in Turkey, 1850–1990', in V. Zamagni and P. Scholliers (eds), *Real Wages in the*

Nineteenth and Twentieth Centuries, B9 Proceedings of the Eleventh International Economic History Congress, Milan: Università Bocconi.

Parker, R. A. C. (1969), *Europe 1919–45*, London: Wiedenfeld and Nicolson.

Pasvolsky, L. (1928), *Economic Nationalism of the Danubian States*, London: Allen & Unwin.

Pasvolsky, L. (1930), *Bulgaria's Economic Position*, Washington DC: Brookings Institution.

Payne, S. G. (1968), *Franco's Spain*, London: Routledge & Kegan Paul.

Pearson, R. (1983), *National Minorities in Eastern Europe 1848–1945*, London: Macmillan.

Pearton, M. (1971), *Oil and the Romanian State*, Oxford: Oxford University Press.

Pelt, M. (1998), *Tobacco, Arms and Politics: Greece and Germany from World Crisis to World War 1929–41*, Copenhagen: Museum Tusculanum Press.

Pentzopoulos, D. (1962), *The Balkan Exchange of Minorities and its Impact on Greece*, Paris: Mouton.

Petrini, E. (1931), 'The agrarian reform in Rumania', *International Review of Agriculture*, **22**.

Political and Economic Planning (1945), *Economic Development in S. E. Europe*, London: Political and Economic Planning.

Pollard, S. (1981), *Peaceful Conquest: the Industrialisation of Europe 1760–1970*, Oxford: Oxford University Press.

Pollard, S. (1997), *Marginal Europe: The Contribution of Marginal Lands Since the Middle Ages*, Oxford: Oxford University Press.

Pollard, S. (1998), 'The peripheral European countries in the 19th century', in J. Batou and T. David (eds), *Uneven Development in Europe: The Obstructed Growth of the Agricultural Countries, 1918–1939*, Geneva: Droz.

Polonsky, A. (1975), *The Little Dictators: The History of Eastern Europe Since 1918*, London: Routledge & Kegan Paul.

Ponikowski, W. (1930), 'Polish agricultural land organisation since the world war', *Annals of the American Academy of Political and Social Science*, **150**.

Prados de la Escosura, L. (1993), *Spain's Gross Domestic Product, 1850–1990*, Madrid: Ministerio de Economía y Hacienda.

Psomiades, H. J. (1965), 'The economic and social transformation of modern Greece', *Journal of International Affairs*, **19**.

Pundeff, M. (1992), 'Bulgaria', in J. Held (ed.), *The Columbia History of Eastern Europe in the Twentieth Century*, New York: Columbia University Press.

Quataert, D. (1994), 'The age of reforms, 1812–1914', in H. Inalcik and D. Quataert (eds), *An Economic and Social History of the Ottoman Empire, 1300–1914*, Cambridge: Cambridge University Press.

Radice, E. A. (1985), 'General characteristics of the region between the wars', in M. C. Kaser and E. A. Radice (eds), *The Economic History of Eastern Europe 1919–1975*. Vol. I. *Economic Structure and Performance Between the Wars*, Oxford: Oxford University Press.

Ranki. G. (1974), 'Has modernity made a difference?', in G. Gati (ed.), *The Politics of Modernization in Eastern Europe*, New York: Praeger.

Ranki, G. (1983a), *Economic and Foreign Policy: the Struggle of the Great Powers for the Hegemony of the Danube Valley 1919–1939*, New York: Columbia University Press.

Ranki, G. (1983b), 'Inflation in Hungary', in N. Schmukler and E. Marcus (eds), *Inflation Through the Ages*, New York: Brooklyn College Press.

Ranki, G. (1985), 'Problems of southern European economic development (1918–38)', in G. Arrighi (ed.), *Seimiperipheral Development: the Politics of Southern Europe in the Twentieth Century'*, Beverly Hills, Ca.: Sage Publications.

Reis, J. (1995), 'Portuguese banking in the inter-war period', in C. H. Feinstein (ed.), *Banking, Currency, and Finance in Europe Between the Wars*, Oxford: Clarendon Press.

Reynolds, L. G. (1985), *Economic Growth in the Third World*, New Haven, Conn.: Yale University Press.

Ritschl, A. O. (2001), 'Nazi economic imperialism and the exploitation of the small: evidence from Germany's secret foreign exchange balances, 1938–1940', *Economic History Review*, **54**.

Roberts, H. L. (1951), *Rumania: Political Problems of an Agrarian State*, New Haven: Yale University Press.

Robinson, J. et al. (1943), *Were the Minorities Treaties a Failure?*, New York: Antin Press.

Rose, W. J. (1939), *Poland*, Harmondsworth: Penguin Books.

Roszkowski, W. (1986), 'Poland's economic performance between the two world wars', *East European Quarterly*, **20**.

Roszkowski, W. (1989), 'The growth of the state sector in the Polish economy in the years 1918–1926', *Journal of European Economic History*, **18**.

Rothschild, J. (1974), *East Central Europe between the Two World Wars*, Seattle: University of Washington Press.

Royal Institute of International Affairs (1936), *The Balkan States: A Review of the Economic and Financial Development of Albania, Bulgaria, Greece, Roumania and Yugoslavia since 1919*, London: Oxford University Press.

Royal Institute of International Affairs (1938), *The Baltic States*, Oxford: Oxford University Press.

Royal Institute of International Affairs (1939), *South Eastern Europe: a Political and Economic Survey*, London: Oxford University Press.

Sandberg, L. G. (1982), 'Ignorance, Poverty and Economic Backwardness in the Early Stages of European Industrialization. Variations on Alexander Gerschenkron's Grand Theme', *Journal of European Economic History*, **11**.

Schönfeld, R. (1975), 'Die Balkanländer in der Weltwirtschaftskrise', *Vierteljahrschrift für Sozial-und Wirtschaftsgeschichte*, **62**.

Senghaas, D. (1985), *The European Experience: a Historical Critique of Development Theory*, Leamington Spa: Berg Publishers.

Seton-Watson, H. (1946), *Eastern Europe Between the Wars 1918–1941*, Cambridge: Cambridge University Press.

Simutis, A. (1942), *The Economic Reconstruction of Lithuania after 1918*, New York: Columbia University Press.

Singleton, F. and Carter, B. (1982), *The Economy of Yugoslavia*, London: Croom Helm.

Smith, G. (1994), *The Baltic States: The National Self-Determination of Estonia, Latvia and Lithuania*, Basingstoke: Macmillan.

Smith, L. (1936), 'The zloty, 1924–35', *Journal of Political Economy*, **44**.

Snooks, G. D. (1996), *The Dynamic Society: Exploring the Sources of Global Change*, London: Routledge.

Spekke, A. (1951), *History of Latvia: An Outline*, Stockholm: M. Goppers.

Spigler, J. (1986), 'Public finance', in M. C. Kaser and E. A. Radice (eds), *The Economic History of Eastern Europe 1919–1975*. Vol. II, *Interwar Policy, the War and Reconstruction*, Oxford: Oxford University Press.

Spulber, N. (1959), 'The role of the state in economic growth in Eastern Europe since 1860', in H. G. Aitken (ed.), *The State and Economic Growth*, New York: Social Science Research Council.

Spulber, N. (1966), *The State and Economic Development in Eastern Europe*, New York: Random House.

Statham, P. (1990), 'A new look at the New South Wales Corps 1790–1810', *Australian Economic History Review*, **30**.

Statham, P. (ed.) (1992), *A Colonial Regiment: New Sources Relating to the New South Wales Corps 1789–1810*, Canberra: ANU.

Svennilson, I. (1954), *Growth and Stagnation in the European Economy*, Geneva: United Nations.

Szlaffer, H. (1990), *Economic Nationalism in East-Central Europe and South America, 1919–1939*, Geneva: Droz.

Taylor, A. J. P. (1948), *The Habsburg Monarchy 1809–1918*, London: Hamish Hamilton.

Taylor, J. (1952), *The Economic Development of Poland 1919–1950*, Ithaca, New York: Cornell University Press.

Teichova, A. (1985), 'Industry', in M. C. Kaser and E. A. Radice (eds), *The Economic History of Eastern Europe 1919–1975*. Vol. I. *Economic Structure and Performance Between the Wars*, Oxford: Oxford University Press.

Teichova, A. (1989), 'East-Central and South-East Europe 1919–1939', in P. Mathias and S. Pollard (eds), *The Cambridge Economic History of Europe*. Vol. VIII. *The Industrial Economies: the Development of Economic and Social Policies*, Cambridge: Cambridge University Press.

Temin, P. (1993), 'Transmission of the Great Depression', *Journal of Economic Perspectives*, **7**.

Temperley, H. W. V. (1920), *A History of the Peace Conference of Paris*, Vol. 1, London: Hodder & Stoughton.

Temperley, H. W. V. (1921), *A History of the Peace Conference of Paris*, Vol. IV, London: Hodder & Stoughton.

Thomas, H. (1961), *The Spanish Civil War*, London: Eyre & Spottiswoode.

Thomas, H. (1977), *The Spanish Civil War*, 3rd edn, London: Hamish Hamilton.

Thornburg, M. W., Spry, G. and Soule, G. (1949), *Turkey: An Economic Appraisal*, New York: The Twentieth Century Fund.

Tilly, C. (1992), *Coercion, Capital and European States, AD 990–1990,* Oxford: Blackwell.

Tiltman, H. H. (1934), *Peasant Europe*, London: Jarrolds.

Timoshenko, V. (1933, 1983), *World Agriculture in Depression*, Ann Arbor: University of Michigan. Reprinted by Garland Publishing, New York, 1983.

Tipton, F. B. and Aldrich, R. (1987), *An Economic and Social History of Europe, 1890–1939*, Basingstoke: Macmillan.

Tomasevich, J. (1949), 'Foreign economic relations', in R. J. Kerner (ed.), *Yugoslavia,* Berkeley, Ca.: University of California Press.

Tomasevich, J. (1955), *Peasants, Politics and Economic Change in Yugoslavia*, Stanford, Ca.: Stanford University Press.

Tortella, G. (1987), 'Agriculture: a slow-moving sector, 1830–1935', in N. Sánchez-Albornoz (ed.), *The Economic Modernization of Spain, 1830–1930*, New York: New York University Press.

Tortella, G. (1994), 'Patterns of economic retardation and recovery in south-western Europe in the nineteenth and twentieth centuries', *Economic History Review*, **47**.

Tracey, M. (1964), *Agriculture in Western Europe: Crisis and Adaptation Since 1880*, London: Cape.

Turnock, D. (1986), *The Romanian Economy in the Twentieth Century*, London: Croom Helm.

Valenta, J. (1974), 'The Drift to Dictatorship', in A. J. P. Taylor and J. M. Roberts (eds), *History of the 20th Century*, London: Phoebes Publishing Company.

Vinski, I. (1955), 'National product and fixed assets in the territory of Yugoslavia 1909–1959', *Income and Wealth*, **9**.

Von Rauch, G. (1974), *The Baltic States: The Years of Independence: Estonia, Latvia, Lithuania, 1917–1940*, London: G. Hurst.

Wallerstein, I. (1985), 'The relevance of the concept of semiperiphery to southern Europe', in G. Arrighi (ed.), *Semiperipheral Development: the Politics of Southern Europe in the Twentieth Century*, Beverly Hills, Ca.: Sage Publications.

Warriner, D. (1964), *Economics of Peasant Farming*, London: Frank Cass.

Warriner, D. (ed.) (1965), *Contrasts in Emerging Societies: Readings in the Social and Economic History of South-East Europe in the Nineteenth Century*, London: The Athlone Press.

Wellisz, L. (1938), *Foreign Capital in Poland*, London: Allen & Unwin.

Wicker, E. (1986), 'Terminating hyperinflation in the dismembered Habsburg Monarchy', *American Economic Review*, **76**.

Williams, D. (1963), 'The 1931 financial crisis', *Yorkshire Bulletin of Economic and Social Research*, **15**.

World Bank (1993), *Annual Report*, Washington DC: World Bank.

Wyatt, S. C. (1934), 'Turkey: the economic situation and the five-year plan', *International Affairs*, **13**.

Wynot, E. D. (1983), *Warsaw Between the World Wars: Profile of the Capital City in a Developing Land, 1919–1939*, East European Monographs, Boulder, Co.: distributed by Columbia University Press, New York.

Yeager, L. B. and Associates (1981), *Experiences with Stopping Inflation*, Washington DC.: American Enterprise Institute.

Yovanovich, D. (1930), *Les Effets Economiques et Sociaux de la Guerre en Serbie*, Paris: Presses Universitaires de France.

Zilinskas, V. L. (1946), 'Independent Lithuania's economic progress', *Baltic Review*, **1**.

Zürcher, E. J. (1998), *Turkey: A Modern History*, London: I. B. Taurus.

Zweig, F. (1944), *Poland Between the Wars: A Critical Study of Social and Economic Changes*, London: Secker & Warburg.

Index